AS-Level Psychology

AS Psychology is seriously tricky — no question about that.
To do well, you're going to need to revise properly and practise hard.

This book has thorough notes on everything you need to know for the
AQA A, Edexcel and OCR specifications, plus plenty of detailed psychological studies.

There are also warm-up and exam-style practice questions for every topic,
with a separate section of advice on how to do well in the exams.

And of course, we've done our best to make the whole thing vaguely entertaining for you.

Complete Revision and Practice

Published by CGP

Editors:
Katherine Craig, Jane Sawers.

Contributors:
Radha Bellur, Richard Carciofo, Dr Karen Goodall, Christine Johnson, Tracey Jones, Denise Say, Simon Venn, Stuart Wilson.

This book is suitable for:

AQA A, Edexcel, OCR.

There are notes at the tops of double pages to tell you if there's a bit you can ignore for your specification.

ISBN 978 1 84762 139 9

With thanks to Glenn Rogers and Hayley Thompson for the proofreading.

Groovy website: www.cgpbooks.co.uk

Jolly bits of clipart from CorelDRAW®
Printed by Elanders, Newcastle upon Tyne.

Based on the classic CGP style created by Richard Parsons.

Contents

Introduction — What is Psychology?

Section One — Cognitive Psychology

Section Two — Developmental Psychology

Section Three — Biological Psychology

Section Four — Social Psychology

Section Five — Individual Differences

Section Six — Research Methods

Do Well in Your Exam

We deliberately haven't put any answers in this book, because they'd just be saying what's already in the book. So instead, here's how to write answers and do well.

What is Psychology?

These two pages give you a very quick intro to psychology. Don't spend ages learning this cos it's really just an overview of stuff you'll cover in detail later on.

Psychology is a Science with Lots of Theories and Few Facts

Psychology is "**the scientific study of experience and behaviour**."
This basically means that psychologists look at what people and animals do, why they do it, and how they feel.

A lot of psychology sounds like **common sense**, but it's a science, so everything's got to be investigated. You've got to come up with a **theory** about something and then **scientifically test** it.

It's difficult to prove things in psychology, so there are loads of disagreements and a lot of theories that sound rubbish. But you can't just say they're rubbish in your exam — that'd be too easy. No, you've got to use other theories and experiments to support your answer.

The different schools of thought are called **approaches**. Each approach has its own explanation for why we do what we do. You'll be looking at the **cognitive**, **biological**, **developmental**, **social**, and **psychodynamic** approaches. Fortunately for you, they're split up into handy little sections.

The Cognitive Approach Focuses on Internal Processes

This section is part of **AQA A Unit 1**, **Edexcel Unit 1**, **OCR Unit 2**.

The brain is a complex information processor.

1) Cognitive psychologists focus on **internal processes** to understand behaviour, such as how we perceive or remember things.
2) They compare the human mind to a **computer** system, so they use **computer models** to try to understand human cognition (thinking).
3) Using concepts from information processing, cognitive psychologists describe the brain as a **processor** — it receives **input**, **processes** it, and produces an **output**. Obviously it's ridiculously more complicated, but the general idea is the same.
4) Cognitive psychology studies are often laboratory-based and **artificial**, so they can lack **validity** in the **real world**. This is known as '**ecological validity**' (see page 6).

Developmental Psychology is About How Humans Develop... Obviously...

This section covers **AQA A Unit 1** and **OCR Unit 2**. You jammy Edexcel people can ignore it altogether. It's a bit of a jumble of ideas from different approaches...

Developmental psychologists look at how people **develop** and **change** over their lifetime.
They place emphasis on the importance of **early experiences** in shaping the rest of a person's life.

Freud (1909) believed that children go through stages of **psychosexual development**.
There are five stages of **psychosexual development** — the oral, anal, phallic, latency and genital stages.
If a child has a serious problem or excessive pleasure in any of these stages, they can become **fixated** with that stage. The **fixations** can continue into adult life and affect their behaviour.

In the second half of the 20th century psychologists started to look at how children are **qualitatively different** to adults in their understanding, abilities and feelings.

Researchers like **Piaget** and **Samuel and Bryant** looked at children's **cognitive** development. They studied the way children approach problems depending on their age and the stage of development they've reached.

They found that the brain appears to have a **timetable** of **what** we can do and **when** we can do it— e.g. children don't start speaking or progress with potty training until they reach a certain stage of development.

Alan won't be able to start growing until the nurse loosens her grip.

What is Psychology?

The **Biological Approach** Explains Behaviour as a Product of **Nature**

Everyone has to do this one, and it's **Unit 2** for all of you. Don't be confused if you're doing **OCR** though — you'll know this bit as the **physiological** approach.

There are three **key assumptions**:

1. **Human behaviour** can be explained by looking at internal, biological stuff, like hormones and the nervous system.

2. Experimental research that uses **animals** can tell us about **human behaviour** because we have similar biological make-ups.

3. **Unwanted behaviour** can sometimes be changed for the better using **biological treatments** — e.g. medication for mental illness.

So, as far as this approach is concerned, it's what's inside that counts...

1) Researchers look at **genetics**, the **brain**, **hormones** and the **nervous system** to explain behaviour.
2) It's very scientific — research is mostly carried out in **laboratory experiments**.
3) Common research techniques include **brain scans** and **correlational studies**.

Individual Differences is About **Differences** Between... erm... **Individuals**

You'll all be doing this bit too, and it's **Unit 2** for everyone. This is another section that's made up of bits from loads of approaches. The main thing that researchers want to find out is **how** and **why** we're all **different** from each other. You might think it's pretty obvious that we're all different, but psychologists have got to find something to fill the day.

We all have different interests.

1) Other areas of psychology tend to assume that people are broadly the same — e.g. developmental psychologists assume that we all go through the same basic stages of development.
2) A big area of research is **abnormality**. Deviation from the norm is okay to a point, but societies have difficulties dealing with people who are considered to be very abnormal.
3) Because of this, an important issue to bear in mind is how **normality** is **defined**, and whether anyone has the right to decide that someone else is **abnormal**.

Social Psychologists Look at How We **Interact** with Each Other

Last one, hurrah. This section is part of **AQA A Unit 2**, **Edexcel Unit 1**, **OCR Unit 2**.

1) This approach is all about how we **influence** each other.
2) Major areas of research include **conformity** and **obedience**.
3) Society needs people to conform and be obedient in order to function properly — e.g. if drivers didn't abide by the rules of the road there would be chaos.
4) This can be a problem though, because people might be more likely to do something they think is wrong if they feel pressured by others.

Probably the most famous experiment in social psychology is **Milgram's Behavioural Study of Obedience** (1963). In the experiment he tested people's obedience by asking participants to give someone electric shocks. Most of his participants carried on giving the shocks, even when they thought they were causing harm. He concluded that most people will follow orders even if it means doing something they don't think is right. Pretty scary stuff. You can find this study on page 78.

It's psychology, Jim, but not as we know it...

There are so many different types of theory that call themselves 'psychology'. Some of them are a bit more like biology, some are more like computing, and some... are Freud's theories. The interesting thing about his weird ideas is that it's hard to prove them wrong. So they're still around and that means you've got to learn them.

The Scientific Process

'How Science Works' is all about the scientific process — how we develop and test scientific ideas. It's what scientists do all day, every day. Well, except at coffee time. Never come between scientists and their coffee.

Science Answers Real-life Questions

Science tries to explain **how** and **why** things happen — it **answers questions**.
It's all about seeking and gaining **knowledge** about the world around us.
Scientists do this by **asking** questions and **suggesting** answers and then **testing** them, to see if they're correct — this is the **scientific process**.

The evidence supported Quentin's Theory of Flammable Burps.

1) **Ask** a question — make an **observation** and ask **why or how** it happens.
2) **Suggest** an answer, or part of an answer, by forming a **theory** (a possible explanation of the observations).
3) Make a **prediction** or **hypothesis** — a **specific testable statement**, based on the theory, about what will happen in a test situation.
4) Carry out a **test** — to provide **evidence** that will support the prediction (or help to disprove it).

Suggesting explanations is all very well and good, but if there's **no way to test** them then it just ain't science.
A theory is **only scientific** if it can be tested.

Science is All About Testing Theories

It starts off with one experiment backing up a prediction and theory. It ends up with all the scientists in the world **agreeing** with it and you **learning** it. Stirring stuff. This is how the magical process takes place:

1) The results are **published** — scientists need to let others know about their work, so they try to get their results published in **scientific journals**. These are just like normal magazines, only they contain **scientific reports** (called papers) instead of celebrity gossip. All work must undergo **peer review** before it's published.

- **Peer review** is a process used to **ensure the integrity** of published scientific work. Before publication, scientific work is sent to **experts** in that field (**peers**) so they can assess the **quality** of the work.
- This process helps to keep scientists **honest** — e.g. you can't **'sex-up'** your conclusions if the data doesn't support it, because it **won't pass** peer review.
- Peer review helps to **validate conclusions** — it means published theories, data and conclusions are more trustworthy. But it **can't guarantee** that the conclusions are 100% right. More **rounds** of predicting and testing are needed before they can be taken as **'fact'**.
- Sometimes **mistakes** are made and bad science is published. Peer review **isn't perfect** but it's probably the best way for scientists to **self-regulate** their work and to ensure **reliable** scientific work is **published**.

2) Other scientists read the published theories and results, and try to **repeat them** — this involves repeating the **exact experiments**, and using the theory to make **new predictions** that are tested by **new experiments**.
3) If all the experiments in all the world provide evidence to back it up, the theory is thought of as scientific 'fact' (**for now**).
4) If **new evidence** comes to light that **conflicts** with the current evidence the theory is questioned all over again. More rounds of **testing** will be carried out to see which evidence, and so which theory, **prevails**.

If the Evidence Supports a Theory, It's Accepted — For Now

Our currently accepted theories have survived this **'trial by evidence'**. They've been tested **over and over and over** and each time the results have backed them up. **BUT**, and this is a big but (teehee), they never become totally undisputable fact. Scientific **breakthroughs or advances** could provide new ways to question and test a theory, which could lead to **changes and challenges** to it. Then the testing starts all over again...
And this, my friend, is the **tentative nature of scientific knowledge** — it's always **changing** and **evolving**.

The Role of Science

Science is all about the search for truth and knowledge. But why bother? We want to know as much as possible so we can use it to try to improve our lives (and because we're nosy).

Science Helps Us Make **Better Decisions**

Lots of scientific work eventually leads to **important discoveries** that could **benefit humankind**. Oh yes. These results are **used by society** (that's you, me and everyone else) to **make decisions** about the way we live. All sections of society use scientific evidence to make decisions:

1) **Politicians** use science to devise policy. E.g. **cognitive behavioural therapy** is available on the NHS because there's evidence to show it can help people with **depression**.
2) **Private organisations** use science to determine what to make or develop — e.g. evidence has shown that the number of people being diagnosed with **depression** is increasing, so drugs companies might put **more money** into this area of research.
3) **Individuals** also use science to make decisions about their **own lives** — e.g. evidence suggests that we should exercise and eat healthily, but it's up to individuals to **decide** whether they take that advice or not.

Other **Factors** Can **Influence** Decision Making

Other factors can influence decisions about science or the way science is used:

Economic factors

- Society has to consider the **cost** of implementing changes based on scientific conclusions — e.g. the **NHS** can't afford the most expensive drugs without **sacrificing** something else.
- Scientific research is **expensive** so companies won't always develop new ideas — e.g. developing new drugs is costly, so pharmaceutical companies often only invest in drugs that are likely to make **money**.

Social factors

- **Decisions** affect **people's lives**. How psychologists decide what's **normal** and what's **abnormal** affects how people are treated — e.g. homosexuality was defined as an **abnormal behaviour** until 1987.

Environmental factors

- Scientists believe **unexplored regions**, like parts of rainforests, might contain **untapped drug** resources. But some people think we shouldn't **exploit** these regions because any interesting finds might lead to **deforestation**, **reduced biodiversity** and **more CO_2** in the atmosphere.

Science Has **Responsibilities**

Yes, you've guessed it — **ethics**. Science has to be **responsible** in many ways. Scientists aren't allowed to test something just because they can. They have to think about the **ethical considerations** surrounding the experiment design and how the results could affect society.

1) **Design** — e.g. experiments involving **animals** are tightly controlled and monitored. **Studies** are checked to ensure they aren't placing individuals in **unnecessary danger**. If a study shows a drug has a highly **beneficial effect**, it's stopped and those in the **placebo** (negative) group are given the drug too.
2) **Results** — e.g. scientists' understanding of some **genetic disorders** could lead to tests to detect members of the population that carry the genes for them. But would people want to know?

Society does have a say in what experiments take place. **Controversial experiments** involving ethical issues have to be approved by scientific and **ethics councils** before they are allowed to be carried out.

So there you have it — how science works...

Hopefully these pages have given you a nice intro to how science works — what scientists do to provide you with 'facts'. You need to understand this, as you're expected to use it to evaluate evidence for yourselves — in the exam and in life.

The Cognitive Approach

If you're doing AQA, just focus on the Research Methods bits. *If you're doing anything else then you have to read the whole ruddy lot. Even if you're just having a flick through and weren't actually thinking about work just yet. Too late I'm afraid. Get yourself and ticket and climb aboard the revision train, cos it's non-stop all the way to Examsville...*

Cognitive Psychology Looks at How We **Interpret** the World

1) Cognitive psychology is all about **how** we think.
2) Cognitive psychologists try to **explain behaviour** by looking at our **perception**, **language**, **attention** and **memory**.
3) **Computers** and computer models are often used to explain how we think and behave. Humans are treated as **information processors** (computers) and behaviour is explained in terms of **information processing** (how computers deal with information). Cognitive psychology is sometimes called the **information processing** approach.
4) But cognitive psychology has **limitations**. Research is often carried out in artificial situations (laboratories, using computer models) and the role of emotion and influence from other people is often ignored. For these reasons some argue that the results aren't valid in the real world.
5) A second criticism is that cognitive psychology fails to take **individual differences** into account by assuming that all of us process stuff in exactly the same way.

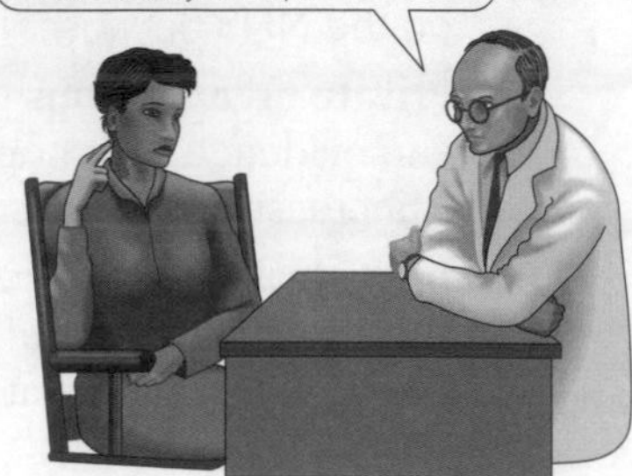

Cognitive Psychology Developed as the **Computer Age Developed**

1) People began to see similarities in how computers and humans make sense of information.
2) Computer terms are often used in cognitive psychology:
The brain is described as a **processor** (the thing that makes things happen) — it has data **input** into it, and **output** from it. Some parts of the brain form **networks** (connections of bits). Other parts work in **serial** (info travels along just one path) or in **parallel** (info travels to and fro along lots of paths at the same time).
3) Cognitive psychologists use computers to create **computational models** of the human mind.

Cognitive Psychologists Use **Four** Main Research Methods

Here's a snappy little phrase for you to learn before you read on: '**ecological validity**' — it's the measure of how much the result of an experiment reflects what would happen in **natural settings**. If a result has **low** ecological validity, it might work fine in the lab. But try and use it to explain real life behaviour, and you'll find yourself up the creek without a paddle. And no-one wants that.

1 — Laboratory Experiments

A lot of research in cognitive psychology happens in **laboratories**. This is very **scientific** and reliable as it is possible to have great control over variables in a lab. However, often this type of research doesn't tell us much about the real world — it has **low ecological validity**.

2 — Field Experiments

Field experiments take place in a **natural** situation (e.g. studies of memory or attention in a school environment), so they have more ecological validity, but there's less control of other variables.

3 — Natural Experiments

Natural experiments involve making observations of a **naturally occurring situation**. The experimenter has little control of the variables, and participants can't be randomly assigned to conditions. Natural experiments have **high ecological validity**, but they're **not massively reliable**, as **uncontrolled** (or **confounding**) variables can affect the results.

4 — Brain Imaging

Brain imaging can now be carried out during a cognitive task. For example, MRI scans have been used to show the blood flow in different brain areas for different types of memory tasks.

The Cognitive Approach

Case Studies Provide Support for the Cognitive Approach

Case studies use patients' behaviour to test a theory. **Brain damaged** patients are often studied — the damaged parts of the brain are linked to observed differences in behaviour. However, it's hard to make **generalisations** from the study of subjects with brain damage to 'normal' individuals. Also, **individual differences** between people mean that one subject may respond in a way that is totally different from someone else. Hmmm, tricky.

Cognitive psychologists believe that the different types of memory are **separate systems** in the brain. The case study of HM supported this by showing that short- and long-term memory must be based in different brain structures.

Milner et al (1957) — case study of HM

Diagnosis: HM was a patient with severe and frequent epilepsy. His seizures were based in a brain structure called the hippocampus. In 1953, doctors decided to surgically remove part of the brain round this area.

Results: The operation reduced his epilepsy, but led to him suffering memory loss.
He could still form short-term memories (STMs), but was unable to form new long-term memories (LTMs). For example, he could read something over and over without realising that he had read it before. He also moved house and had difficulty recalling the new route to his house. However, he could still talk and show previous skills (**procedural memory**). From tests, they found HM's **episodic memory** (for past events) and **semantic memory** (for knowledge, e.g. word meanings) was affected more than his **procedural memory**.

Cognitive Psychologists Apply **Animal Research** to Humans

The results of **non-human** studies can be **applied** to human cognitive abilities. For example, discovering whether chimpanzees can learn language helps psychologists develop theories about how humans learn language.

However, there are so many **differences** between humans and animals that results can be explained wrongly. For example, you might conclude that chimpanzees can't learn a **spoken** language because they lack the **cognitive** abilities. But it's actually more likely to be because they lack the **physiological** attributes, like a voice box.

I know the following study doesn't really generalise to humans, but if you're doing **OCR** you need to know about it.

Savage-Rumbaugh (1986) — symbol communication in chimps

OCR Core Study

Method: Two pygmy chimpanzees and two common chimpanzees were taught to communicate using symbols on a keyboard. A mixture of training and observation of others was used. All communications were recorded.

Results: Common chimps needed training to form symbol-object associations. However, pygmy chimps spontaneously used symbols to communicate after observing others. The pygmy chimps were also able to understand and respond to spoken English, unlike the common chimps.

Conclusion: Two closely related species differ greatly in their ability to develop a symbolic communication system.

Evaluation: There are **ethical** considerations, in that the chimps were taken from their natural environment and taught to do something that was extremely unnatural to them. There are also issues of **external validity** — it's not possible to accurately generalise results from chimpanzees to humans.

Practice Questions

Q1 Why is cognitive psychology sometimes called the information processing approach?

Q2 Why are laboratory experiments more reliable than field experiments?

Q3 How is brain imaging useful in cognitive psychology?

Exam Questions

Q1 Explain how the study of HM provided support for cognitive psychological thinking. [4 marks]

Q2 Explain why animal studies have been criticised as lacking validity. [3 marks]

Syntax error. Funny line does not compute. Insert file 'humour for books'.

If your brain goes wrong just turn it off and on again. That normally works for me. One day we'll probably know enough about the brain to be able to build computer people. Then you could make a computerised version of yourself and amaze your friends and family by projecting illegally downloaded TV out of your own face. Imagine that. They'd be so proud...

Short-Term and Long-Term Memory

Ignore these pages if you're doing OCR.

I used to worry that I could remember where I was in, say, May '98, but I couldn't recall why I'd just walked into a room. But it's due to the difference between short-term and long-term memory. Or something... I forget the exact reason.

*Memory is a **Process** in Which Information is **Retained** About the Past*

Memories are thought to have a physical basis or '**trace**'. Most psychologists agree that there are three types of memory — **sensory memory (SM)**, **short-term memory (STM)** and **long-term memory (LTM)**.
SM is visual and auditory information that passes through our senses very briefly. SM disappears quickly through **spontaneous decay** — the trace just fades. SM isn't around for very long, so most studies are on LTM and STM.

STM and LTM differ in terms of:
1) **Duration** — How long a memory lasts.
2) **Capacity** — How much can be held in the memory.
3) **Encoding** — Transferring information into code, creating a 'trace'.

STM has a **limited capacity** and a **limited duration** (i.e. we can remember a little information for a short time).
LTM has a pretty much **unlimited capacity** and is theoretically **permanent** (i.e. lots of information forever).

*Research Has Been Carried Out into the Nature of **STM and LTM***

***Peterson and Peterson** (1959) Investigated STM Using Trigrams*

Peterson and Peterson (1959) investigated the duration of STM.

Method: Participants were shown **nonsense trigrams** (3 random consonants, e.g. CVM) and asked to recall them after either 3, 6, 9, 12, 15 or 18 seconds. During the pause, they were asked to count backwards in threes from a given number. This was an **'interference task'** — it prevented them from repeating the letters to themselves.

Results: After **3 seconds**, participants could recall about **80%** of trigrams correctly.
After **18 seconds,** only about **10%** were recalled correctly.

Conclusion: When rehearsal is prevented, **very little** can stay in STM for longer than about **18 seconds**.

Evaluation: The results are likely to be reliable — it's a **laboratory experiment** where the variables can be tightly controlled. However, nonsense trigrams are artificial, so the study lacks **ecological validity** (see page 37 for more about reliability and validity). Meaningful or 'real-life' memories may last longer in STM. Only one type of **stimulus** was used — the duration of STM may depend on the type of stimulus. Also, each participant saw **many different trigrams**. This could have led to confusion, meaning that the first trigram was the only realistic trial.

***Bahrick et al** (1975) Investigated LTM in a Natural Setting*

Bahrick et al (1975) studied very long-term memories (VLTMs).

Method: 392 people were asked to list the names of their ex-classmates. (This is called a **'free-recall test'**.)
They were then shown photos and asked to recall the names of the people shown (**photo-recognition test**) or given names and asked to match them to a photo of the classmate (**name-recognition test**).

Results: Within 15 years of leaving school, participants could **recognise** about **90%** of names and faces. They were about **60%** accurate on **free recall**. After 30 years, **free recall** had declined to about **30%** accuracy.
After 48 years, name-recognition was about **80%** accurate, and photo-recognition about **40%** accurate.

Conclusion: The study shows evidence of **VLTMs** in a **'real-life'** setting. Recognition is better than recall, so there may be a huge store of information, but it's not always easy to **access** all of it — you just need help to get to it.

Evaluation: This was a field experiment and so had **high ecological validity**. However in a 'real-life' study like this, it's hard to **control** all the variables, making these findings less reliable — there's no way of knowing exactly **why** information was recalled well. It showed better recall than other studies on LTM, but this may be because **meaningful** information is stored better. This type of information could be rehearsed (if you're still in touch with classmates, or if you talk to friends about memories of classmates), increasing the rate of recall.
This means that the results can't be generalised to other types of information held in LTM.

Short-Term and Long-Term Memory

STM and LTM Have Very **Different Capacities**

Jacobs (1887) studied the capacity of STM.

Method: Participants were presented with a string of letters or digits. They had to repeat them back in the same order. The number of digits or letters increased until the participant failed to recall the sequence correctly.

Results: The majority of the time, participants recalled about **9 digits** and about **7 letters**. This capacity increased with **age** during childhood.

Conclusion: Based on the range of results, Jacobs concluded that STM has a **limited storage capacity** of **5-9 items**. Individual differences were found, such as STM increasing with age, possibly due to increased brain capacity or use of memory techniques, such as **chunking** (see below). Digits may have been easier to recall as there were only 10 different digits to remember, compared to 26 letters.

Evaluation: Jacobs' research is **artificial** and **lacks ecological validity** — it's not something you'd do in real life. More meaningful information may be recalled better, perhaps showing STM to have an even greater capacity. Also, the previous sequences recalled by the participants might have confused them on future trials.

Miller (1956) reviewed research into the capacity of STM. He found that people can remember about seven items. He argued that the capacity of STM is **seven, plus or minus two** — 'Miller's magic number'. He suggested that we use '**chunking**' to combine individual letters or numbers into larger more meaningful units. So 2,0,0,3,1,9,8,7 is about all the digits STM can hold. 'Chunked' into the meaningful recent years of 2003 and 1987, it's much easier to remember. STM could probably hold about seven such pieces of chunked information, increasing STM's capacity.

Encoding is About the Way Information is Stored in Memory

In **STM**, we sometimes try to keep information active by repeating it to ourselves. This means it generally involves **acoustic** coding. In **LTM**, encoding is generally **semantic** — it's more useful to code words in terms of their meaning, rather than what they sound or look like (although encoding in LTM **can** also be visual or acoustic).

Encoding can be visual (pictures), acoustic (sounds, e.g. 'chunky' and 'monkey' are acoustically similar) or semantic (meanings, e.g. 'chunky' and 'beefy' are semantically similar).

Baddeley (1966) investigated encoding in STM and LTM.

Method: Participants were given four sets of words that were either **acoustically similar** (e.g. man, mad, mat), **acoustically dissimilar** (e.g. pit, cow, bar), **semantically similar** (e.g. big, large, huge) and **semantically dissimilar** (e.g. good, hot, pig). The experiment used an **independent groups** design (see page 130) — participants were asked to recall the words either immediately or following a 20-minute task.

Results: Participants had problems recalling acoustically similar words when recalling the word list immediately (from **STM**). If recalling after an interval (from **LTM**), they had problems with semantically similar words.

Conclusion: The patterns of confusion between similar words suggest that **LTM** is more likely to rely on **semantic** encoding and **STM** on **acoustic** encoding.

Evaluation: This is another study that **lacks ecological validity**. Also, there are **other types** of LTM (e.g. episodic memory, procedural memory) and **other methods** of encoding (e.g. visual) which this experiment doesn't consider. The experiment used an **independent groups** design, so there wasn't any control over participant variables.

Practice Questions

Q1 What is meant by encoding?

Q2 What is chunking?

Exam Question

Q1 Identify one flaw in the design of a study into the duration of STM.
How could this flaw have been overcome? [4 marks]

Remember the days when you didn't have to remember stuff like this...

Whether you're going to remember something depends a lot on how much it means to you personally. So trivial things that have no bearing on your life whatsoever are forgotten pretty quickly. But more important things like the Hollyoaks theme tune tend to go round and round in your head forever. Or is that just because you've got it on in the background...

Models of Memory

Ignore these pages if you're doing OCR.

This page is all about why you can't remember the last page. Maybe you didn't rehearse it enough, or maybe you only looked at the letters instead of trying to understand the facts. Or maybe you spilt tea on it and couldn't read the words...

Atkinson and Shiffrin (1968) Created the **Multi-Store Model**

1) The multi-store model proposes that memory consists of three stores — a **sensory store**, a **short-term store** and a **long-term store**.
2) Information from our environment (e.g. visual or auditory) initially goes into **sensory memory**. You don't really notice much of this stuff. However, if you pay attention to it, or think about it, the information will be encoded and will pass into **short-term memory**.
3) Short-term memory has a **finite** capacity and duration. But if information is processed further (rehearsed) then it can be transferred to **long-term memory**. In theory, the information can then remain there forever. Unless you really really need to remember it, in which case it'll probably stay there until something more interesting comes along, like a bee or a cloud.

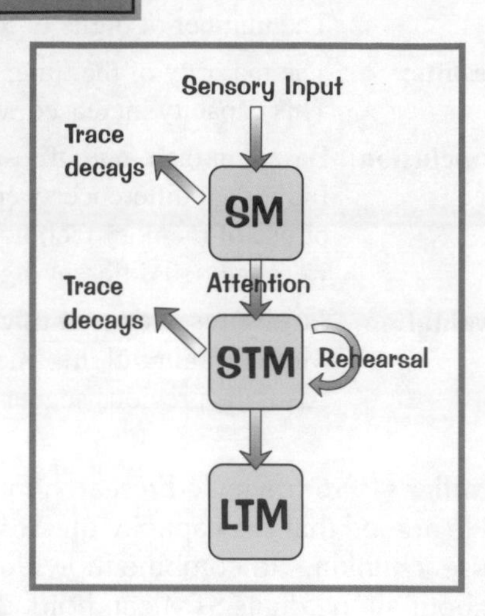

Many Studies **Support** the Multi-Store Model...

Several studies have been carried out that show that memory is made up of separate stores.

1) The **Primacy Effect** — Research shows that participants are able to recall the first few items of a list better than those from the middle. The multi-store model explains this because **earlier** items will have been **rehearsed** better and transferred to **LTM**. If rehearsal is prevented by an interference task, the effect disappears, as the model predicts.

2) The **Recency Effect** — Participants also tend to remember the last few items better than those from the middle of the list. Earlier items are rehearsed, so transfer to LTM, whilst **later** items are recalled because they're still in **STM**.

3) People with **Korsakoff's Syndrome** (amnesia that's mostly caused by chronic alcoholism) provide support for the model. They can recall the **last** items in a list (unimpaired recency effect), suggesting an unaffected **STM**. However, their **LTM** is very poor. This supports the model by showing that STM and LTM are **separate stores**.

...But There Are Also Many **Limitations** of the Model

Although there's lots of support for the model, there's plenty of criticism too.

1) In the model, information is transferred from the STM to LTM through **rehearsal**. But in **real life** people don't always spend time rehearsing, yet they still transfer information into LTM. Rehearsal is not always needed for information to be stored and some items can't be rehearsed, e.g. smells.

2) The model is **oversimplified**. It assumes there is only one long-term store and one short-term store. This has been disproved by evidence from **brain damaged** patients, suggesting several **different** short-term stores, and other evidence suggesting different long-term stores.

Models of Memory

Baddeley and Hitch (1974) Developed the **Working Memory Model**

Baddeley and Hitch developed a multi-store model of STM called the 'working memory model'.
Their model proposed that STM is made up of several different stores.

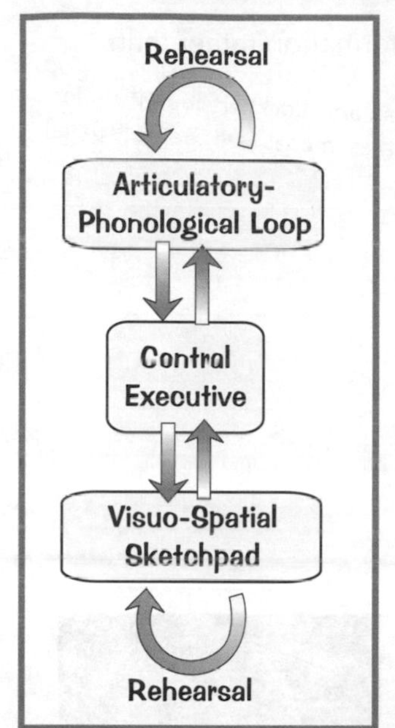

The **central executive** is the key component and can be described as attention.
It has a **limited capacity** and controls two 'slave' systems that also have **limited capacity**:

1) The **articulatory-phonological loop** holds speech-based information. It contains a **phonological store** (the inner ear) and an **articulatory process** (the inner voice).
2) The **visuo-spatial sketchpad** deals with the temporary storage of visual and spatial information.

Baddeley and Hitch based their model on results from studies that used **'interference tasks'**:

1) If participants are asked to perform two tasks simultaneously that use the same system, their performance will be affected e.g. saying 'the the the' while silently reading something is very difficult.
2) According to the working memory model, both these tasks use the articulatory-phonological loop. This has limited capacity so it can't cope with both tasks. Performance on one, or both tasks, will be affected.
3) However, if the two tasks involve different systems, performance isn't affected on either task (e.g. saying 'the the the' whilst tracking a moving object).

As Usual the Model has **Strengths** and **Weaknesses**

Shallice and Warrington (1974) found **support** for the working memory model through their case study of KF.

KF was a brain damaged patient who had an impaired STM. His problem was with immediate recall of words presented **verbally**, but not with visual information. This suggested he had an impaired **articulatory loop**, therefore providing evidence for the working memory model's view of STM.

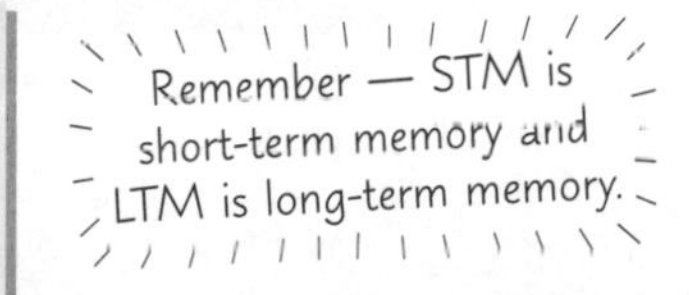

However, many psychologists have **criticised** this model — they think that Baddeley and Hitch's idea of a central executive is **simplistic** and **vague**. Their model doesn't really explain exactly what the central executive is, apart from being involved in attention.

Practice Questions

Q1 What is the primacy effect?

Q2 Name the components of the multi-store model of memory.

Q3 Who came up with the working memory model?

Q4 How did the study of KF provide support for the working memory model?

Q5 What have I drawn on my visuo-spatial sketchpad? That's right, it's a house.

Exam Questions

Q1 Evaluate Atkinson and Shiffrin's multi-store model of memory. [8 marks]

Q2 How did Baddeley and Hitch use the results from studies involving interference tasks to develop their model? [4 marks]

Memory, all alone in the moonlight... something about the moon... la la la...

I don't know about you, but I find these pages pretty boring. Kind of learnable, but still boring enough that you find yourself face-down on your desk in a pool of dribble, with a biscuit stuck to your forehead. Don't fret though — it's not long before you can start learning about the gory experiments with electric shocks and nastiness. Much better than this stuff...

Models of Memory

You only need to look at these pages if you're doing Edexcel.
Just when you thought you'd seen the last memory model... Well, here's one more. It's the last one, I promise.

Craik and Lockhart (1972) Developed the **Levels of Processing Model**

Craik and Lockhart's levels of processing model focuses on the **processing** of incoming information rather than suggesting the existence of particular memory structures.

They discussed three levels of processing:

Craik and Lockhart found support for their model (see the next page).

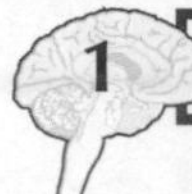

1 Physical processing

Physical processing occurs at a '**shallow**' level and analyses information in terms of its **physical** qualities, e.g. **some words are typed in black ink**. Apart from the words '**black ink**' just here, which have been typed in purple ink just to confuse you.

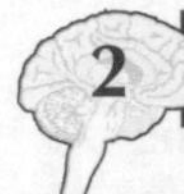

2 Phonemic processing

Phonemic processing occurs at a '**deeper**' level than physical processing. It focuses on the **sound** of information, e.g. **pea rhymes with bee.**

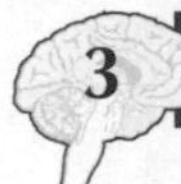

3 Semantic processing

Semantic processing occurs at the '**deepest**' level and analyses the **meaning** of information, e.g. **a pea is a vegetable.**

Harry worked on various levels of processing at the doughnut factory.

The levels of processing theory suggests that information **processed** at a **deeper** level should be **recalled** better.

The *First Levels of Processing Model* was a bit *Simplistic*

1) The idea of deep and shallow processing was thought to be a bit **simplistic** — so Craik and Lockhart also added ideas of **elaboration**, **organisation** and **distinctiveness**.
2) They predicted that information will be recalled better if it has been **elaborated** (e.g. explained more, perhaps with examples), or **organised** (e.g. if participants had to sort information into categories), or made **distinctive** (e.g. said with a funny voice).

Research supported their ideas of elaboration, organisation and distinctiveness.

For example, a study by **Eysenck and Eysenck** (1980) supported **distinctiveness**. Participants in a recall experiment were either asked to say words in a distinctive way (e.g. by pronouncing letters that are usually silent) or in the normal way. They found that subsequent recall of the words was **better** in the condition where they'd been pronounced distinctively.

A study by **Craik and Tulving** (1975) investigated **elaboration**. Participants had to judge whether a word would fit into a gap in a sentence. The sentences were either simple or fairly elaborate and complex. In a subsequent test, it was found that memory was **better** for words judged with **complex** sentences than simple sentences.

One criticism that applies to both of these studies is that saying a word distinctively, or reading a more elaborate sentence, will take **longer** than reading the word normally or reading a shorter sentence. So, it could just be that the **extra time** spent **encoding** the words causes **better memory**.

Models of Memory

Craik and Tulving's Work Supported the Levels of Processing Model

Craik and Tulving (1975) did a series of experiments that supported the levels of processing model. They found that words that had been processed **semantically** were remembered best, **phonemically** second best and **physically** worst.

Craik and Tulving (1975) studied levels of processing.

Method: Participants were given a list of words. For each word, they were asked one of three types of question:

1. **Shallow physical processing** — e.g. is the word in upper case letters?
2. **Intermediate phonemic processing** — e.g. does the word rhyme with hat?
3. **Deep semantic processing** — e.g. does the word fit into the following sentence?

The experimental design was **repeated measures** — each participant did all three types of processing task (see page 130). Participants were then given a **surprise** recognition test. They were given a word list and had to identify which words were in the original list.

Results: Recognition was better for the words which had been processed more **deeply**

Conclusion: The findings **support** the levels of processing theory — memory was better for words that had been processed more deeply.

Evaluation: The participants **weren't told** that their memory was going to be tested. This meant that the results weren't affected by participants trying to remember the words by processing them in other ways. However, the study **lacks ecological validity**. You wouldn't normally be told how to process a piece of information — it happens automatically. Also, deeper processing takes **longer** than shallow processing. So, it could be the time taken to process something, not the depth of processing, that affects memory.

Yep, You Guessed it — the Theory has been *Criticised*

1) There is a **circular argument** over what **depth** really is. In the levels of processing model, the definition of good recall is something that comes from deep processing. But the definition of deep processing is 'something that leads to good recall'. However, with elaboration, organisation and distinctiveness added to the model, this criticism doesn't work so well.
2) The model doesn't acknowledge that **separate memory stores** may exist.
3) The model may also be confusing **effort** with **depth**.

Practice Questions

Q1 What is meant by phonemic processing?

Q2 What is meant by semantic processing?

Q3 What does the levels of processing theory propose?

Q4 What three ideas did Craik and Lockhart add to their more simplistic model?

Exam Questions

Q1 Describe the weaknesses of Craik and Lockhart's levels of processing model. [4 marks]

Q2 Describe and evaluate Craik and Tulving's (1975) levels of processing research. [8 marks]

All this criticism — I don't know why people bother...

As you've probably gathered from these pages about models of memory, someone comes up with a theory and there's some experimental evidence to support it. Then, although some people support the model, others plain criticise it. Anyway, for your exam, you've got to be good at evaluating stuff — that is, pointing out the strengths and weaknesses of something.

Forgetting

These three pages are just for Edexcel. *Forgetting is great — such an easy way to not answer difficult questions. Just screw your eyes up, point your head towards the sky, wibble and say, 'Ooh, I know it, it's in there, err, I can't remember'.*

Forgetting is When Learnt Information **Can't Be Retrieved**

Experiments on memory assume that if you can't retrieve a memory, it's forgotten. Forgetting is thought to happen when information is **unavailable** in **STM** and **inaccessible** and/or **unavailable** in **LTM**.

In other words, we can forget because:

1) The information was never **stored** — an **availability** problem, e.g. you didn't pay attention when the information was presented.
2) The information was stored, but is hard to **retrieve** — an **accessibility** problem, e.g. you read something once, a long time ago, and now need a lot of help to recall it.
3) The information is **confused** — there is an **interference** problem, e.g. two pieces of learnt information are too similar, and you can't tell them apart easily.
4) I'm sure there was one more... (that's a funny joke about forgetting).

Decay and Displacement are Theories Explaining Forgetting in **STM**

Theories suggest that information in STM might either just disappear with time, or get pushed out by new information:

Trace Decay Theory

Memories have a physical basis or '**trace**'.
Trace decay theory suggests that this trace **decays** over time unless it is passed to LTM. This explains the findings from the **Peterson and Peterson (1959)** experiment — when rehearsal of information was prevented, very little information stayed in STM for longer than about 18 seconds (see page 8). However, we can't be sure that the trace really decayed instead of being overwritten by new information (**displacement**).

Reitman (1974) gave participants words to learn, then made them listen for a tone as an interference task, preventing rehearsal. There was no new information to push out the old. So if recall was impaired this would suggest the reason was decay, not displacement. There was a slight, but not huge, reduction in recall so we have some evidence for decay.

Displacement Theory

Displacement theory suggests that new information physically overwrites old information in a limited capacity system like STM. This makes sense — if STM is full, then any new information will push out information already there. It'll then be forgotten, unless it has been rehearsed and transferred to LTM.

Waugh and Norman's (1965) study involved participants hearing a list of digits. They were then told a digit from the list, and asked to recall the one that came after it. Participants were much better at recalling digits that came from the **end** of the list. This supports **displacement theory**.

However, in different conditions of the experiment, the digits were either presented 1 per second or 4 per second. It was found that recall improved when digits were presented faster, which suggests that **decay** rather than displacement was to blame.

Seeing as there's evidence for both the decay and displacement theories of forgetting in STM, a possible explanation could be that **both** are true. There's no reason why **decay and displacement** can't both cause forgetting in STM.

Forgetting

Forgetting in **LTM** Could Be Due to **Interference**

Interference theory suggests that one piece of learned information can block the recall of another piece of learned information, resulting in forgetting.
Long-term memories might also be forgotten because of **decay**. However, studies of **LTM** have found more problems in recall if you take in new information rather than just having a relatively information-free break.
Therefore, **interference** is a more likely explanation than decay, as new information affects the recall of old information.
Interference can happen in two ways:

Retroactive interference

This is where **new** information interferes with the ability to recall **older** information.
E.g. if you've changed your telephone number, learning the new number may interfere with your ability to remember your old phone number.

Proactive interference

This is where **older** information interferes with the ability to recall **new** information.
E.g. if you've moved your cups to a new cupboard in your kitchen, you might keep going back to the old cupboard by mistake. This interference can be removed, though, if useful information is given as a prompt (a **cue**). (However, this explanation has been criticised as it suggests forgetting is better explained as **retrieval failure**.)

Tulving (1974) Came Up with the **Cue-Dependent Theory**

Tulving reckoned that forgetting is due to a **lack of appropriate retrieval cues**, not due to the original information being lost or interfered with. Tulving proposed that we have more chance of retrieving a memory if the **cue** for recall is **appropriate**.
Cues can either be **state dependent** or **context dependent**:

State dependent cues are **internal**, such as your **mood**.
Context dependent cues are **external**, such as the **surroundings** or **situation**.

Learning snooker is cue-dependent.*

Cue-dependent theory states that we remember more if we are in the same **context** or **state** as we were in when we encoded the information originally. This is known as **cue-dependent learning**.

Godden and Baddeley Studied **Cue-Dependent Forgetting**

Godden and Baddeley provided support for the cue-dependent theory.

Godden and Baddeley (1975) studied cue-dependent forgetting.

Method: Godden and Baddeley used an **independent groups design** (see page 130) in their study. Participants either learned word lists on **land** or **underwater**. They were then given a recall test in the same place as the learning took place or in the opposite setting.

Results: Recall was better when learning and testing took place in the **same setting** rather than in different settings.

Conclusion: This study **supports** Tulving's cue-dependent theory. Forgetting was due to a **lack of context-dependent retrieval cues**.

Evaluation: The study **lacks ecological validity**. You wouldn't normally be asked to learn or recall words underwater. Also, the differences between the two environments were much more **extreme** than they would be in real life. In normal learning and recall situations, the differences are much less extreme — e.g. in a classroom and an exam hall. Some words were **forgotten** even when learning and recall were in the **same context**. This means that cue-dependent theory **doesn't tell the whole story**.

* Here at CGP we value our customers' opinions. How did you rate that joke? Do you love snooker and also humour? Have you been waiting for the two disciplines to be combined ever since the days of Big Break? Or do you feel personally offended that such a terrible joke should be allowed into this otherwise quite good book? Post your comments on our guestbook.

Forgetting

Still just Edexcel...

Tulving and Psotka Investigated Forgetting in LTM

Tulving and Psotka also carried out research into forgetting in LTM. They compared the theories of interference and cue-dependent forgetting. Like Godden and Baddeley, they found support for **cue-dependent theory**.

Tulving and Psotka (1971) — forgetting in LTM

Method:	Tulving and Psotka compared the theories of **interference** and **cue-dependent forgetting**.
	Each participant was given either 1, 2, 3, 4, 5 or 6 lists of 24 words. Each list was divided into 6 categories of 4 words. Words were presented in category order, e.g. all animals, then all trees etc.
	The study used an **independent groups** design (see page 130). After the lists were presented, in one condition participants had to simply recall all the words — **total free recall.**
	In another condition, participants were given all the category names and had to try to recall words from the list – **free cued recall**.
Results:	1) In the **total free recall** condition there was strong evidence of **retroactive** interference. Participants with 1 or 2 lists to remember had higher recall than those with more lists to remember, suggesting the later lists were **interfering** with remembering the earlier lists.
	2) In the **cued recall** test the effects of retroactive interference **disappeared**. It didn't matter how many lists a participant had — recall was still the same for each list (about **70%**).
Conclusion:	The results suggest that interference had not caused forgetting. Because the memories became accessible if a cue was used, it showed that they were available, but just inaccessible. Therefore, the forgetting shown in the total free recall condition was **cue-dependent forgetting**.
Evaluation:	Cue-dependent forgetting is thought to be the best explanation of forgetting, as it has the **strongest** evidence. Most forgetting is seen to be caused by **retrieval failure**. This means that virtually all memory we have is available in LTM — we just need the right cue to be able to access it. However, the evidence is **artificial** (e.g. recalling word lists), lacking meaning in the real world — the study **lacks ecological validity**. Also, it would be difficult, if not impossible, to test whether all information in LTM is accessible and available, and just waiting for the right cue.

Jasper couldn't quite recall what his mother had told him about these things.

Practice Questions

Q1 What is forgetting?

Q2 Name two theories of forgetting in STM.

Q3 Name the two types of interference.

Q4 Outline the cue-dependent theory of forgetting.

Exam Questions

Q1 Outline and evaluate trace decay theory. [4 marks]

Q2 Describe and evaluate Godden and Baddeley's (1975) research into cue-dependent forgetting. [8 marks]

Remember, remember the 5th of October...

These are great pages for playing psychologist. You can easily make up lists of words and then get your friends to read them. Give them an interference task and then test them. What fun. I love psychology experiments. I'm always doing experiments on my friends, though they've gone off the idea a bit since that incident with the misplaced electrode.

Eyewitness Testimony

This topic is for everybody. *If you witness a crime or an accident, you might have to report what you saw, and your version of events could be crucial in prosecuting someone... But your memory isn't as accurate as you might think...*

Eyewitness Testimony Can Be ***Inaccurate*** *and* ***Distorted***

1) **Eyewitness testimony** (EWT) is the **evidence** provided by people who **witnessed** a particular event or crime. It relies on **recall** from memory.
2) EWT includes, for example, **descriptions** of criminals (e.g. hair colour, height) and crime scenes (e.g. time, date, location).
3) Witnesses are often **inaccurate** in their recollection of events and the people involved. As you can probably imagine, this has important implications when it comes to police interviews.
4) Many cognitive psychologists focus on working out what **factors** affect the accuracy of eyewitness testimony, and how accuracy can be **improved** in interviews.

Eyewitness Testimony Can Be Affected by ***Misleading Information***

Loftus and Palmer (1974) investigated how EWT can be **distorted**.
They used **leading questions**, where a certain answer is subtly implied in the question:

Loftus and Palmer (1974) studied eyewitness testimony.

	Loftus and Palmer carried out two experiments in their study.
	Experiment 1:
Method:	Participants were shown a film of a multiple car crash. They were then asked a series of questions including 'How fast do you think the cars were going when they **hit**?' In different conditions, the word 'hit' was replaced with **'smashed'**, **'collided'**, **'bumped'** or **'contacted'**.
Results:	It was seen that participants given the word **'smashed'** estimated the **highest speed** (an average of 41 mph), and those given the word **'contacted'** gave the **lowest** estimate (an average of 32 mph).
	Experiment 2:
Method:	The participants were split into three groups. One group was given the verb 'smashed', another 'hit', and the third, control group wasn't given any indication of the vehicles' speed. A week later, the participants were asked **'Did you see any broken glass?'**.
Results:	Although there was no broken glass in the film, participants were more likely to say that they'd seen broken glass in the **'smashed'** condition than any other.
Conclusion:	**Leading questions** can affect the **accuracy** of people's memories of an event.
Evaluation:	This has implications for questions in **police interviews**. However, this was an artificial experiment — watching a video is not as **emotionally arousing** as a real-life event, which potentially affects recall. In fact, a later study found that participants who thought they'd witnessed a **real** robbery gave a more **accurate** description of the robber. The experimental design might lead to **demand characteristics**, where the results are skewed because of the participants' expectations about the purposes of the experiment. For example, the leading questions might have given participants **clues** about the nature of the experiment (e.g. they could have realised that the experiment was about susceptibility to leading questions), and so participants might have acted accordingly. This would have reduced the **validity** and **reliability** of the experiment.

Loftus and Zanni (1975) also considered **leading questions**. They showed participants a film of a car accident, then asked them either 'Did you see **the** broken headlight?' or 'Did you see **a** broken headlight?' There was no broken headlight, but **7%** of those asked about '**a**' broken headlight claimed they saw one, compared to **17%** in the group asked about '**the**' broken headlight. So, the simple use of the word 'the' is enough to affect the accuracy of people's memories of an event.

Eyewitness Testimony

The *Accuracy* of Eyewitness Testimony is *Affected* by *Many Factors*

If you're doing **AQA A**, you don't need to know about reconstructive memory.

The *Age* of the *Witness* can Affect the *Accuracy of Recall*

Studies have shown that the **age** of the witness can have an effect on the accuracy of eyewitness testimony.

Valentine and Coxon (1997) studied the effect of age on EWT.

Method: 3 groups of participants (children, young adults and elderly people) watched a video of a kidnapping. They were then asked a series of leading and non-leading questions about what they had seen.

Results: Both the elderly people and the children gave more incorrect answers to non-leading questions. Children were misled more by leading questions than adults or the elderly.

Conclusion: Age has an effect on the accuracy of eyewitness testimony.

Evaluation: This has **implications** in law when children or elderly people are questioned. However, the experiment was **artificial** and so wasn't as emotionally arousing as the same situation would have been in real life — the study **lacks external validity**. The study could have seemed like an experiment into how well people remember things from **TV**, which isn't the same as real life.

Anxiety can Affect *Focus*

Psychologists tend to believe that **small increases** in anxiety and arousal may **increase the accuracy** of memory, but **high levels** have a **negative effect** on accuracy. In **violent crimes** (where anxiety and arousal are likely to be high), the witness may focus on **central details** (e.g. a weapon) and neglect other peripheral details.

Loftus (1979) studied weapon focus in EWT.

Method: In a study with an **independent groups** design, participants heard a discussion in a nearby room. In one condition, a man came out of the room with a pen and grease on his hands. In the second condition, the man came out carrying a knife covered in blood. Participants were asked to identify the man from 50 photographs.

Results: Participants in condition 1 were 49% accurate. Only 33% of the participants in condition 2 were correct.

Conclusion: When anxious and aroused, witnesses focus on a weapon at the expense of other details.

Evaluation: The study has **high ecological validity**, as the participants weren't aware that the study was staged. However, this means that there are also **ethical** considerations, as participants could have been very stressed at the sight of the man with the knife.

Reconstructive Memory Can Play a Part in EWT

Reconstructive memory is about filling the gaps in our memories. **Bartlett** believed that when we remember something, we only store **some** elements of the experience. We **reconstruct** events using these elements, filling in the **gaps** in the memory with our own **schemas**, to form **reconstructive memories**. Schemas are **ready-stored opinions** and **expectations** which we use for quick judgements to deal with the world.

Bartlett (1932) demonstrated reconstructive memory.

Method: Participants were shown a short story from a different culture, which therefore contained **unfamiliar** material. Participants were asked to **recall** the story several different times over a number of days.

Results: The recalled stories were always **shorter** than the original. Many parts were recalled from the participants' own cultural perspectives, with certain facts **changed** to fit. For example, 'canoe' was changed to 'boat'. The recalled version soon became very **fixed** over time with only minor variations.

Conclusion: The **meaning** of a story is remembered, but the gaps are filled in with more familiar material to make the story **easier** to remember. This has an effect of **skewing** (shaping) information to make it fit our schemas.

Comment: It is possible that errors occurred from **conscious guessing** rather than participants actually believing that their recalled stories were the same as the original. Later studies have found that if participants were told from the beginning that accurate recall was required, errors dropped significantly.

Eyewitness Testimony

The **Cognitive Interview** was Developed to **Increase Accuracy**

Cognitive psychologists have played a big part in helping to **increase the accuracy** of eyewitness testimony. As you've seen, research shows that the accuracy of eyewitness testimony is affected by many factors. The **cognitive interview technique** was developed by **Geiselman et al (1984)** to try to increase the accuracy of witnesses' recall of events during police questioning.

Here's basically what happens in cognitive interviews:

1) The interviewer tries to make the witness **relaxed** and tailors his/her **language** to suit the witness.
2) The witness recreates the environmental and internal (e.g. mood) **context** of the crime scene.
3) The witness reports absolutely **everything** that they can remember about the crime.
4) The witness is asked to recall details of the crime in **different orders**.
5) The witness is asked to recall the event from various **different perspectives**, e.g. from the eyes of other witnesses.
6) The interviewer avoids any **judgemental** and **personal comments**.

There is **Research** to **Support** the Cognitive Interview

Research has shown that people interviewed with the cognitive interview technique are much more **accurate** in their recall of events. For example:

Geiselman et al (1986) studied the effect of the cognitive interview.

Method: In a staged situation, an intruder carrying a **blue** rucksack entered a classroom and stole a slide projector. Two days later, participants were questioned about the event. The study used an **independent groups** design — participants were either questioned using a standard interview procedure or the cognitive interview technique. Early in the questioning, participants were asked 'Was the guy with the **green** backpack nervous?'. Later in the interview, participants were asked what colour the man's rucksack was.

Results: Participants in the cognitive interview condition were less likely to recall the rucksack as being green than those in the standard interview condition.

Conclusion: The cognitive interview technique **enhances memory recall** and **reduces the effect of leading questions**.

Evaluation: The experiment was conducted as though a real crime had taken place in the classroom — it had **high ecological validity**. The experiment used an **independent groups** design (see page 130). The disadvantage of this is that the participants in the cognitive interview condition could have been naturally less susceptible to leading questions than the other group.

Practice Questions

Q1 What is eyewitness testimony?

Q2 What are leading questions?

Q3 Give two factors that can affect the accuracy of eyewitness testimony.

Exam Questions

Q1 Explain why Loftus' (1974) studies of EWT have been criticised for lacking validity. [4 marks]

Q2 Outline the techniques used in the cognitive interview. [4 marks]

A tall thin man, quite short, with black, fair hair — great fat bloke she was...

Well, now I haven't a clue what I've really experienced in my life. Did that man I saw shoplifting really have stubble, scars, a pierced chin and a ripped leather jacket, or is that just my shoplifter stereotype kicking in? In fact, come to think of it, I couldn't actually tell you whether my granny has a hairy chin or not. I think she does, but then I think all grannies do...

Strategies for Memory Improvement

This topic is only for AQA.
This stuff might actually come in handy when you're revising for your exams. You can't say we never try to help you...

Mnemonics are Internal Memory Strategies

We often avoid having to remember things by making **notes** and **lists**. However, sometimes this isn't possible — say, when you're learning stuff for an **exam**. This is where **mnemonics** come in useful. These use things like **visual imagery** and **associations** to **cue** your recall.

There are Loads of Different Mnemonics

Here are just a few...

Organising Material Makes it Easier to Remember

Research has shown that when we're learning something, we often automatically **organise** the material in a way that makes it easier to remember.

For example, **Jenkins and Russell** (1952) studied the recall of **word lists**. The word lists contained words that were **highly associated** (e.g. knife and fork). They found that participants tended to **group** the associated words together in recall even though they'd been **separated** in the original presentation. So, if 'knife' and 'fork' had been separated by other words in the original list, they'd be recalled together.

Tulving (1962) repeatedly gave his participants a list of words to learn. He changed the **order** that the words were presented in each trial. He found that the **order** of the participants' recall became increasingly **consistent** — they were **organising** and **chunking** the material to be learnt into easily remembered groups. E.g. if the word list contained cat, daisy, sock, giraffe, shoe, scarf, dog and rose, it's likely that no matter what order they were presented in, the words would be grouped together into categories for recall — animals, clothes and flowers.

Some Strategies Use Imagery

Method of Loci

1) It's useful for remembering a **list of words or objects**, e.g. the items on a shopping list.
2) The items to be remembered are associated with **locations** (**loci**) in a **well-known place**, e.g. your house:

- So, for example, say the shopping list contains **milk**, **bread**, **chocolate**, **apples** and **bananas**.
- You'd take a **mental tour** around your house, **visually placing each object** at a **specific place**.
- You could place the bottle of milk at your front door, hang the bread from a coat hook, put the chocolate on a table in the hall, put the apples on the sofa in the living room and, finally, put the bananas in the kitchen sink.
- When you get to the supermarket, all you'd need to do is **mentally repeat the tour** around your house, remembering which items were placed where.

Peg-Word Technique

This is another technique that uses imagery to remember a set of objects or words.
Take the shopping list example again — milk, bread, chocolate, apples and bananas.
First of all, you use a set of peg-words which are **already stored in memory**.

The peg-words rhyme with the numbers — this helps you to remember them.

1) So, for this list of five objects, you'd need five peg-words:

One is a bun	Two is a shoe	Three is a tree	Four is a door	Five is a hive

2) Then, **each item** on the shopping list is **linked to a number**. So, you could imagine a bar of chocolate inside a bun, bananas poking out of a shoe, apples hanging on a tree, and so on...
3) In the supermarket, you'd just need to remember each peg-word and picture the item associated with it.

Strategies for Memory Improvement

The First Letter Mnemonic Helps with Learning Something's Order

The trick here is to use the **first letter** of each word to create a new sentence.
Say you're trying to learn the order of the **planets**:

Mercury, **V**enus, **E**arth, **M**ars, **J**upiter, **S**aturn, **U**ranus, **N**eptune

You could turn this into...

My **V**olkswagen **E**ats **M**ouldy **J**am **S**andwiches **U**ntil **N**oon

(...or something even funnier, cos I'm not that funny).

Narrative Stories Link Words Together

This method involves **linking** together all the items that need remembering. This is done by putting them into a **story**.
So, say the list of words to be learnt is **bicycle**, **duck**, **ice cream**, **tree** and **house** — you could turn this into...

Bob got onto his **bicycle** and rode down to the **duck** pond at the park. He bought an **ice cream** and sat under a **tree** to eat it. After a while, he cycled back to his **house**.

Bower and Clark (1969) studied narrative stories.

Method: The study used an independent groups design — participants were split into two conditions. Each group was given 12 lists, each containing 10 words. In one condition, the participants were advised to come up with stories to link the 10 words together. The second group of participants was a control group — they were simply asked to learn the word lists.

Results: Both groups recalled the lists equally well immediately after learning each one. However, when it came to recalling all 12 lists, recall was much better in the group that had created stories with the words.

Conclusion: Creating narrative stories aids recall from long-term memory.

Evaluation: This links to the **multi-store model** (page 10) — the words are moving into long-term memory because they are being **rehearsed** during the creation of stories. The study used a **control condition**, which meant that the effect of the independent variable (the stories) could be measured. However, it **lacks ecological validity** — learning word lists isn't something that you'd normally do in real life.

Mnemonic Strategies have Limitations

1) The above strategies work best when you're learning a list, or trying to learn the order of something. This isn't much use if it's equally important to **understand** something whilst you're learning it.
2) You've still got to be able to **remember** the mnemonic — e.g. the **peg-words**. If you forget those, you've got **no link** to the stuff you were trying to remember.

Practice Questions

Q1 What are mnemonics?

Q2 What is a peg-word?

Q3 Describe the narrative story strategy.

Exam Questions

Q1 Evaluate two strategies that could be used to improve the recall of a list of words. [6 marks]

Q2 Describe two limitations of mnemonic strategies. [4 marks]

Mnemonics — I can't even say the damn word...

Just make sure that you don't wander around the supermarket claiming that there's a banana in your shoe — or you might have some explaining to do once security have finished strip-searching you. Oh, and don't get too engrossed in trying to turn this whole book into bizarre sentences. It might be amusing, but it won't be so funny when it comes to your exam...

Variations in Cognitive Performance

Just for OCR. That's all.
We're not all equally good at everything — that'd be boring. Cognitive performance can differ between people because of disorders (e.g. autism and Asperger syndrome) and because of individual differences.

People with **Autism** Have Communicative, Social and Linguistic Problems

1) A person with autism will tend to have the following characteristics:
   - Be **withdrawn** and poor at forming relationships.
   - Be less likely to **respond** to environmental stimuli, especially people.
   - Have **communication difficulties**, such as abnormal speech.
   - Have **compulsive** and **ritualistic behaviour**, including an obsession with **sameness**.
2) **Very occasionally**, people with autism are **exceptionally gifted**, in areas such as music, mathematics and art.
3) There are thought to be two types of autism:
   a) The **Asperger** type (**Asperger syndrome**) tend to have normal or above normal intelligence and some neurological problems (e.g. motor difficulties).
   b) The **Kanner** type tend to have **learning disabilities** and additional **problems**, such as epilepsy.

Someone with Autism may **Lack a "Theory of Mind"**

1) A **theory of mind** is our understanding that other people see the world in **different ways** from us.
2) **Very young children** don't have theory of mind — they don't understand that other people think or see things differently.
3) To have a social or emotional **relationship** with another person, it's important to understand their different emotional state or point of view — you need to have a theory of mind.
4) If autistic children don't develop a theory of mind, it may explain why they may find **social contact** difficult.

The chocolate cake was Amy's — she didn't care what anyone else's point of view was.

Baron-Cohen et al (1985) studied theory of mind in autistic children.

Method: Three groups of children were studied — children with autism with an average age of 12 years, children with Down Syndrome with an average age of 11 years, and 'normal' children with an average age of 4 years. The experimenter had two dolls, Sally and Anne. Sally had a basket, Anne a box. Children were asked to name the dolls (the **naming question**). Then Sally was seen to hide a marble in her basket and leave the room. Anne took the marble and put it in her box. Sally returned and the child was asked, 'Where will Sally look for her marble?' (**belief question**). The correct response is to point to the basket, where Sally believes the marble to be. They were also asked, 'Where is the marble really?' (**reality question**) and 'Where was the marble in the beginning?' (**memory question**). Each child was tested twice, with the marble in a different place the second time.

Results: **100%** of the children got the **naming** question, **reality** question and **memory** question correct. In the **belief** question, the children with Down Syndrome scored **86%**, the 'normal' children **85%**, but the children with autism scored **20%**.

Conclusion: The results were not due to **learning disabilities**, as both the autistic children and those with Down Syndrome had similar mental ages. The findings therefore seem to suggest that autistic children have **under-developed theories of mind**. They seem unable to predict or understand the beliefs of others.

Evaluation: Dolls were used throughout the study, causing it to lack **ecological validity**. Also, as **dolls** were used, it may be that children with autism had a more highly developed theory of mind and understood that dolls did not have beliefs. Repeating the study by acting out the scenes with **humans** might show an increase in ability on theory of mind tasks. However, when **Leslie and Frith (1988)** did a similar study with real people and not dolls, the same pattern of results was obtained.

Variations in Cognitive Performance

Asperger Syndrome is a Form of Autism

1) A person with Asperger syndrome will tend to have the following characteristics:
   - difficulties with **social interaction**.
   - **communication difficulties**, e.g. difficulty understanding gestures, facial expressions and tones of voice.
   - **narrow interests**, and a preoccupation with them.
   - **motor difficulties** (clumsiness).

Baron-Cohen followed the traditional dress of his family on his days off.

2) Unlike the Kanner type of autism, people with Asperger syndrome:
   - **don't** have **language difficulties**,
   - **don't** have a **delay in their cognitive development**.

*Some Research has Focused on **Adults** with **Autism** or **Asperger Syndrome***

Although a lot of work is focused on theory of mind in **children**, some studies explore theory of mind in **adults**.

OCR Core Study

Baron-Cohen et al (1997) studied theory of mind in adults.

Method: The researchers tested theory of mind ability in adults with **high-functioning autism** or **Asperger syndrome**. People with autism or Asperger syndrome aren't usually able to reason about what another person thinks. However, people with high-functioning autism or Asperger syndrome can do this. Participants were given photographs of faces with just the eyes showing and were asked to assess the person's **mental state**. Two **control tasks** were also used — recognising a person's gender from a photograph of their eyes, and recognising basic emotions from a whole face. The experiment used a **repeated measures** design (see page 130) — all participants did all the tasks. Two **control groups** were used — **age-matched normal controls** and a group with **Tourette's syndrome**.

Results: It was seen that participants with high-functioning autism or Asperger syndrome were significantly **impaired** at inferring a person's **mental state**. However, they were **unimpaired** on both **control tasks**.

Conclusion: Individuals with high-functioning autism or Asperger syndrome are impaired on a subtle theory of mind test.

Evaluation: The use of **control tasks** and **control groups** allowed the researchers to make comparisons with their results. Although the test is an advanced test of theory of mind, it's still much **simpler** than the demands of interaction and communication in **everyday life**. The stimuli are **still photographs** — the real world is hardly ever still. Gestures and expressions happen very **quickly** with **little time for interpretation**. A better set of stimuli would therefore be **film clips**, which would better represent real life and improve the study's **ecological validity**.

Practice Questions

Q1 Describe the characteristics of someone with autism.

Q2 Name the two types of autism.

Q3 What is a 'theory of mind'?

Q4 Describe the characteristics of someone with Asperger syndrome.

Exam Questions

Q1 Outline the method of Baron-Cohen et al's (1997) study. [4 marks]

Q2 Describe one limitation of Baron-Cohen et al's (1997) study. How could this have been overcome? [4 marks]

One thing's for sure — you're gonna need a theory of psychology...

As you've probably noticed, there's another Core Study on this page for all you OCR types — you can probably expect to get a question on it in your exam. So, make sure you know what the researchers did and what they found out. And just to top it all off, make sure you've got a few points on evaluation up your sleeve to pull out at the appropriate moment.

The Developmental Approach

*OCR and AQA A only. Developmental psychologists focus on how we change and develop throughout our lives. Describing **how** we change isn't enough though — they also try to explain **why** the changes take place. Show-offs.*

*Different **Research Methods** Are Used **Depending** On What's Being Studied*

(There's more general stuff on research methods on pages 126-127, for those of you who can't get enough of 'em...)

Observational Studies Can Be Naturalistic or Controlled

1) **Naturalistic observation** takes place in the child's own environment and none of the variables are manipulated — e.g. a parent might note down their child's behaviour in a diary.

Advantage

Ecological validity — behaviour will be natural because the subject is in a real-life, familiar setting.

Disadvantage

Extraneous variables — there's no control over the variables, so you can't be sure what caused your results.

2) With **controlled observation** the child is observed by a researcher, usually in a laboratory setting. Some of the variables are controlled — e.g. a child might be given a certain toy to play with and observed through a one-way mirror, like in Bandura et al's study (see page 29).

Advantage

Control — the effect of **extraneous variables** is minimised, so you're more likely to be able to establish cause and effect.

Disadvantage

Observer bias — the observer's expectations may affect what they focus on and record, so the reliability of the results might be a problem. Another observer might have come up with very different results.

Correlational Studies Look for Relationships Between Variables

Variables often rise and fall together — e.g. height and weight usually rise together as a child grows. But this doesn't mean that one variable **causes** the other to change — that's pretty important to remember. The data for correlational studies often comes from surveys, questionnaires and interviews.

Advantage

Ethical — you can study variables that would be unethical to manipulate, e.g. whether there's a relationship between smoking during pregnancy and low birthweight.

Disadvantage

Causal relationships — these can't be assumed from a correlation. Results may be caused by a third, unknown variable.

Case Studies Are Detailed Descriptions of One Person

Case studies allow researchers to analyse unusual cases in lots of detail — e.g. Freud's study of **Little Hans** (page 27).

Advantage

Rich data — researchers have the opportunity to study rare phenomena in a lot of detail.

Disadvantage

Generalisation — only using a single case makes generalising the results extremely difficult.

Interviews Are like Conversations

1) **Clinical interviews** are used loads in developmental psychology. They're **semi-structured**, meaning that the researcher asks some specific questions, but also lets the participant ramble on about stuff.
2) Participants could be children, or their carers, teachers or parents.
3) Face-to-face interviews can include **open-ended** (non-specific) or **fixed** (specific) questions.

Advantage

Rich data — especially from open-ended questions.

Disadvantage

Participants — children can have implicit knowledge but be unable to verbalise it, so their skills can be underestimated.

The Developmental Approach

Experiments *Can Have a* ***Longitudinal*** *or* ***Cross-Sectional Design***

Two main kinds of experimental design are used to work out how behaviour changes with age — **longitudinal** and **cross-sectional**. These are used **alongside** the **research method**.

1) A **longitudinal design** tests the **same people** repeatedly as they get older and wrinklier.
2) This means you can plot the **group average** as a function of age. It also allows you to look at the development of **individuals** within the group.
3) Researchers can then look at whether the data shows a **gradual change**, or a more sudden shift that suggests **stage-like development**.
4) Longitudinal designs can be **retrospective**. This involves looking back over a period of time — e.g. looking at a child's medical history.

Advantage — you get detailed data about the same people, and individual differences are taken into account.

Disadvantage — studying the development of the same people can take years, so it's time-consuming and costly.

1) A **cross-sectional design** tests different people of **different ages**. For example, if you wanted to look at how vocabulary increases with age, you could measure the vocabulary of children in different year groups.
2) Their performance is then **averaged** over different individuals at each age.

Advantage — they provide a quick estimate of developmental changes, and are much less time-consuming than a longitudinal design.

Disadvantage — they don't take individual differences into account. Different people are measured at each age, so you can't be sure they all developed in the same way.

Researchers *Have to Think About* ***Ethics***

Psychologists have to be extra careful when they're conducting research with children.

See pages 136-137 for more about ethics in general.

1) Under-16s might not understand the implications of participating in a study, so researchers have to get **informed consent** from their parents or guardians.
2) It's important that researchers get the **power balance** right because children generally view adults as more powerful than them. Extra care has to be taken to inform children of their rights — e.g. the right to **withdraw**.
3) Researchers need to make sure that a study won't cause the participants physical or psychological **harm**. They have to use the **least stressful** procedure possible, and **abandon** the study if the child seems distressed.

Animal studies have provided **valuable information** for developmental research. But there's debate about whether they're ethical or not.

Advantage — Some **research designs** couldn't have been conducted on humans ethically — e.g. Harlow's study of attachment, where young monkeys were separated from their mothers (see page 30).

Disadvantages — Some see it as **unethical** to inflict suffering on animals, especially when they can't give consent. Animals and humans are different, so you can't **generalise** results from one species to the other.

Practice Questions

Q1 Give one advantage of correlational studies.

Q2 Give one disadvantage of longitudinal designs.

Q3 What ethical considerations are important when children are involved in a study?

Exam Question

Q1 A researcher conducts a study to find out how children in different stages of development play with a particular toy.

a) Identify a research method and an experimental design that could be used for this study. [2 marks]

b) Evaluate the experimental design you identified in part a). [4 marks]

*I once did an experiment on my luggage...**

Basically there are loads of different ways to test your theory, so all you need to do is pick the one that best fits whatever you're studying. Or you could just shut your eyes, point at the page, and see what comes up. A word of advice though — if you end up trying to do clinical interviews on babies, then maybe have a rethink. Or try monkeys instead...

* It was a case study.

Theories of Child Development

OCR only. *Things are going to get theory-tastic in this section, so strap yourself in and prepare for take-off...*

Piaget's Theory is the Most *Well Known* Theory of *Cognitive Development*

A child's mental abilities and skills develop with time — things like paying attention, learning, thinking and remembering. But as with so much in psychology, there are loads of theories to explain how this happens.

Piaget suggested four major stages of cognitive development

1. The **sensorimotor stage** (birth to 2 years) — At first, a child only performs simple **reflex** activities such as sucking. Gradually, through repetition, the child learns more complex routines. After about 8 months, the child has **object permanence** — it realises that objects continue to exist even when it can't see them. At about 18 months, the child shows **representational thought** — it searches for missing objects (showing that it can think about things that it can't see), and shows the beginnings of language.
2. The **pre-operational stage** (2 to 7 years) — The child starts **constructing** and **using** mental symbols (e.g. language) to think about **situations**, **objects** and **events**. However, it can't **conserve** — it can't understand that the properties of something don't change if its appearance changes (e.g. that there's still the same amount of liquid even if it's poured into a taller glass). Piaget thought that children at this stage hadn't yet acquired the ability to **think logically**, hence this is the **pre-**operational stage. Piaget divided the pre-operational stage into:
   a) The **pre-conceptual period** (2 to 4 years) — The child shows **animism** (assigning qualities of living things to non-living things), **transductive reasoning** (concentrating only on one aspect to work something out, e.g. if a car has wheels, and a random thing has wheels, then that thing must be a car) and **egocentrism** (only viewing the world from their own perspective).
   b) The **intuitive period** (4 to 7 years) — The child becomes **less egocentric** and better at classifying objects due to their perceptual attributes, e.g. size, colour.
3. The **concrete operational stage** (7 to 11 years) — The child learns **new ways of thinking** about **new objects**, **events** and **situations**. It can **conserve** and think **logically**, but only about **real** situations.
4. The **formal operational stage** (11 years and up) — The child is now able to think about **abstract** ideas (e.g. 'justice'). It can also think about **hypothetical** events.

Samuel and Bryant tested Piaget's theory of conservation

In Piaget's standard conservation task, children are shown two rows of counters, each with the same number, and asked if each row contains the same amount of counters. Then one row is spread out, and they're asked the question again. Samuel and Bryant investigated whether younger children fail Piaget's conservation task because they think that if a question's asked twice, then two different answers are required.

OCR Core Study

Samuel and Bryant (1984) varied conservation tasks.

Method: Samuel and Bryant carried out a **laboratory experiment** with an **independent groups** design. 252 children aged between 5 and 8½ years were split into four groups according to their age. Each group was then divided into 3 subgroups:
a) The **standard group** — standard conservation task using counters. Two questions.
b) The **one judgement** task — only one question was asked, after the counters were moved.
c) The **fixed array control** — they only saw the display **after** it had been changed.

Results: They found that younger children did better in the **one judgement** condition than the standard condition, but **older children** always did better overall.

Conclusion: The study supports Samuel and Bryant's argument that two questions may confuse children. But, it still shows that conservation improves with age, so it doesn't disprove Piaget.

Evaluation: This was a **laboratory experiment** so there was good **control** of the variables. However, lab experiments also lack **ecological validity** — the participants were not in a natural situation, so the results can't be **generalised** to real life. It's also possible that the results were affected by a third variable — e.g. younger children may have performed worse because they were more **intimidated** by the experimental situation.

Theories of Child Development

Freud (1909) Talked About '*Psychosexual Development*'

Freud claimed that a lot of our development is determined by unconscious forces (things in your mind that you're not aware of). The three main parts of the personality are the **id**, the **ego** and the **superego**:

1) The **id** is the basic animal part of the personality that contains our innate, aggressive and sexual instincts. It wants to be satisfied by whatever means possible, and obeys the **pleasure principle**.
2) The **ego** is the conscious, rational mind. It negotiates between the id and the superego to work out if you can have what you want — it works on the **reality principle**.
3) The **superego** is your conscience. It's the moral part of the personality and includes ideas about how to behave that were learnt from your parents.

The ego and the superego develop as the child goes through **five stages** of **psychosexual development** — the **oral**, **anal**, **phallic**, **latent**, and **genital** stages. Is anyone starting to think he was a bit nuts...?

Comments on Freud's theory of development:

1) Freud's theory places emphasis on how experiences in early childhood can affect later development. This has formed the basis for lots of other important theories — e.g. Bowlby's theory of attachment (page 31).
2) Because they're based on the **unconscious mind**, Freud's theories are **unfalsifiable** (can't be **proved** wrong).
3) The theory is based on case studies of people in 'distress', so the findings can't be **generalised** to everyone else.
4) The unscientific research methods mean it's not possible to establish **cause and effect**.

Freud (1909) — The case study of Little Hans

OCR Core Study

Method: Freud carried out a **case study** of a child called Hans who had a phobia of horses. Hans was observed by his father, who made notes of Hans's dreams and stuff he said, and then relayed his findings to Freud for analysis.

Results: Hans was afraid of horses because he thought they might bite him or fall on him. During the study he developed an interest in his 'widdler'. His mum had told him not to play with it or she'd cut it off. Hans told his dad about a dream where he was married to his mum and his dad was now his grandfather.

Conclusion: Freud's interpretation of these findings was that Hans had reached the **phallic stage** of development and showed evidence of the **Oedipus complex** — he wanted to have an exclusive relationship with his mother and was jealous of his father. Hans had sexual feelings for his mother, shown partly by his dream of marrying her. The horse symbolised Hans's father because, to him, they both had big penises. His fear of horses is an example of **displacement** — a **defence mechanism** that protected him from his real fear of his father. Hans suffered from **castration anxiety**. He was afraid that he would be castrated by his father if he found out about his feelings for his mother. This was symbolised by Hans's fear that a horse would bite him.

Evaluation: This was a **case study**, meaning that it provided lots of detailed data about the subject. The findings provided evidence to support Freud's theories. However, the results were based entirely on observation and interpretation. This means they could have easily been caused by a third variable (e.g. Hans's castration anxiety might have come from his mother threatening to cut his penis off...). Also, before the study Hans had been frightened by a horse falling down in the street, which could explain his fear of them. Freud analysed information from Hans's father, so the results could be **biased**. As this was a study of one person, the results can't be **generalised**.

Practice Questions

Q1 Describe the main characteristics of children's thinking at the pre-operational stage.

Q2 What is conservation?

Q3 What are Freud's five stages of psychosexual development?

Exam Questions

Q1 Outline Samuel and Bryant's (1984) method for the study of conservation. [6 marks]

Q2 Compare and contrast two theories of development. [12 marks]

Stages of development — crying, shouting, sulking, drinking...

Personally, I think Freud was a nutter. A funny thing about him is that a lot of his ideas came from studying himself. You'd think he'd be a bit embarrassed to admit to all the mother-fancying and general obsession with genitals...

The Effects of Early Childhood Experience

This is for OCR only. *Behaviourists think that they can explain how children learn and develop by conditioning. No, not by using a 2-in-1 to make their hair soft and sleek — a different type of conditioning. Read on...*

The **Behaviourist** Approach to Development is Pretty Scientific

Behaviourism developed in early 1900s America and remained influential during most of the century. It was pioneered by **John Watson** who proposed the three main assumptions that the approach is based on:

1) Virtually all behaviour is **learnt** from the environment. The only exceptions are inborn reflexes and instincts, e.g. the reflex to blink when you get dirt in your eye.
2) **Both humans** and **animals** learn behaviour using the same principles of learning.
3) For psychology to be **scientific** we should only study **observable behaviour** which can be analysed in quantitative terms, e.g. how many times a person does something. The 'mind' can't be seen or measured, so it can't be scientifically studied.

Following these assumptions, behaviourists would usually do **experiments on animals** to study how they learn. They'd then **generalise** these results to us **humans** to explain how we learn.

Behaviourists Proposed **Two Types** of Conditioning:

Classical Conditioning

In early 1900s Russia, **Ivan Pavlov** was studying how dogs' salivation helps them to digest food, when he noticed that they would sometimes salivate before they got food. Instead of just thinking they were hungry, he realised they had **associated** food with another stimulus, such as the sound of the door opening. He later made the dogs associate food with bells, lights and other abstract stimuli. This process of learning can be applied to human development:

Pavlov's dogs got pretty hungry waiting for the food to arrive.

1) Having needs dealt with and gaining comfort naturally makes a baby happy — it hasn't **learnt** to be happy, it's an **inborn reflex**.

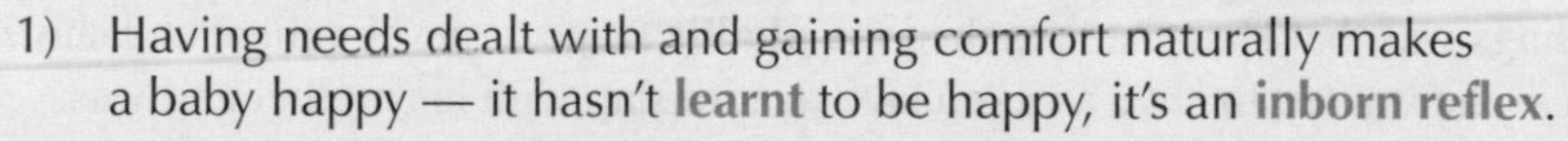

2) So, comfort is an **unconditioned stimulus (UCS)** that produces happiness — an **unconditioned response (UCR)**.
3) The baby's mother will talk to it while she feeds it and changes its nappy, etc. So, the baby hears its mother's voice every time it's made comfortable and happy.
4) The sound of its mother's voice is paired with having needs met and being comfortable **(UCS)**, so the mother's voice becomes the **conditioned stimulus (CS)**.
5) Eventually the sound of the mother's voice alone will make the baby feel happy, even when it isn't paired with having its needs met. The **CS** (voice) now causes a **conditioned response (CR)** — the baby has **learnt** to be pleased at the sound of its mother's voice.

Operant Conditioning

Classical conditioning only applies to reflexive responses. **B.F. Skinner** studied how animals can learn from the **consequences of their actions**. Consequences can be classified as follows:

1) **Positive reinforcement**. This is when something 'desirable' is obtained in response to doing something e.g. after murmuring, the baby gets attention (the positive reinforcer). The baby is likely to murmur again.
2) **Negative reinforcement**. This is when something 'undesirable' (the negative reinforcer) is removed when something happens, e.g. after crying, a dirty nappy is removed. The child is likely to cry the next time the nappy is filled with digested baby food.
3) **Punishment**. This is when something 'undesirable' (the 'punisher') is received after doing something, e.g. after picking up something dangerous, the child is shouted at. The child is less likely to do it again.

There's a lot of evidence to show that animals and humans can learn by conditioning (see pages 112-113) but conditioning can't explain all human behaviour. We also learn by observation, as shown by **social learning theory**.

The Effects of Early Childhood Experience

Social Learning Theory (SLT) Accepts that Cognitive Processes are Important

SLT developed in the 1950s. It agrees with behaviourism that people can learn by conditioning but also claims that they learn a lot by **observation** and **imitation** of role models. This involves **cognitive processes**. People must focus their **attention** on the role model, **perceive** what they do and **remember** it in order to learn how to do it too.
A study by Bandura shows how children imitate adult role models.

OCR Core Study

Bandura et al (1961) — imitation of aggressive models

Method:	36 girls and 36 boys with a mean age of 52 months took part in the study. The study had a **matched participants design** (children were matched on ratings of aggressive behaviour shown at their nursery school) and had **three conditions**. In the first condition, children observed **aggressive adult models** playing with a Bobo doll — e.g. hitting it with a mallet. In the second, children observed **non-aggressive models** playing with other toys and ignoring the Bobo doll. The third condition was a **control condition** in which children had no exposure to the models. The children's behaviour was then observed for 20 minutes in a room containing aggressive toys (e.g. a Bobo doll, a mallet) and non aggressive toys (e.g. a tea set, crayons).
Results:	Children exposed to aggressive models imitated a lot of their aggressive behaviour. Children in the non-aggressive and control conditions showed barely any aggressive behaviour. Aggressive behaviour was slightly higher in the control condition than in the non-aggressive condition.
Conclusion:	Aggressive behaviour is learned through **imitation** of others behaving aggressively.
Evaluation:	This study provides evidence for **social learning theory**. There was **strict control** of the variables, meaning that the results are likely to be **reliable** and the study can be **replicated**. However, it has **low ecological validity** because the participants weren't in a natural situation. It's also difficult to **generalise** the results because a limited sample was studied — the children were all from the same school. The study encouraged aggression in children — this could be an **ethical problem**.

*Some **Comments** on SLT, Behaviourism and Bandura's Research:*

See page 114 for extra info on SLT.

1) Bandura's study shows that **reinforcement is not needed for learning**. We can learn just by **observing**. However, the reinforcement the model is seen to receive may have an effect — for example, if you see a model punished for an action, you're unlikely to copy it (see page 114).
2) Bobo dolls are designed for 'aggressive' play — you're **supposed** to hit them. As well as this, the children were shown how to play with the doll, so this study might actually be a test of **obedience** (see page 78) rather than observational learning.
3) Behaviourism and SLT emphasise learning as the cause of behaviour and so are on the '**nurture**' side of the **nature-nurture debate**. This has implications for society. For example, children may imitate aggression from media role models. However, potential **genetic influences** are not taken into account.

Practice Questions

Q1 What are the main assumptions of the behaviourist approach?
Q2 What is the difference between negative reinforcement and punishment?
Q3 Why do Bandura's results support SLT?
Q4 Identify the dependent and independent variables in Bandura's study.

Exam Questions

Q1 Outline two types of conditioning. [8 marks]

Q2 Evaluate Bandura's (1961) study of observational learning. [6 marks]

Walk away from the Bobo doll with your mallet in the air...

These psychologists are an interesting lot. Pavlov rang a bell over and over again to get a dog to dribble and Bandura and his gang beat up toys in front of children — whatever floats your boat I guess. Anyway, what you need to do is remember what they did — and more importantly what conclusions they drew from their results.

Explanations of Attachment

This is for AQA A only. *These pages deal with the different psychological explanations for how and why attachments develop between infants and their carers. Simple eh — you'd think, but this is psychology...*

Attachment is a Strong Emotional Bond

Attachment is a close emotional relationship between infants and their caregivers.
'Attached' infants will show a desire to be **close** to their **primary caregiver** (usually their biological mother).
They'll show **distress** when they're **separated**, and **pleasure** when they're **reunited**.

Learning Theory Links Attachment to Pleasure

This is also known as **behaviourist theory**, and focuses on the baby wanting its needs fulfilled.
Conditioning is given as an explanation for how attachments form.

Classical Conditioning. This is about learning **associations** between different things in our environment. Getting food naturally gives the baby **pleasure**. The baby's desire for food is fulfilled whenever its mother is around to feed it. So an **association is formed between mother and food**. So, whenever its mother is around, the baby will feel pleasure — i.e. 'attachment'.

Operant Conditioning. **Dollard and Miller (1950)** claimed that babies feel discomfort when they're hungry and so have a desire to get food to **remove the discomfort**. They find that if they cry, their mother will come and feed them — so the discomfort is removed (this is '**negative reinforcement**'). An easy life. The mother is therefore associated with food and the baby will want to be close to her. This produces 'attachment behaviour' (distress when separated from the mother, etc.).

Harlow Showed That Comfort is Important in Attachment

Just because babies spend most of their time either eating or sleeping, it doesn't mean they automatically attach to the person who feeds them. **Schaffer and Emerson (1964)** found that many babies didn't have strong attachments with their mother, even though she fed them. **Good quality interaction with the baby seemed more important** — the baby will attach to whoever is the most sensitive and loving. This is also shown in **Harlow's** study, **'Love in Infant Monkeys'**.

	Harlow (1959) showed the need for 'contact comfort'.
Method:	Harlow aimed to find out whether baby monkeys would prefer a source of **food** or a source of **comfort** and **protection** as an attachment figure. In **laboratory experiments** rhesus monkeys were raised in isolation. They had two 'surrogate' mothers. One was made of wire mesh and contained a feeding bottle, the other was made of cloth but didn't contain a feeding bottle.
Results:	The monkeys spent most of their time clinging to the cloth surrogate and only used the wire surrogate to feed. The cloth surrogate seemed to give them **comfort** in new situations. When the monkeys grew up they showed signs of **social** and **emotional disturbance**. The females were bad mothers who were often violent towards their offspring.
Conclusion:	Infant monkeys formed more of an attachment with a figure that provided comfort and protection. Growing up in isolation affected their development.
Evaluation:	This was a **laboratory experiment**, so there was strict control of the variables. This means that it's unlikely the results were affected by an unknown variable. The findings of this study were **applied to real life**. They led to a change in hospital procedure — human babies in incubators are now given soft blankets. However, it can be argued that you can't **generalise** the results of this study to human beings, because humans and monkeys are **qualitatively different**. There were also **ethical problems** with this study — the monkeys were put in a stressful situation, and later they showed signs of being psychologically damaged by the experiment. Monkeys are social animals, so it was unfair to keep them in isolation. The fact that they were in isolation also means that the study lacked **ecological validity** — the monkeys weren't in their natural environment, so the results can't be reliably applied to real life. Laboratory experiments can usually be **replicated**, but ethical guidelines now in place mean that you couldn't repeat this study today to see whether you'd get the same results.

Mummy?

Explanations of Attachment

We're Not Done Yet — There's the *Ethological Approach*...

Lorenz wasn't an experienced father, but his geese loved him.

1) Ethology is the study of animals in their natural environment. **Konrad Lorenz (1935)** found that geese automatically 'attach' to the first moving thing they see after hatching, and follow it everywhere (I bet this gets quite annoying). This is called **imprinting**.
2) Normally the geese would imprint onto their mother, but Lorenz managed to get them to attach to him because he was the first thing they saw.
3) Imprinting seems to occur during a **'critical period'** — in this case, the first few hours after hatching. It's a **fast, automatic** process.
4) It's unlikely to occur in humans. Our attachments take a **longer** time to develop and we don't automatically attach to particular things — quality care seems more important in human attachment formation.

...and *John Bowlby's Evolutionary* Theory...

Bowlby (1951) argued that something like imprinting occurs in humans. He developed several main claims.

1) We have **evolved** a biological need to attach to our main caregiver — usually our biological mother. Having one special attachment is called **monotropy**. Forming this attachment has survival value as staying close to the mother ensures food and protection.
2) A strong attachment provides a **'safe base'**, giving us confidence to explore our environment.
3) It also gives us a **'template'** for all future relationships — we learn to trust and care for others.
4) The first 3 years of life are the **critical period** for this attachment to develop — otherwise it might never do so.
5) If the attachment doesn't develop (e.g. because of separation or death), or if it's broken, it might seriously damage the child's social and emotional development (see pages 34-35).

Comments on Bowlby's theory:

1) There is some **evidence** for his claims. **Harlow's** study supports the idea that we have evolved a need to attach. It also suggests that social and emotional development might be damaged if an attachment isn't formed. See pages 34 and 35 for more studies that support Bowlby's theory.
2) **Schaffer and Emerson (1964)** provided evidence against Bowlby's claims about monotropy. They found that many children form **multiple attachments**, and may not attach to their mother.
3) **Harlow's** study of monkeys raised in isolation also goes against the idea of **monotropy**. Other monkeys who didn't have a mother, but who grew up together, didn't show signs of social and emotional disturbance in later life. They didn't have a primary caregiver, but seemed to attach to each other instead.
4) There is **mixed evidence** for claims of a **critical period** for attachments to develop (pages 36-37).
5) The effect of attachment not developing, or being broken, may not be as bad as Bowlby claimed (pages 34-37).

Practice Questions

Q1 What is 'attachment'?

Q2 What is meant by 'imprinting'?

Q3 What is 'monotropy'?

Exam Question

Q1 a) Outline one theory of attachment. [6 marks]

b) Explain two criticisms of the theory outlined in part a). [4 marks]

Monkey lovin'...

Hanging around a pond waiting for the geese to hatch always seems like a nice idea at the time. We'd all love to have some instant gosling children following us round. But a word of warning — it's not quite so much fun when you're having to regurgitate worms into their beaks at four in the morning. And then they break your arm with their big wings. Or is that swans...

Types of Attachment

This bit's just for AQA A. *As you know, an 'attachment' is a strong, emotional bond between two people. Psychologists are interested in how our first attachments form and what influences them.*

Attachments Can Be Secure or Insecure

Secure Attachments

In a secure attachment, there's a **strong bond** between the child and its caregiver. If they're separated, the infant becomes **distressed**. However, when they're reunited, the child is **easily comforted** by the caregiver. The majority of attachments are of this type. Secure attachments are associated with a healthy cognitive and emotional development.

Insecure Attachments

Attachments can also be insecure. Here, the bond between child and caregiver is **weaker**. Ainsworth et al came up with **two types** of insecure attachment:

Insecure-avoidant

If they're separated from their caregiver, the child **doesn't** become particularly distressed, and can usually be comforted by a **stranger**. This type of insecure attachment is shown by children who generally **avoid** social interaction and intimacy with others.

Insecure-resistant

The child is often **uneasy** around their caregiver, but becomes **upset** if they're separated. Comfort can't be given by strangers, and it's also often **resisted** from the caregiver. Children who show this style of attachment both **accept** and **reject** social interaction and intimacy.

There are many ways to form a strong attachment with your child.

An Infant's **Reaction** in a **Strange Situation** Shows if It's **Securely** Attached

Ainsworth came up with the concept of the **strange situation**. She used it to assess how children react under conditions of **stress** (by separation from the caregiver and the presence of a stranger) and also to **new situations**.

Ainsworth et al (1978) — The Strange Situation

Method: In a **controlled observation**, 12-18 month old infants were left in a room with their mother. Eight different scenarios occurred, including being approached by a stranger, the infant being left alone, the mother returning, etc. The infant's reactions were constantly observed.

Results: About 15% of infants were **'insecure-avoidant' (type A)** — they ignored their mother and didn't mind if she left. A stranger could comfort them.
About 70% were **'securely attached' (type B)** — content with their mother, upset when she left, happy when she returned and avoided strangers.
About 15% were **'insecure-resistant' (type C)** — uneasy around their mother and upset if she left. They resisted strangers and were also hard to comfort when their mother returned.

Conclusion: Infants showing different reactions to their carers have different types of attachment.

Evaluation: The research method used allowed control of the variables, making the results reliable. However, the laboratory-type situation made the study artificial, reducing the ecological validity. The parents may have changed their behaviour, as they knew that they were being observed. This could have had an effect on the children's behaviour. Also, the new situation in the experiment may have had an effect on the children's behaviour — the study might not accurately represent their behaviour in real life. Another problem is that the mother may not have been the child's **main attachment figure**.

Types of Attachment

*Similar Studies Have Taken Place in **Different Cultures***

Ainsworth et al's (1978) findings have been shown many times in the **USA**, but it wasn't then known whether they could be applied to other **cultures**. **Cross-cultural studies** have since taken place:

Van Ijzendoorn and Kroonenberg (1988) — cross-cultural studies

Method:	Van Ijzendoorn and Kroonenberg carried out a meta-analysis (page 92) of 32 studies of 'the strange situation' in different countries (e.g. Japan, Britain, Sweden, etc.). They were analysed to find any overall patterns.
Results:	The percentages of children classified as secure or insecure were very **similar** across the countries tested. Secure attachments were the most common type of attachment in the countries studied. Some differences were found in the distribution of insecure attachments. In Western cultures, it was seen that the dominant type of insecure attachment was avoidant. However, in non-Western cultures, the dominant type was resistant.
Conclusion:	There are cross-cultural similarities in raising children, producing common reactions to the 'strange situation'.
Evaluation:	Children are brought up in different ways in different cultures. This might result in different types of attachment in different cultures. Because of this, the 'strange situation' might not be a suitable method for studying cross-cultural attachment. Using a **different type** of study may have revealed different patterns or types of attachment in different cultures. Also, the study assumes that different **countries** are the same thing as different **cultures**. One problem with the research method is that meta-analyses can **hide** individual results that show an unusual trend.

*There are Important **Findings** from Strange Situation Research*

1) **Some cultural differences are found. Grossman et al (1985)** claimed that more 'avoidant' infants may be found in Germany because of the value Germans put on independence — so 'avoidance' is seen as a good thing.
2) **The causes of different attachment types are debatable.**
   The causes may be the sensitivity of their carers and/or their inborn temperament.
3) **The strange situation experiment doesn't show a characteristic of the child.** The experiment only shows the child's relationship with a specific person, so they might react differently with different carers, or later in life.

Attachment type may influence later behaviours. Securely attached children may be more confident in school and form strong, trusting adult relationships. 'Avoidant' children may have behaviour problems in school and find it hard to form close, trusting adult relationships. 'Resistant' children may be insecure and attention-seeking in school and, as adults, their strong feelings of dependency may be stressful for partners.

Practice Questions

Q1 What is a secure attachment?

Q2 What are the two types of insecure attachment?

Q3 Who came up with the 'strange situation'?

Q4 What have cross-cultural studies shown about attachments?

Exam Questions

Q1 Outline and evaluate Ainsworth's (1978) 'strange situation' study. [12 marks]

Q2 Explain two disadvantages of using the 'stange situation' in a study of attachment. [4 marks]

Try to get all these ideas firmly attached to the inside of your head...

Next time you're in trouble at school and your parents are called in to 'discuss your behaviour', try sobbing gently under your breath, 'I think it's all my anxious-resistant attachment formation, it's left me insecure and needy of attention'. It's a desperate attempt, but it might just make your parents feel bad enough to let you off. This holds no guarantees though...

Disruption of Attachment

Just for AQA A. *The attachments we form are pretty important — there can be serious consequences if they're broken...*

Attachment Can be Disrupted by **Separation** or **Deprivation**

Separation is where a child is away from a **caregiver** they're attached to (such as their mother). The term's used when it's a **relatively short** time, just hours or days — not a longer or permanent separation.

Deprivation describes the loss of something that is **wanted or needed**. So, 'maternal deprivation' is the loss of the mother (or other attachment figure). A more **long-term** or even **permanent** loss is implied.

Separation Can Have **Major Effects**

According to several studies, infants or children who have been separated may react through the following stages. The stages are referred to as the **'PDD model' — Protest, Despair, Detachment**:

1) **Protest** — During the first few hours, the child will **protest** a lot at being **separated** from its mother (or other attachment figure), by crying, panicking, calling for its mother, etc.

2) **Despair** — After a day or two, the child will start to lose interest in its surroundings, becoming more and more **withdrawn**, with occasional crying. They may also eat and sleep less.

3) **Detachment** — After a few days, the child will start to become more **alert** and interested again in its surroundings. It will cry less and may seem to have **'recovered'** from its bad reaction to the separation. However, its previous attachment with its carer may now be permanently **damaged** — the trust and security may be lost.

Robertson and Robertson (1968) — evidence for the PDD model

Method:	In a naturalistic observation, several children who experienced short separations from their carers were observed and filmed. For example, a boy called John aged around 18 months stayed in a residential nursery for nine days while his mother had another baby.
Results:	John showed the signs of passing through **'protest'** for the first day or two. Then he showed **despair** — he tried to get attention from the nurses but they were busy with other children so he 'gave up' trying. Then he showed **detachment** — he was more active and content. However, when his mother came to collect him, he was reluctant to be affectionate.
Conclusion:	The short-term separation had very **bad effects** on John, including possible **permanent damage** to his attachment with his mother.
Evaluation:	John's reaction might not have been due to separation — it could have been down to his new environment or the fact that he was getting much less attention than he was used to. There will have been little control of **variables**, and it would be difficult to replicate each **individual situation**. However, as the study took place in a natural setting, the results will have **ecological validity** but will be less **reliable**.

Some comments on the PDD model include:

1) These findings suggest that **separating a child from its carers should be avoided** whenever possible. This has important implications for childcare practice, e.g. children should be allowed to visit, or remain with, their mothers during a stay in hospital. Sounds fair enough to me.
2) **Many factors** influence how a child reacts to a separation. These include age (older children will cope better), the quality of the care received during the separation, the individual temperament of the child and how often it has experienced separations. So, **separations do not necessarily produce the PDD effects**. They may even be good for the child (see pages 38-39).
3) Studies have shown that there's a difference between children placed in an **institutionalised setting** and those in **foster care**. It would seem that as long as children are still receiving **emotional support**, they manage to cope with the separation.

Disruption of Attachment

*John Bowlby (1953) Studied Longer-Term Maternal **Deprivation***

Even if short-term separation may not necessarily be bad for a child, **John Bowlby** argued that long-term **deprivation** from an attachment figure could be harmful. He produced his **maternal deprivation hypothesis**:

1) Deprivation from the main carer during the **critical period** (the first 3-5 years), will have harmful effects on a child's emotional, social, intellectual and even physical development. Not so good.
2) Long-term effects of deprivation may include **separation anxiety** (the fear of another separation from the carer). This may lead to problem behaviour, e.g. being very clingy, and avoiding going to school. Future relationships may be affected by this emotional insecurity. Bowlby's research showed evidence for this.

	Bowlby (1944) — The 44 Juvenile Thieves
Method:	**Case studies** were completed on the backgrounds of 44 adolescents who had been referred to the clinic where Bowlby worked because they'd been stealing. There was a **control group** of 44 'emotionally disturbed' adolescents who didn't steal.
Results:	17 of the thieves had experienced frequent separations from their mothers before the age of two, compared with 2 in the control group. 14 of the thieves were diagnosed as 'affectionless psychopaths' (they didn't care about how their actions affected others). 12 of these 14 had experienced separation from their mothers.
Conclusion:	Deprivation of the child from its main carer early in life can have very **harmful long-term consequences**.
Evaluation:	The results indicate a link between deprivation and criminal behaviour. However, it can't be said that one **causes** the other. There may be **other factors** that caused the criminal behaviour. Although case studies provide a lot of **detailed information**, the study relied on **retrospective data**, which may be unreliable.

This study, and others on institutionalisation and hospitalisation, suggested that long-term effects of separation included:

1) **Affectionless psychopathy** (as seen in the 44 Juvenile Thieves study).
2) **Anaclitic depression** — involving appetite loss, sleeplessness and impaired social and intellectual development.
3) **Deprivation dwarfism** — infants are physically underdeveloped due to emotional deprivation.

Some comments on Bowlby's maternal deprivation hypothesis:

1) Other evidence supports Bowlby's claims. **Goldfarb (1943)** found that orphanage children who were socially and maternally deprived were later less intellectually and socially developed.
2) The evidence has **criticisms**: Bowlby linked the thieves' behaviour to maternal deprivation, but **other things were not considered**, e.g. whether the poverty they grew up in led them to steal. The children in Goldfarb's study may have been most harmed by the **social deprivation** in the orphanage rather than the maternal deprivation.

Even when deprivation has harmful effects, these may be reversed with appropriate, **quality care**. For example, **Skeels and Dye (1939)** found that children who had been socially deprived (in an orphanage) during their first two years of life quickly improved their IQ scores if they were transferred to a school where they got one-to-one care.

Practice Questions

Q1 What is the PDD model?

Q2 What does Bowlby's maternal deprivation hypothesis propose?

Exam Questions

Q1 Evaluate one study into the effects of separation. [4 marks]

Q2 Outline research into the long-term effects of disruption of attachment. [8 marks]

The PDD model can also be applied as a reaction to excessive study...

So, if your mum leaves you alone for a while when you're little you might well become a bank robber — sounds like a pretty poor excuse to me, but there you go. It's certainly interesting stuff. Even if you don't agree, the bottom line is you have to learn the theories, who came up with them, and what their pros and cons are — it's a world of pain.

Failure to Form Attachments — Privation

***These pages are just for AQA A. Maternal privation** is when a child has **never** had an attachment to its mother or another caregiver. (In contrast to deprivation where an attachment has formed but is broken.)*

*Privation Means **Never** Forming a **Bond** with a **Caregiver***

Rutter (1981) claimed that the effects of **maternal privation** are more likely to be **serious** than the effects of **maternal deprivation**. Evidence for this comes from **case studies** of children who have suffered difficult conditions or cruel treatment. Some nasty stuff coming up...

*Some **Case Studies** of **Privation** Include:*

Curtiss (1977) — The Case of Genie

This reported the case of a girl who suffered **extreme cruelty** from her parents, and never formed any attachments. Her father kept her strapped to a high chair with a potty in the seat for most of her childhood. She was beaten if she made any sounds, and didn't have the chance to play with toys or with other children.

She was finally discovered when she was 13 years old. She was **physically underdeveloped** and could only speak with **animal-like sounds.**

After a lot of help she later learned some language but her **social and intellectual skills never seemed to fully develop.**

Koluchova (1976) — The Case of the Czech twin boys

This is the case of **twin boys** whose mother died soon after they were born. Their father remarried and their stepmother treated them very cruelly. They were often kept locked in a cellar, beaten, and had no toys.

They were found when they were seven with rickets (a bone development disease caused by a lack of vitamin D), and **very little social or intellectual development.**

They were later adopted and made lots of progress. By adulthood they had above average intelligence and had normal social relationships.

*There are a Number of **Limitations** to this Evidence*

1) The children didn't just suffer **maternal privation** — they also had very little **social and intellectual stimulation**, and were generally treated horribly. So all of these factors have to be taken into account when we're looking at their development.
2) The case studies show **mixed results** for how much children can **recover** from privation early in life. Some recovered well (the Czech twins) but others didn't (Genie).
3) **Differences between the cases** might explain why some recovered better than others. We should consider:
   a) Length of privation and how **old** they were when they were discovered (the Czech twins were much younger than Genie, so still had time to develop once they were in a better environment).
   b) Experiences during the isolation (**the twins may have attached to each other**).
   c) Quality of care after the isolation (the twins were adopted, but Genie was passed between psychologists and eventually put in an institution).
   d) Individual differences, including ability to recover.
4) There are problems with **generalising** the findings because they only focus on individual cases (see page 24, and also have a look at page 127 for more general stuff on case studies).

The evidence suggests that **recovery from privation is possible**. However, because of the lack of information about what had happened to the children, we can't know for sure exactly what they experienced, e.g. whether they had ever had even a brief attachment. So we can't ever be sure why the twins recovered more than Genie.

More controlled, scientific evidence is needed, but it would be **ethically wrong** to actually put children in situations of privation to see what might happen. Some studies of children raised in institutions have provided evidence of the effects of privation, although we still can't be precisely **sure** of the **reasons** behind these effects.

Failure to Form Attachments — Privation

*Hodges and Tizard (1989) Studied Early **Institutional Care***

Studies of children raised in **institutions** (e.g. orphanages) may provide **more accurate records** of what the children experienced, seeing as they can be properly scientifically observed over a long period of time.

Hodges and Tizard (1989) studied children raised in institutions.

Method: This was a **longitudinal** (long-term) study of 65 children who had been placed in a residential nursery before they were four months old. They hadn't had the opportunity to form close attachments with any of their caregivers. By the age of four, some of the children had returned to their birth mothers, some had been adopted, and some stayed in the nursery.

Results: At 16 years old, the **adopted** group had **strong** family relationships, although compared to a control group of children from a 'normal' home environment, they had weaker peer relationships. Those who stayed in the **nursery** or who returned to their **mothers** showed **poorer** relationships with family and peers than those who were adopted.

Conclusion: Children can **recover** from early maternal privation if they are in a good **quality**, **loving** environment, although their social development may not be as good as children who have never suffered privation.

Evaluation: This was a **natural experiment**, so it had **high ecological validity**. However, the sample was quite **small** and more than 20 of the children couldn't be found at the end of the study, so it's hard to **generalise** the results. **Rutter et al (1998)** studied 111 Romanian orphans adopted by British families before they were two years old. Their development was compared to a control group of British children. They were initially below normal development, but by four years of age their development had caught up. However, the **older** the children were when they were adopted, the **slower** their development was.

*Research Suggests Two **Long-Term Effects** of **Privation***

Privation of attachments early in life will damage a child's development, although how much it's damaged depends on several factors, such as age. Children can recover to some extent, but some of the effects of privation might be permanent:

1) **Reactive attachment disorder** **Parker and Forrest (1993)**
This is a rare but serious condition in which children seem to be permanently damaged by early experiences such as privation of attachment. The symptoms include an inability to give or receive affection, poor social relationships, dishonesty and involvement in crime.
2) **The cycle of privation**. Some evidence (e.g. **Quinton et al 1985)**, suggests that children who experienced privation may later become less caring parents. Therefore their children are deprived of a strong maternal attachment and may then be less caring to their children, and so on.

Practice Questions

Q1 Explain the difference between deprivation and privation.
Q2 Explain a limitation of case study evidence.
Q3 Why might the Czech twins have recovered better than Genie?
Q4 Outline the strengths and weaknesses of Hodges and Tizard's (1989) study.
Q5 What is reactive attachment disorder?

Exam Questions

Q1 Define the terms deprivation and privation. [2 marks]

Q2 Outline the results of two studies on the effects of privation. [8 marks]

Developmental problems — enough to make you develop mental problems

There are some pretty grisly case studies of seriously abused children on these pages. Not the nicest of topics to be studying, though it is interesting to see how these theories of severe privation fit in with the earlier ones about children separated from their carers. My advice would be to get the theories and case studies in your head quickly and move on to the next bit.

The Effects of Day Care on Child Development

AQA A only. 'Day care' refers to any ***temporary care*** *for a child provided by someone other than the parents or guardians they live with. Lots of studies have been done to test whether day care has an effect on social development.*

Day Care Might Affect Social Development

It may be necessary for children to form a strong attachment with their main carer before they can learn social skills and have relationships with others (see pages 34-37). Here are some studies that explore the impact of day care on attachment, peer relations and aggression.

Clarke-Stewart et al (1994) — positive effects of day care

Method: This study was made up of a series of separate **observations**, to examine the effects of day care. One experiment looked at the **peer relationships** of 150 children aged 2-3 years, who came from different social backgrounds.
In another experiment, the **strength of attachment** in a group of 18-month-old children was studied. These children had at least 30 hours of day care per week. The 'strange situation' was used. The results were compared with those of children who had 'low intensity' day care (less than 10 hours per week).

Results: The 2-3 year olds who had experienced day care were good at coping with social situations and negotiating with each other.
In the 'strange situation' experiment, the 18-month-olds who had high intensity day care were just as distressed when separated from their mothers as those who had low intensity day care.

Conclusion: Day care can have a positive effect on the development of peer relationships in 2-3 year olds. Attachment in 18-month-olds is not affected by temporary separation.

Evaluation: The observations were **controlled**, so the study could easily be replicated. However, because the situation was artificial, the study lacks **ecological validity** and the results can't be **generalised** to other children.

Shea (1981) — positive effects of day care

Method: Infants aged between 3 and 4 were videotaped in the playground during their first 10 weeks at nursery school. Their behaviour was assessed in terms of **rough-and-tumble play**, **aggression**, **frequency of peer interaction**, **distance from the teacher** and **distance from the nearest child**.

Results: Over the 10 weeks the children's peer interaction increased and their distance from the teacher decreased. There was a decrease in aggression and an increase in rough-and-tumble play. The increase in sociability was more evident in children who attended day care 5 days a week than in those who went 2 days a week.

Conclusion: Day care causes children to become more sociable and less aggressive.

Evaluation: This was a **naturalistic observation**, meaning that the study has high **ecological validity** because none of the behaviour was manipulated. However, it means that the results could have been affected by **extraneous variables**. The behaviour was open to interpretation, so the findings could be biased — e.g. it could be difficult to differentiate between 'aggression' and 'rough-and-tumble play'.

Belsky and Rovine (1988) — negative effects of day care

Method: Infants were placed in the '**strange situation**' to assess how secure their attachments with their mothers were (see page 32). One group had experienced no day care and one had experienced at least 20 hours of day care per week before their first birthday.

Results: The infants who had received day care were more likely to have an **insecure** attachment type.
They were either **'insecure-avoidant' (type A)** — ignored their mother and didn't mind if she left, or **'insecure-resistant' (type C)** — uneasy around their mother and upset if she left.
Those who hadn't had day care were more likely to be **securely attached** (type B).

Conclusion: Day care has a **negative** effect on an infant's social development.

Evaluation: The 'strange situation' is a **controlled observation**, so there was **good control** of the variables. However, this means that the study lacks **ecological validity**, because it creates an artificial situation.
DiLalla (1998) also found negative effects on children's **peer relationships** — the more day care children had, the **less prosocially** they behaved, i.e. the less they helped, shared, etc.

The Effects of Day Care on Child Development

Research into How Day Care Affects Development Varies Widely

It seems that nobody can really decide whether day care is good or bad for children.
Here are some of the reasons why the findings vary so much:

1) The studies focus on slightly different things (e.g. quality of care, age of child), and use different **samples**.
2) There are **methodological problems** with the studies that might lead to inconsistent results.
E.g. Clarke-Stewart has admitted that the '**strange situation**' isn't a good way of assessing attachment in infants who have day care (despite using it in her study). They're used to temporary separation so might respond indifferently and be wrongly classed as '**insecure**'.
3) All of these studies rely on **correlations**, so it's not possible to establish **cause and effect.**
4) The studies don't take **individual differences** like temperament into account.

Research Has Affected Day Care Practices

Research into child development and day care has influenced decisions about what might be best for children in day care. **Scarr (1998)** identified several factors that make for good day care:

1) Good **staff training**
2) Adequate **space**
3) Appropriate **toys** and **activities**
4) A good **ratio of staff to children**
5) **Minimising staff turnover** so that children can form **stable attachments** with carers

Arnold had made lots of friends since being in day care.

Vandell et al (1988) found that children who had **good quality** day care were more likely to have **friendly interactions** with others compared to those receiving **lower quality** day care.

Scarr (1998) and Vandell et al's (1988) studies show that **high quality day care** can have a **positive effect** on **social development**.

Practice Questions

Q1 Why might day care affect a child's social development?
Q2 Evaluate a study that shows the negative effects of day care on social development.
Q3 Why might the results from studies into the effects of day care differ from each other?
Q4 So, how do you make a great day care centre?

Exam Questions

Q1 Outline research findings on the effects of day care on social development. [6 marks]

Q2 Evaluate research findings on the effects of day care on social development. [6 marks]

If this is all getting too difficult you can always blame it on your day care...

Let me see if I've got this — if a child is stuck in poor quality day care their social skills won't develop very well. But if the day care is good and stimulating, it can have positive effects on the child's development. I don't mean to knock these guys' hard work — but it's not exactly rocket science. Anyway, no complaints — it makes it all easier to learn...

The Biological Approach

These 2 pages are for everyone. *The biological (or physiological, if you're doing OCR) approach is all about looking at how physical, squidgy bits cause behaviour and determine experience. Yep, there's a shed-load of biology coming up...*

There Are Three Basic **Assumptions** of the Biological Approach

1) Human behaviour can be explained by looking at biological stuff such as **hormones**, **genetics**, **evolution** and the **nervous system**.
2) In theory, if we can explain all behaviour using **biological causes**, unwanted behaviour could be **modified** or **removed** using **biological treatments** such as medication for mental illness.
3) Experimental research conducted using **animals** can inform us about human behaviour and biological influences, because we share a lot of biological similarities.

Genetics Is Used to Explain Behaviour

First of all, here's a speedy recap of the basic genetic knowledge that'll be handy in this section:

1) At conception, the egg and sperm join up to give a total of **46 chromosomes**.
2) Each chromosome is made up of a coil of **DNA**, which in turn is made up of loads and loads of **genes**.
3) The genes contain the information that make us **unique** in appearance (e.g. hair, skin and eye colour).

Darwin's theory of evolution suggests that over time, individuals who are **better adapted** to their environment through having **better genes** are more likely to survive to reproduce and pass on their useful genes. Those who are **less well-adapted** will be less likely to survive to reproduce and pass on their genes. Eventually, their less useful genes will be eliminated from the gene pool for that species. Through this process of **natural selection**, early humans **became better adapted** to their environments.

Biological psychologists reckon that **genetics** can explain "**psychological traits**". These are things like gender behaviour (things that men and women do differently), intelligence, personality and sexual orientation. They also study genetics to see which genes make some people more likely to develop things like mental illness or addictions. **Twin studies** and **adoption studies** are useful for investigating these areas (see page 42).

The **Nervous System** Controls What We Do and How We Do It

Biology recap time again — this time for the nervous system. Just when you thought the fun was all over...

1) The nervous system allows parts of the body to **communicate** with each other.
2) The **central nervous system** (CNS) consists of the **brain** and the **spinal cord**.
3) The **peripheral nervous system** (PNS) is all the **nerves** connecting the CNS with the rest of the body.
4) In the body, **neurones** are organised into nerves — spinal and cranial nerves.

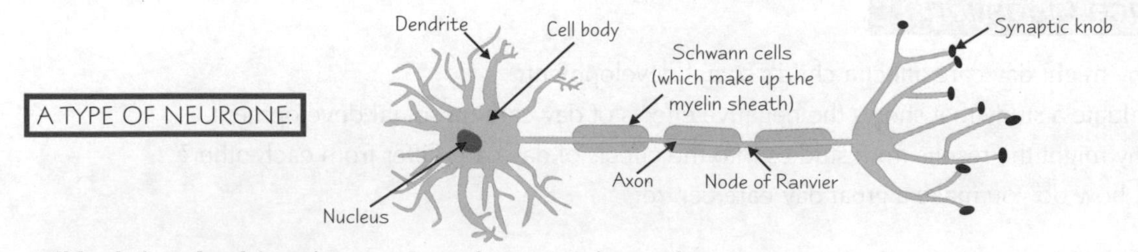

5) The **cell body** has **dendrites** that receive information from other neurones.
6) This info passes along the **axon** in the form of an **electrical wave** that ends up at a **synaptic knob**.
7) There's a small gap before the next neurone called a **synapse**.
8) **Neurotransmitters** are chemicals that are released from the synaptic knob. They pass across the synapse, to pass on the signal to the dendrites of the next neurone.

Biological psychologists spend loads of time working out what different neurotransmitters do and how they can be influenced by things like **diet**, **exercise** and **drugs**. They also work out how to manipulate neurotransmitters with **medications**, to control different behaviours. For example, if a medication or diet was developed to reduce the neurotransmitters that signal stress, this could help people who get stressed out too easily.

The Biological Approach

Brain Scanning is Used to Investigate Possible **Abnormalities**

There are various types of brain scanning out there — some just look at the **structure** and others look at **function**.

1) Magnetic Resonance Imaging (MRI)

MRI scans use **magnetic fields** to produce a **detailed image** of the brain that can show up abnormalities such as tumours and structural problems. It can also show **brain activity** by monitoring **blood flow** to different areas.

2) Positron Emission Tomography (PET)

PET scans measure **brain activity** using sensors placed on the head, which track a radioactive substance that has been injected into the person. PET scans can show which areas of the brain are more **active** when the person performs an activity such as counting. This helps us to understand about **function** and **communication** within the brain.

Both techniques are pretty **expensive** to use during research. However, it's useful to be able to see which parts of the brain are activated during certain activities, as different **functions** are performed in different parts of the brain. Certain functions, such as speech, problem solving and language processing, are generally localised more in one of the two **hemispheres** of the brain. This is known as **brain lateralisation**.

The Biological Approach Has **Strengths** and **Weaknesses**

Strengths:

1) The approach can provide **evidence** to support or disprove a theory — it's a very **scientific** approach.
2) If a biological cause can be found for mental health problems or for unwanted behaviour such as aggression, then **biological treatments** can be developed to help individuals.

Weaknesses:

1) The approach doesn't take into account the influence of people's **environment**, their **family**, **childhood experiences** or their **social situation**. Other approaches see these as being important factors in explaining behaviour.
2) Using a biological explanation for negative behaviour can lead to individuals or groups avoiding taking **personal** or **social responsibility** for their behaviour.

Practice Questions

Q1 What are the basic assumptions of the biological approach?

Q2 What does the CNS consist of?

Q3 What does PET stand for?

Q4 Why is the biological approach described as being a very scientific approach?

Exam Questions

Q1 Explain how information is passed through the nervous system. [6 marks]

Q2 Evaluate the biological approach in psychology. [12 marks]

MRI scans have shown that a student's brain patterns were identical when reading this page and when sleeping — coincidence...

Actually I think this is pretty interesting stuff. I mean the way your brain works must be one of the biggest remaining mysteries in medical science — sure, they can start to recognise areas of the brain and stuff — but there's a long way to go.

The Biological Approach

These 2 pages are for everyone — don't worry, there's plenty to go around...
Biological psychologists aren't just happy with one research method. Pure greediness if you ask me...

There are **Two Main Ways** to Study **Genetic Influences**

Twin Studies

1) Twin studies use **identical (monozygotic — MZ) twins** because they have **identical genes**.
2) They can be compared to see if there are any similarities in their **behaviour**.
3) For example, if both twins get very similar scores on an IQ test, that indicates a possible genetic cause for intelligence.
4) **Non-identical (dizygotic — DZ) twins** only share **half** their genes so it's less likely that their behaviour will be similar.
5) However, all twins are likely to have similar **environmental experiences** if they're raised in the same family.

Adoption Studies

1) Adoption studies are used to compare family members with **close genetics** (ideally identical twins) who have been brought up in **different environments**.
2) Research into schizophrenia has found that adopted children are at a **higher risk** of developing the disorder if a **biological parent** had it, even if no-one in the adopted family has this type of mental disorder.
3) This indicates that the genetic influence is strong.

Twin and Adoption Studies Have Some **Limitations**

1) MZ twins who are raised in the **same family** also share the **same environmental influences** so ideally MZ twins raised in different families should be used in research. Unfortunately though, there's not a massive number of people in these circumstances.
2) If there's a purely genetic reason for behaviour then in **all** sets of MZ twins where one twin has a certain behaviour, the other should also have it. However, research looking at areas such as mental health, intelligence and personality always finds MZ twins where this **isn't the case**. This means that there must also be factors other than genetics.

Gottesman and Shields (1966) Investigated **Schizophrenia in Twins**

Gottesman and Shields found evidence to support a genetic cause for schizophrenia.

Gottesman and Shields (1966) — schizophrenia in twins

Method:	Hospital records for the past 16 years were examined to identify people with schizophrenia who had a **twin**. Around 40 sets of twins agreed to take part in the study, which was a **natural experiment** using **independent measures**. If it was uncertain whether a set were MZ or DZ twins, they were excluded from the study as a control of an extraneous variable.
Results:	The concordance rate (the amount of twins who both had schizophrenia) was about **48%** for **MZ** twins and about **17%** for **DZ** twins. The exact figures vary depending on thc type of schizophrenia, but overall, MZ twins had a much higher concordance rate than DZ twins.
Conclusion:	DZ twins only share half of their genes and MZ twins share all of their genes. As the results for MZ twins are much higher, this suggests a **genetic cause** for schizophrenia.
Evaluation:	The results for MZ twins don't show 100% concordance, which means that there must be **other important factors** that influence schizophrenia. Although the researchers had a large amount of data covering a long period of time, it's unlikely the study could be **replicated** until new data existed.

The Biological Approach

Biological Research Uses a Variety of Research Methods

Experiments (also see page 126)

1) Experiments try to establish **cause and effect** by comparing groups and analysing any **differences** between them.
2) For example, the **Gottesman and Shields (1966)** study compared schizophrenia concordance rates in MZ and DZ twins.
3) Experiments are useful in this area because they can investigate possible **biological causes** of behaviour.
4) However, other **variables** have to be very tightly **controlled**, as they can affect the results of a study.

Correlations (also pages 146-147)

1) Correlations describe the **relationship** between two variables.
2) For example, **Holmes and Rahe (1967)** (page 48) found a positive correlation between the amount of **stressful life events** and **ill health** experienced. As one variable increases, so does the other.
3) Correlations only show a relationship, **not** a cause and effect — e.g. we can't say that the stressful life events themselves caused the health problems.
4) They're useful for establishing relationships between variables and often lead to **further research**.

Case Studies (also see page 127)

1) Case studies are used to investigate things that couldn't be investigated any other way.
2) For example, **Money** (1972) reported a case study of a boy who was raised as a girl after his penis was damaged during surgery (see page 67).
3) Case studies are useful for investigating a situation in **great depth**.
4) However, they can't be **generalised** to other people as they're often unique situations.

Questionnaires and Interviews (also see page 127)

1) Questionnaires and interviews are used to collect information from people **directly**.
2) For example, **Holmes and Rahe (1967)** used these techniques to get people to rate how stressful individual events were to them (see page 48).
3) They rely on the **honesty** of the person but can provide **very detailed information**.

Animals are often used in biological psychology experiments. There's loads more information about this on page 66.

Practice Questions

Q1 Which two techniques can be used to test for genetic influences?

Q2 Which of these methods was used by Gottesman and Shields (1966)?

Q3 Give three research methods used in the biological approach.

Exam Questions

Q1 Outline and evaluate the use of twin and adoption studies within the biological approach. [12 marks]

Q2 Evaluate the use of experimental studies and correlational studies within the biological approach. [6 marks]

Concordance — isn't that the name of a fancy old plane...

Remember though, it's pretty rare to be able to say that something has a definite genetic cause. Like with the Gottesman and Shields study, even if there's a stong case supporting a genetic influence, other factors always creep in — like environment and upbringing, or even what you had for tea last Thursday. A lot more research still needs to be done.

Stress as a Bodily Response

Just for AQA A. In fact, the next 14 pages are just for you.
I'm sure you all know what stress is. It's having 3 hours left to revise before an exam, or having to visit your girlfriend or boyfriend's parents. We all feel it — but this is psychology, so it needs a proper scientific explanation.

Stress is a Response to Stimuli in the Environment

Stress is one of those annoying words with two meanings... How helpful.

1) It can be the environmental **stimulus** that triggers a stress response, e.g. a giant cockroach dancing towards you. In other words, it's the thing that causes you to act stressed.
2) But it can also be the **response** to the stimulus — our reaction, e.g. running for the hills.

However, the white-coated ones have agreed to explain stress as '**the response that occurs when we think we can't cope with the pressures in our environment**'. This is shown in the diagram below:

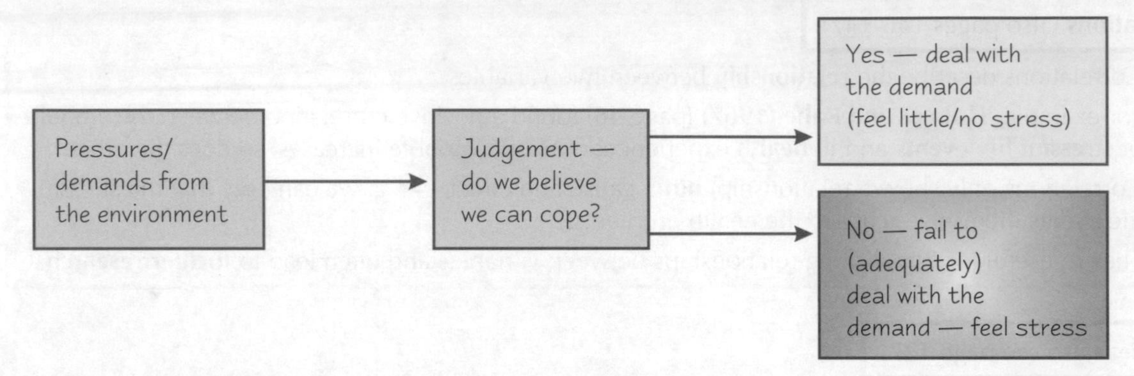

So, stress is the response that occurs when we think the demands being placed on us are greater than our ability to cope. These are our **own judgements** — so we could **over** or **underestimate** the demands, or our ability to cope. Whether the stress is justified or not doesn't matter — if we **think** we can't cope we get stressed. And when we get stressed something physically changes in us.

The Hypothalamus is the Bit of the Brain that Responds to Stress

The evaluation of whether something is a **stressor** occurs in the **higher brain centres** — the **cerebral cortex**. When there's a stressor in the environment, these higher areas send a signal to the **hypothalamus**. This tiny part of the brain makes up for its size by having many functions — including controlling the **physiological activities** involved in stress. In response to the higher areas, the hypothalamus triggers **two processes** in the body:

The activation of the sympathomedullary pathway...

1) In the **initial shock response**, the **hypothalamus** triggers activity in the **sympathetic branch** of the **autonomic nervous system** — which is a branch of the **peripheral nervous system** (see page 40).
2) The sympathetic branch becomes more active when the body is **stressed** and **using energy**.
3) It stimulates the **adrenal medulla** within the **adrenal glands**, which releases **adrenaline** and **noradrenaline** into the bloodstream.
4) These affect the body in several ways, including:

- **Blood pressure** and **heart rate** increase to get blood quickly to areas of the body where it's needed for activity.
- **Digestion decreases** so that blood can be directed to the brain and muscles.
- **Muscles** become more **tense** so that the body is physically responsive.
- **Perspiration increases** so that the body can cool down and burn more energy.
- **Breathing rate increases** so that more oxygen can be sent to the muscles.

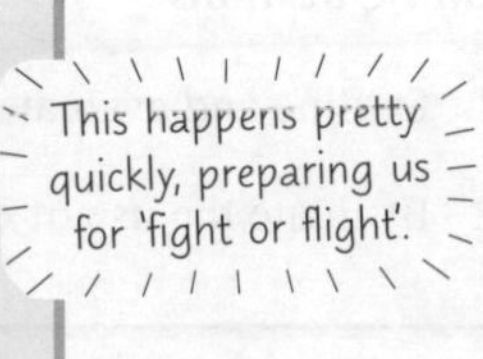

5) The result of these changes is that the body is **ready to use energy** to deal with the stressful situation, e.g. running away from the rhino that's escaped from the zoo.

Stress as a Bodily Response

... Followed by the activation of the **pituitary-adrenal system**

If the stress is **long-term**, say several hours or more, then the sympathomedullary response will start to use up the body's **resources**. So, a second system produces a **countershock response** — which supplies the body with more fuel. It's like putting your body on red alert.

1) The hypothalamus also triggers the release of **CRH** (corticotropin-releasing hormone).
2) CRH stimulates the **anterior pituitary gland**.
3) This then releases a hormone called **ACTH** (adrenocorticotropic hormone).
4) ACTH travels through the body and then stimulates the **adrenal cortex**, which is near the kidneys.
5) The adrenal cortex then releases **corticosteroids** which give us energy by converting **fat** and **protein**.
6) This energy is needed to replace that used up by the body's initial reaction to the stress, e.g. running away.

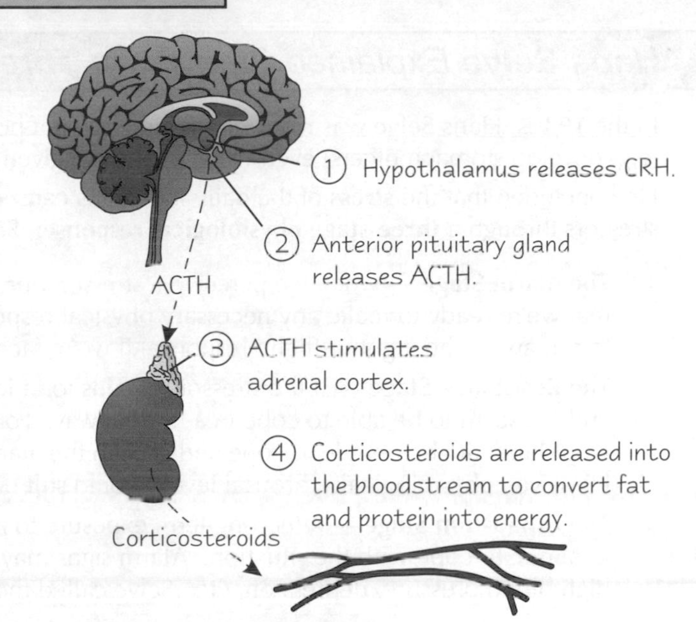

Changes in the Body Can Be Seen as Having **Survival Value**

1) During our evolution many threats to us would have been from **predators** or other **physical dangers**.
2) So, to successfully respond to them, we would have required **energy** to fight or run away — the **'fight or flight'** response.
3) However, in **modern society** stressors are more likely to be **psychological** than physical and are more **long-term**, e.g. the stresses of working at a desk, commuting, noisy neighbours, etc.
4) Therefore the physical stress response is not really needed, and in the long term it may actually be harmful to our bodies — the next two pages explain how.
5) Some stress can be positive and exhilarating — this is known as **eustress**, e.g. a parachute jump might lead to this kind of arousal.

Leo was finding the journey to work increasingly stressful.

Practice Questions

Q1 What is stress?

Q2 When does the sympathetic branch of the nervous system become more active?

Q3 Why does digestion decrease when the body is under stress?

Q4 What function do corticosteroids perform?

Exam Questions

Q1 A dog runs out into the road and Michael has to brake suddenly. He feels his heart start to pound. Explain why this happens. [6 marks]

Q2 Outline the response of the pituitary-adrenal system to long-term stress. [6 marks]

Well, as bodily responses go, I guess stress isn't so bad...

Stress is a natural reaction in response to anything which threatens you. In the past, it would have been a lion chasing you. Now it's more likely to be a deadline or late train. So next time you see someone getting stressed about something, try telling them, "relax, it could be worse — at least you're not being chased by a lion" — that'll soon calm them down.

Stress and Physical Illness

Only for people doing AQA A. *The last couple of pages made it blindingly obvious that stress isn't just something in your head — it's a physical response. These pages cover what stress can do to your physical state in the long run.*

Hans Selye Explained Stress as a *Three-Stage Response*

In the 1930s, Hans Selye was researching the effects of hormones when he noticed that rats would become ill (e.g. develop stomach ulcers) even when they were given harmless injections (can't have been that harmless).

He concluded that the **stress** of the daily injections **caused the illness** and suggested that all animals and humans react to stressors through a **three-stage physiological response**. Selye called this the **General Adaptation Syndrome (GAS)** (1936).

1) **The Alarm Stage** — when we perceive a stressor, our body's first reaction is to increase arousal levels so that we're ready to make any necessary physical response (described on page 44). These mean we're able to run away (the 'fight or flight' response) if we're faced with a big-toothed hairy monster.
2) **The Resistance Stage** — if the stressor remains for a long time, our bodies can adapt to the situation and we seem to be able to cope in a normal way. For example, if we start a high-pressure job we would initially be unable to cope and go into the alarm stage, but after time we would seem to adapt. However, physiologically, arousal levels would still be higher than normal to cope with the situation.
3) **The Exhaustion Stage** — after long-term exposure to a stressor our bodies will eventually be unable to continue to cope with the situation. Alarm signs may return and we may develop illnesses, e.g. ulcers, high blood pressure, depression, etc. Selye called these 'diseases of adaptation'.

Comment — the stages Selye identified are supported by a lot of scientific research. However, the GAS theory describes a single type of response and so neglects the fact that the body's reaction to stress does vary, e.g. how much adrenaline is released depends on how the stressor is perceived by the person (how frightening it is, etc.). Also, a certain bacterium has been found to be involved in the formation of ulcers. It could still be the case, though, that stress weakens the immune system making ulcers more likely.

Long-Term Stress Can Affect the *Cardiovascular System*

The "cardiovascular system" is just a fancy name for the **heart** and **blood vessels**.
A **long-term stress response** may have a direct effect on this system:

Krantz et al (1991) — stress and the heart

Method:	In a **laboratory experiment**, 39 participants did one of three stress-inducing tasks (a maths test, a Stroop test and public speaking). Their **blood pressure** and the extent to which the vessels around their heart **contracted** (low, medium or high myocardial ischaemia) was measured. Participants were instructed not to take any prescribed heart medication prior to the study.
Results:	Participants with the greatest myocardial ischaemia showed the highest increases in blood pressure. A small number of participants who showed mild or no myocardial ischaemia only had a very moderate increase in blood pressure.
Conclusion:	Stress may have a **direct influence** on aspects of body functioning, making cardiovascular disorders more likely.
Evaluation:	Although the effects were clearly **linked** to stress, it can't be said that one causes the other. Also, it wasn't shown whether the effects also occur at other times. They might sometimes happen even if the person feels relaxed — and therefore couldn't just be linked to feeling stressed. Not everybody showed the same reaction, which suggests that **individual differences** between the participants may also have played a role. The **ecological validity** of the study was reduced because it took place under **laboratory conditions** that weren't fully representative of real-life stress. However, the findings of the study are supported by **Williams (2000)** — it was seen that people who got angry easily or reacted more angrily to situations had a higher risk of cardiovascular problems.

Stress and Physical Illness

Stress Can Also Affect the **Immune System**

The immune system is made of cells (e.g. white blood cells) and chemicals that **seek and destroy bacteria** and **viruses**. When someone experiences stress over a long time (a **long-term stress response**) their immune system stops functioning properly. Loads of studies have tested whether long-term stress makes us more vulnerable to infection and illness.

Brady et al (1958) — stress and the development of ulcers

Method: Monkeys were put in pairs and given electric shocks every 20 seconds for 6 hour sessions. One monkey of each pair (the 'executive') could push a lever to postpone each shock. The other could not delay them.

Results: The 'executive' monkeys were more likely to develop illness (ulcers) and later die.

Conclusion: The illness and death was not due to the shocks but due to the stress that the executives felt in trying to avoid them. In the long term, this stress reduced the immune system's ability to fight illness.

Evaluation: The experiment has **ethical** issues — the experiment was very cruel and would not be allowed today. Also, we can't **generalise** results from monkeys to humans. Furthermore, we know that people with **little control** over their own lives (such as those with low-level jobs and the long-term unemployed), can experience **high levels of stress**, which this research cannot explain.

The same **Immune System Suppression** happens in **Humans**

Research on humans (fortunately not quite as unethical as the monkey study) has also supported the theory that stress can reduce the effectiveness of the immune system. Take the following study, for example:

Kiecolt-Glaser et al (1995) — stress and wound healing

Method: In a study with an **independent measures** design, a punch biopsy was used to create a small wound on the arms of 13 women who cared for relatives with Alzheimer's disease (a very stressful responsibility). A control group of 13 people also took part.

Results: Wound healing took an average of 9 days longer for the carers than those in the control group.

Conclusion: Long-term stress impairs the effectiveness of the immune system to heal wounds.

Evaluation: **Sweeney (1995)** also found that people caring for relatives with dementia took longer than a control group to heal their wounds. However, for both studies the two groups may have **varied in other ways** apart from the stress of being a carer. The effects on the carers could be due to poor diet, lack of sleep, etc, and not just the stress they experienced. The study only contained a small number of participants — for more reliable results it should be repeated with a larger number.

Practice Questions

Q1 What are the three stages of Selye's general adaptation syndrome?

Q2 What were the results of the Brady et al (1958) study?

Q3 Who were the experimental group in the Kiecolt-Glaser et al (1995) study?

Exam Questions

Q1 Sarah was promoted to team leader in a busy call centre and has noticed that she is experiencing more illness than she used to. Use psychological theories and studies to explain this. [10 marks]

Q2 Evaluate the strengths and weaknesses of studying stress under laboratory conditions. [12 marks]

No more exams thanks — can't be doing with ulcers...

If you think about it, it kind of stands to reason that being really stressed out all the time will have some effect on your body. You need to remember the actual physiological facts about how this happens, and as usual you need to know some criticisms of the studies too. Although, whilst you're at it, do take in the lessons for life on these pages — just chill out dude.

Sources of Stress — Life Changes

These pages are only for AQA A. *There are loads of sources of stress — for some unfortunate individuals it's the thought of peanut butter sticking to their teeth, but for normal folk the two real biggies are **major life changes** and things at **work**.*

Life Changes are a Source of Stress

Throughout our lives, we all experience **major life events** — like the death of a close relative, getting married or moving house. These events and the adjustments they cause us to make can be a major source of stress. When psychologists want to find out what level of stress these events cause, they look at health because it's likely to be linked to stress.

Holmes and Rahe (1967) studied whether the stress of life changes was linked to illness

1) Holmes and Rahe assumed that both positive and negative life events involve change, and that change leads to experiencing stress.
2) To test this assumption, they studied approximately 5000 hospital patients' records and noted any major life events that had occurred before the person became ill.
3) It was found that patients were **likely** to have experienced life changes prior to becoming ill and that **more serious life changes** seemed to be more **linked to stress and illness.**

They ranked life events on the Social Readjustment Rating Scale (SRRS)

1) **Holmes and Rahe** made a list of 43 common life events and asked loads of people to give each one a score to say how stressful it was. They called the numbers that made up each score the **Life Change Units (LCU)**. The higher this number of LCUs, the more stressful it was.

2) Then they **ranked** the events from most stressful to least stressful and called it the **Social Readjustment Rating Scale (SRRS)**. Examples are shown in the table below.

Life Event	Rank	Score (LCU)
Death of a spouse	1	100
Divorce	2	73
Retirement	10	45
Change in school	17	37
Christmas	42	12

Retirement stressful — pah, I can't wait...

3) They found a **positive correlation** between the likelihood of illness and the score on the SRRS — as one variable increases, so does the other. So, the more stress a person experienced, the more likely they were to suffer illness.

Further Correlational Research Supported Their Findings

See above for a reminder of what LCU scores are.

Rahe et al (1970) — LCU score and illness

Method: In a **correlational study**, more than 2500 American Navy seamen were given a form of the SRRS to complete just before they set sail on military duty. They had to indicate all of the events that they had experienced over the previous six months.

Results: Higher LCU scores were found to be linked to a higher incidence of illness over the next seven months.

Conclusion: The stress involved in the changes that life events bring is linked to an increased risk of illness.

Evaluation: The results are **not representative** of the population and can only be **generalised** to American Navy seamen. Also, the results don't explain **individual differences** in response to stress. There are also limitations associated with using correlational research. You can't assume a **causal relationship** between the variables — the correlation might be caused by a third unknown variable. As well as this, there are problems with using the SRRS to rank stressful events (see the next page).

Sources of Stress — Life Changes

There are Some **Issues** with the SRRS

1) The SRRS doesn't separate **positive and negative life events**. Stress and illness might be more linked to negative life changes. For example, a wedding might be stressful, but positive overall, while the death of a spouse might have a very negative stressful effect.
2) Long-term, minor sources of stress, such as everyday **hassles** at work (see page 50), are not considered.

Despite criticisms the SRRS was useful for showing that changes in life may link to stress and illness.

The Research is **Correlational**, Not Experimental

1) **Correlational studies** aim to establish if two variables are **related** to each other.
2) They're useful because they allow us to investigate **relationships** between stress and lots of other variables.
3) For example, it's likely that our stress levels are the result of many **interrelated factors**, rather than one single factor.

Cynthia didn't need any experiments — she knew exactly what was causing her stress.

On the other hand...
1) **Experiments** aim to establish if a change in one variable **causes a change** in another.
2) They have an advantage if we want to find out exactly what is **causing** stress.

Several of the life changes within the SRRS could be **related** to each other. For example, a big change in **job conditions** or getting **fired** are likely to affect a person's **financial situation. Pregnancy** or a change in **personal habits** and **living conditions** may affect **personal health**. This means that life changes could be both the cause **and** effect of stress.

Practice Questions

Q1 What did Holmes and Rahe study?
Q2 What does SRRS stand for?
Q3 Which research method was used in the Rahe et al (1970) study?
Q4 What is the difference between correlational studies and experiments?
Q5 Suggest some life changes that could be related to each other.

Exam Questions

Q1 Explain how the SRRS was devised and evaluate the use of this technique. [10 marks]

Q2 Geoff lost his job, leading to financial difficulties. His doctor also recently diagnosed him as having high blood pressure. Explain how research into life events could explain his medical condition. [10 marks]

The sauces of stress — feels like you're always playing ketchup...

As a quick break, make your own SRRS by putting these stressful situations in order: 1) meeting your girl/boyfriend's parents, 2) walking into a job interview and realising your fly's undone, 3) feeling a spider run across your face in bed, 4) knowing that what you're writing will be read by thousands of cynical A-Level students and you can't think of anything funny to write.

Sources of Stress — In Everyday Life

Just AQA A. Sometimes it's just the little things in life that get us down. If these start getting to us, and cause us to feel stressed, we can become ill. But I won't tell you too much, or you won't bother reading the rest of the page...

Daily Hassles are Everyday Events that are Stressful

Kanner et al (1981) suggested that stress is related to more **mundane events** than the major life events put forward by Holmes and Rahe. Examples of these daily hassles, which they named **irritants**, include having too many things to do, misplacing objects, and getting stuck in traffic.

Kanner et al (1981) — stress and daily hassles

Method: 100 adults completed a questionnaire each month which asked them to choose which hassles they had experienced that month from a list of 117. They then had to rate each hassle to show how severe it had been for them. This was repeated for 9 months.

Results: Certain hassles occurred more frequently than others, such as worrying about weight, family health and the rising cost of living. They found that those with high scores were more likely to have physical and psychological health problems. They also found that scores on an uplifts scale (containing events that make you feel good, e.g. finishing a task or getting on well with a partner) were negatively related to ill health — these events may reduce stress or protect us from it.

Conclusion: Daily hassles are linked to stress and health, with a stronger correlation than that found with the SRRS (see page 48).

Evaluation: The weaknesses of **correlational methods** are relevant here — it isn't possible to establish a cause and effect relationship between the variables. Using questionnaires resulted in **quantitative data**, which is useful for making comparisons, but they don't allow participants to explain why certain experiences are stressful to them, so potentially useful data is missed. They rely on **honesty** in order for the results to be valid — participants may not be completely truthful about admitting mundane daily events that they find stressful. They also rely on the participants' **recall** being accurate.

The Workplace is a Massive Source of Stress

Unfortunately, most people need to work. Some aspects of the **work they do**, **where they work**, or **who they have to work with**, become a source of stress. This is important because if a person is very stressed at work they may be more likely to get ill. This is not only bad for them, but also for their employer because they will take more days off sick.

Stress in the workplace comes from FIVE key areas

- **Relationships at work** — our relationships with our bosses, colleagues and customers may be stressful. For example, we might feel **undervalued** and that we **lack support**.
- **Work pressures** — having a large **workload**, maybe with **strict deadlines.**
- **The physical environment** — where we work may be very noisy, overcrowded, or too hot or cold (aren't we fussy...). Also, our work may involve health risks or unsociable working hours.
- **Stresses linked to our role** — worrying about **job security** or our **prospects for promotion**. Also, the range of our responsibilities may be unclear, and we may experience conflict, e.g. trying to please our bosses and the people who work for us.
- **Lack of control** — we may not have much **influence over the type and amount of work** we do, or where and when we do it. Check out the study by Marmot et al (1997) on the next page.

Sources of Stress — In Everyday Life

A **Lack of Control** in the Workplace is Stressful

Feeling that we don't have much influence over the type and amount of work we do can lead to stress.
This can be seen in Marmot et al's (1997) study:

	Marmot et al (1997) — lack of control and illness in the workplace
Method:	Over 7000 civil service employees working in London were surveyed. Information was obtained about their grade of employment, how much control they felt they had, how much support they felt they had, etc.
Results:	When the medical histories of these employees were followed up 5 years later, those on lower employment grades who felt less control over their work (and less social support) were found to be more likely to have cardiovascular disorders. Participants on the lowest grade of employment were four times more likely to die of a heart attack than those on the highest grade.
Conclusion:	Believing that you have little control over your work influences work stress and the development of illness.
Evaluation:	The study only looked at '**white collar**' work (office-type jobs), so the results may not apply to other jobs. **Smoking** was found to be common in those who developed illnesses. So, perhaps those who felt less control at work were more likely to smoke and the smoking caused the heart problems rather than stress. Other **factors** (e.g. diet and exercise) may be linked to job grade and could be causing illness rather than the perceived lack of control. The research is **correlational**, so it isn't possible to establish a cause and effect relationship between lack of control and illness. Data was obtained using **questionnaires**. This may have encouraged the participants to be more truthful than they would have been if interviewed. However, some people may have been concerned about admitting to experiencing stress at work in case it harmed their job prospects.

Frankenhaeuser (1975) also investigated the link between lack of control and stress in the workplace:

	Frankenhaeuser (1975) — stress levels in sawmill workers
Method:	Frankenhaeuser studied 2 groups of workers at a sawmill. One group had the repetitive task of feeding logs into a machine all day. The job was very noisy and the workers were socially isolated. They didn't have much control over their work as the machine dictated how quickly they should feed the logs in. The other group had a different task which gave them more control and more social contact. Stress levels were measured by testing urine samples and blood pressure.
Results:	The workers who had minimal control and social contact had higher levels of stress hormones (adrenaline and noradrenaline) in their urine. They were more likely to suffer from high blood pressure and stomach ulcers.
Conclusion:	A lack of control and social contact at work can lead to stress.
Evaluation:	This was a field experiment, so it has high **ecological validity**. The findings are **supported** by Marmot's study. However, it doesn't take individual differences into account — some individuals may just be more prone to stress. The results could have been affected by extraneous variables, such as how much the workers were paid.

Practice Questions

Q1 Give one reason why the workplace might be a source of stress.

Q2 Who were the participants in Marmot's (1997) study?

Q3 Give an advantage of using questionnaires in this area of research.

Exam Questions

Q1 Describe a study investigating the relationship between daily hassles and stress. [6 marks]

Q2 Evaluate a piece of research into lack of control in the workplace and work-related stress. [6 marks]

Stress at work — I don't believe it — I live to work...

You might think that the bits about research methods are really boring and not worth learning. They are boring — I'll give you that. But they are worth learning. You'll pick up marks in the exam if you can identify what research method a study uses, and there's plenty more up for grabs if you can evaluate it. Don't go saying I never tell you anything useful.

Stress — Individual Differences

These 2 pages are just for AQA A. *The last few pages have shown how stress affects the body, but that doesn't mean it affects everyone in the same way. If you stick two people in a pit and drop spiders on them, it's unlikely they're going to react in exactly the same way. Psychologists call different personal reactions 'individual differences'.*

*Different **Personalities** Can Lead to Different Stress Levels*

Psychologists love sticking people into groups. One theory about personality is that you can split everyone into three groups called '**Type A**', '**Type B**' or '**Type X**'. Type A people are competitive and ambitious. Type Bs are non-competitive, relaxed and easy-going. Type Xs have a balance of Type A and Type B behaviours. Friedman and Rosenman (1974) tested how these different types of personality affect the likelihood of CHD (coronary heart disease) — one of the most obvious effects of stress.

Friedman and Rosenman (1974) — Type A personality and illness

Method: Approximately 3000, 39-59 year old American males were assessed to class their personality characteristics into Type A, Type B or Type X using interviews and observation. At the start of the study none of them had CHD (coronary heart disease).

Results: Eight years later, 257 of them had developed CHD. 70% of these were classed as Type A personality. This includes being 'workaholic', extremely competitive, hostile to others, and always in a rush. Participants classed as Type B were less competitive and less impatient. They were found to have half the rate of heart disease of Type A. These results were found even when the extraneous variables of weight and smoking were taken into account.

Conclusion: Type A personalities seem to be at a **higher risk** of stress-related illnesses, such as CHD.

Evaluation: Having only three personality types seems a bit **simplistic**. The study doesn't prove that personality characteristics can **cause** stress and illness. It could be the other way round. For example, Type A personality may develop as a **response** to being under stress (from work etc.). Also, the **sample** used in the study was quite limited — middle-aged, male Americans. This means that it's not that easy to **generalise** the results to the rest of the population. In addition, participants may not have been completely **honest** in their interviews so that their characteristics appeared desirable to the researcher (**social desirability bias**).

Later research also identified **Type C** personalities — mild-mannered, easy-going people who may not react well to stressful situations and suppress their emotions. These people seem to have a higher risk of **cancer**. **Type D** personalities were identified as very negative/pessimistic people who worry too much about things and lack social skills. These people seem more at risk from **heart attacks**.

*Kobasa (1979) Identified **Hardiness** as an Important **Individual Difference***

Kobasa described people as being **hardy** or **non-hardy**. There are three main characteristics of hardy personalities:

1) Hardy personalities are very involved in what they do, and show a high level of **commitment**. This means that they work hard at relationships, jobs and other activities in life.
2) They view change in a positive rather than a negative way, seeing it as an opportunity for **challenge**. Hardy personalities enjoy a challenge and see it as an opportunity to develop themselves.
3) They have a strong feeling of **control** over their life and what happens to them. This is known as having an **internal locus of control**.

In comparison, **non-hardy** personalities view any life experiences in a much more **negative** way and feel that they're **unable to cope** with situations. They feel that **external agencies** have control over what happens to them and that it isn't worth trying to become more powerful. They **give up** easily and don't see any value in trying to change what's happening around them.

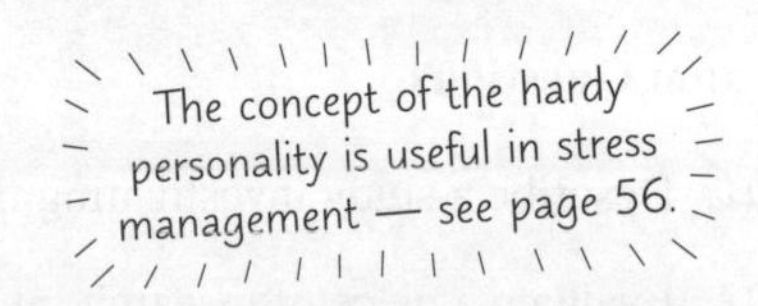

It's difficult to **quantify** what's meant by a hardy personality and therefore difficult to **measure** and test it. We also need to avoid making assumptions about **cause and effect** — it could be that some people have hardy personalities because of a lack of stress in their lives, rather than low stress being the result of personality. It could be that levels of hardiness **fluctuate** and may decrease when the person is experiencing lots of stress, such as after a bereavement.

Stress — Individual Differences

Stress can also be Related to **Gender**

Men and woman are pretty different in loads of ways, so psychologists (who don't miss a trick) thought that maybe these differences could affect what kinds of things men and women find stressful and how they cope. They looked at how **biological**, **social** and **cognitive** differences between males and females influence their response to stress.

Biological Explanation — through evolution, men in their role of 'hunter-gatherer' may have developed a stronger 'fight or flight' response than women, who had the role of caring for the kids. In this way, males and females may have developed different physiological responses to stress.

Taylor et al (2000) suggest that women produce a calmer response to stress due to a hormone. Oxytocin is released in response to stress and has been shown to lead to maternal behaviour and social affiliation. Taylor called this the 'tend and befriend' response (instead of the 'fight or flight' response) and thought it might make females more likely to seek social support to help them cope with stress.

Social Explanation — a Western stereotypical social role is that men are less open about their feelings than women. This means they're less likely to discuss stressful experiences with others and may use harmful coping methods instead, e.g. smoking and drinking.

Carroll (1992) found that women do generally make more use of social support to deal with stress. However, coronary heart disease has increased in women — but this could just be because a change in social roles means that it's now more acceptable for women to drink and smoke.

Cognitive Explanation — **Vogele et al (1997)** claim that women are better able to control anger and therefore respond more calmly to stressful situations. Men may feel that anger is an acceptable way to respond, and feel stress if they cannot show it. These cognitive differences could be the result of biology **or** the roles we are taught to follow, or a bit of both.

Stress Can be Related to **Culture**

1) **Culture** is a really vague term that is used to group people by **beliefs**, **behaviours**, **morals** or **customs** they share.
2) It influences how people live and how others react to them.
3) Variables such as **low socio-economic status** can lead to **poor living conditions** and experience of **prejudice** — which could lead to **negative thinking**.
4) Also, some people believe that **biological factors** could influence the link between culture, stress and illness.

Practice Questions

Q1 Explain the differences between the personality types A and B.

Q2 Give a criticism of Friedman and Rosenman's (1974) research.

Q3 What are the three characteristics associated with a hardy personality?

Exam Questions

Q1 Describe and discuss one explanation of how personality factors are associated with stress. [8 marks]

Q2 Sally has developed CHD. Use Friedman and Rosenman's (1974) study to explain how this could be a result of her personality. [8 marks]

We are all individuals, we are all individuals, we are all individuals...

This is an important thing to remember throughout psychology. People are divided into groups to show how different things affect people — but there are also individual differences, which means that when put in the same situation, people will often react differently. This seems pretty obvious but it's easy to forget if you get too wrapped up in all the theories.

Stress Management — Biological Approach

Just AQA A. *Biological methods of stress management help people cope with stress by changing the way the body responds to it. Drug treatments, biofeedback and exercise have been found to be effective. Best learn about them then.*

Drug Treatments Work in Two Ways

1) They **slow down** the activity of the **central nervous system** (CNS).
   Anti-anxiety drugs called **benzodiazepines** (BZs) increase the body's reaction to its own natural anxiety-relieving chemical **GABA** (gamma-aminobutyric acid), which slows down the activity of neurones and makes us feel relaxed.

OR...

2) They **reduce** the activity of the **sympathetic nervous system** (SNS).
   The SNS increases heart rate, blood pressure and levels of the hormone **cortisol.**
   High levels of cortisol can make our immune system **weak** and also cause heart disease.
   The group of drugs called **beta blockers** reduce all these unpleasant symptoms.

Biofeedback Uses Information About What's Happening in the Body

Biofeedback gives people information about **internal physical processes** that they wouldn't otherwise be aware of, e.g. muscle tension. The idea is to give them more **control** over these internal processes and the ability to **alter** them. For example, if they can **modify** the physical aspects of stress then this may make them more **relaxed** in stressful situations. The process takes place as **training** in a **non-stressful** environment, which the person is then encouraged to use in real-life stressful situations.

There are 4 steps involved:

1) The person is attached to a machine that monitors and gives **feedback** on internal physical processes such as **heart rate**, **blood pressure** or **muscle tension.**
2) They are then taught how to **control** these symptoms of stress through a variety of techniques. These can include **muscle relaxation** — muscle groups are tensed and relaxed in turn until the whole body is relaxed. This teaches people to notice when their body is becoming tense. Other techniques include actively clearing the mind using **meditation**, or **breathing control** exercises.
3) This feeling of relaxation acts like a **reward** and encourages the person to repeat this as an involuntary activity.
4) The person learns to use these techniques in **real-life** situations.

Trisha didn't need biofeedback — she had stress totally sorted

Exercise is Another Biological Method of Managing Stress

1) **Exercise** and being physically active reduces the likelihood of stress-related illness.
2) **Morris (1953)** compared **bus conductors** and **bus drivers** and found that the conductors had lower rates of cardiovascular problems.
3) This could be the result of having a more **active job** or the stress of **driving**.
4) Or, it could be caused by any number of **other variables**...
5) However, it's difficult to get a clear idea of the relationship because active people may be less likely to engage in **harmful behaviours** like smoking and drinking. Active people are likely to **sleep better**, which will have both a **biological** and a **psychological** influence on levels of **stress**.

Stress Management — Biological Approach

The Biological Approach Has **Strengths** and **Weaknesses**

Both drugs and biofeedback are **effective**:

Drugs are **quick** and **effective** in reducing dangerous symptoms such as high blood pressure. **Kahn et al (1986)** found that benzodiazepines were superior to a placebo (sugar pill) when they tracked around 250 patients over an 8-week period.

Attanasio et al (1985) found that biofeedback helped teenagers and children with stress-related disorders to gain **control** over the symptoms of **migraine** headaches. They also showed an increase in **enthusiasm** and a more positive attitude.

Placebos are pills that do nothing at all. They're used to test if any effect happens just because people think they're being treated.

BUT both treat **symptoms** rather than the underlying causes of stress:

Drugs only help with the **symptoms** and only so long as the drugs are taken.

Biofeedback also aims to **reduce** symptoms, but using relaxation techniques can also give the person a sense of **control** and have more **long-lasting** benefits.

Drugs have **side effects**, biofeedback **doesn't**:

Drugs can have minor **side effects** such as dizziness and tiredness or more serious effects such as blurred vision and changes in sex drive. **Withdrawal symptoms** when people come off medication, such as increased anxiety, seizures, tremors and headaches, can be distressing. Benzodiazepines can be **addictive**, and are generally limited to a maximum of 4 weeks' use.

There are no side effects of biofeedback — just **relaxation**. This method's advantage is that it's **voluntary** and not invasive.

Drugs are **easier** to use than biofeedback:

Drugs are relatively **easy** to prescribe and use.

Biofeedback needs specialist **equipment** and expert **supervision**. Some argue that the benefits of biofeedback could be gained from other relaxation techniques and so this is an unnecessary expense.

Practice Questions

Q1 What is GABA?

Q2 What are the steps involved in biofeedback?

Q3 Give one problem of using drugs to deal with stress.

Q4 Why is biofeedback a more expensive form of treatment than drugs?

Exam Questions

Q1 Describe how drugs can help in the management of stress. [6 marks]

Q2 Explain and evaluate two different biological methods of managing stress. [12 marks]

Stress management — quite the opposite of traditional management...

This ridiculously stressed and hectic lifestyle we choose to live is turning us all into ill people. I can't understand it myself — personally I choose the more Caribbean attitude to time management. I'm quite confident I'll never need to take BZs or teach myself to think differently. But then again, I might get into trouble for not finishing this book on time. Hmmm...

Stress Management — Psychological Approach

Just AQA A. *You often can't control what causes the stress, but you can control how it affects you.*

Psychological *Methods Involve Learning to* ***Think Differently***

The psychological approach helps you to cope better by **thinking differently** about the stressful situation. The techniques have been shown to be **effective** and deal with the **source** of the problem rather than just the symptoms. They provide **skills** that have more lasting value — like the **confidence** to cope with future problems and the belief of being in **control** and seeing life as a challenge rather than as a threat. (And other cheesy, upbeat things like that.)

Meichenbaum's Stress Inoculation Training (SIT):

This works like immunisation. Just like you might be inoculated against any attack from disease, you can protect yourself from the harmful effects of stress.

Training involves preparation so that you can deal with stress before it becomes a problem. 3 steps are involved:

1) **Conceptualisation**: Identify fears and concerns with the help of a therapist.
2) **Skill acquisition and rehearsal**: Train to develop skills like positive thinking and relaxation in order to improve self-confidence.
3) **Application and follow-through**: Practise the newly acquired skill in real-life situations with support and back-up from the therapist.

Meichenbaum (1977) found that SIT works both with short-term stressors such as preparing for public speaking, and longer-term stressors such as medical illness, divorce or work-related stress.

Hardiness Training:

Kobasa suggests that a strong and hardy person shows **3 Cs**: **Control** over their lives, **commitment** (a sense of purpose in life) and **challenge** (life is seen as a challenge and opportunity rather than as a threat).
See page 52 for more about this.

Maddi introduced a training programme to increase hardiness, arguing that the more hardy the person, the better they cope with stress. This training has 3 steps:

1) **Focusing**: Learn to **recognise** physical symptoms of stress, e.g. increase in heart rate, muscle tension and sweating.
2) **Reliving stressful encounters**: Learn to **analyse** stressful situations to better understand possible coping strategies.
3) **Self-improvement**: Take on **challenges** that can be coped with and build **confidence**, thereby gaining a greater sense of **control**.

Threat? Nah — just another of life's great opportunities.

Maddi et al (1998) got 54 managers who went on a hardiness training programme to report back on their progress. They recorded an increase in hardiness and job satisfaction and a decrease in strain and illness.

Despite proven effectiveness, there are **weaknesses** with psychological methods:

1) Psychological methods only suit a narrow band of individuals who are **determined** to stick to the technique.
2) Research tends to be based on white, middle-class business folk and so can't necessarily be **generalised** to others.
3) The procedures are very lengthy and require considerable **commitment** of time and effort.
4) The **concepts** may be too complex. For example, a lack of hardiness might be just another label for negativity. It could be argued that it's just as effective to relax and think positively.

Stress Management — Psychological Approach

Cognitive Behavioural Therapy (CBT) Aims to Alter Thought Processes

1) CBT techniques were developed to treat abnormality using concepts from the **cognitive approach**.
2) The idea is that changing the way information is cognitively **processed** will result in a change in **behaviour**.
3) These techniques can be used in stress management — by changing the way we **think** in stressful situations we can **cope** better and **behave** in ways that help to minimise or remove the stressor.

Rational-Emotive Therapy (RET) was Developed by Ellis (1962)

Ellis (1962) suggested an **ABC model**:

1) It begins with an **activating event** (A) which leads to a **belief** (B) about why this happened.
2) This then leads to a **consequence** (C). If the beliefs are **irrational**, they will lead to maladaptive consequences — such as depression, anxiety or symptoms of stress.
3) For example, if somebody fails to get a promotion at work (A), they may believe that it happened because they're useless (B), and the emotional consequence (C) may be feeling depressed.
4) RET focuses on encouraging people to change irrational beliefs into rational beliefs, for a more **positive consequence**.
5) In this example, believing that they didn't get the promotion because it's not possible to always perform well in an interview may lead to a more positive cognitive mood and less stress.

Beck's Cognitive Restructuring Therapy Also Features Negative Beliefs

Beck (1963) identified a **cognitive triad** of types of negative thought which can be applied to stress management. These are thoughts about:

1) **Themselves** — "I'm useless at everything."
2) **The future** — "Nothing will change and I won't improve."
3) **The world** — "You need to be better than I am to succeed in life."

The therapist's goal is to **disprove** the negativity in a person's thinking. After a while they should be able to use **different cognitive processes**, leading to a more **positive belief system**. Beck initially developed the therapy for use with depression, but it's been adapted for use beyond this. For example, Proudfoot et al (1997) found that cognitive therapies were effective when used to deal with the psychological effects of unemployment.

Practice Questions

Q1 What does SIT stand for?

Q2 What are the three parts of Ellis's ABC model?

Q3 Who identified a cognitive triad of negative thoughts?

Exam Questions

Q1 Outline and evaluate the use of SIT for managing stress. [8 marks]

Q2 Explain how cognitive behavioural therapy can be used to help people cope with stressful experiences. [10 marks]

Aaaaaaaaaaaaaaaaaaaaaarrrrrrrrrrrrrrrrrrrrrrgggggggggghhhhhh...

Makes sense, doesn't it? You get bossed around, told to write huge essays, told to write them again, told you can't go out until you've done your essay — of course you're going to feel stressed, it's only natural. But if you insist to yourself that it's all your own choice because it's the only path to a good job and lots of money, then you'll feel better. In theory anyway...

Localisation of Function

Just OCR. *Yep, it's a page about brains. Interesting things. I mean, really, they're just a pile of gooey, squidgy, messy bits of meat. They probably taste quite nice, but how on earth can they see, think, feel, create consciousness, play chess...*

Localisation of Function — Certain Bits of the Brain Do Certain Things

Certain areas of the brain are thought to be responsible for particular functions, e.g. vision, language, coordination... This is known as **localisation of function**.

The brain is split into two **hemispheres** (halves) — the right hemisphere and the left hemisphere.

View from above

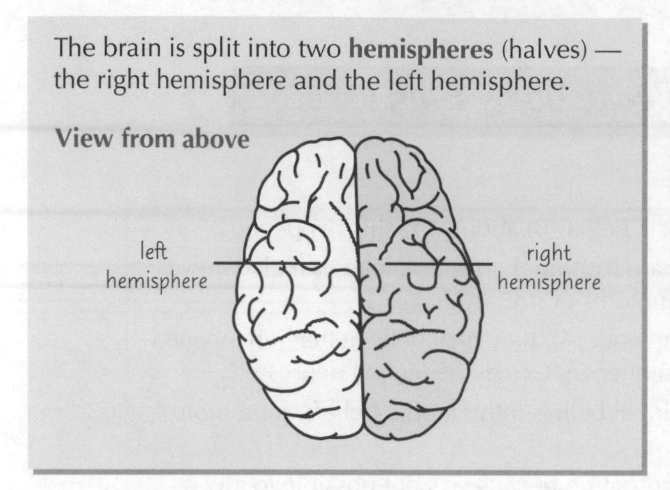

Within each hemisphere, there are four **lobes** — the **frontal** lobe, the **parietal** lobe, the **temporal** lobe and **occipital** lobe.

Side view from left

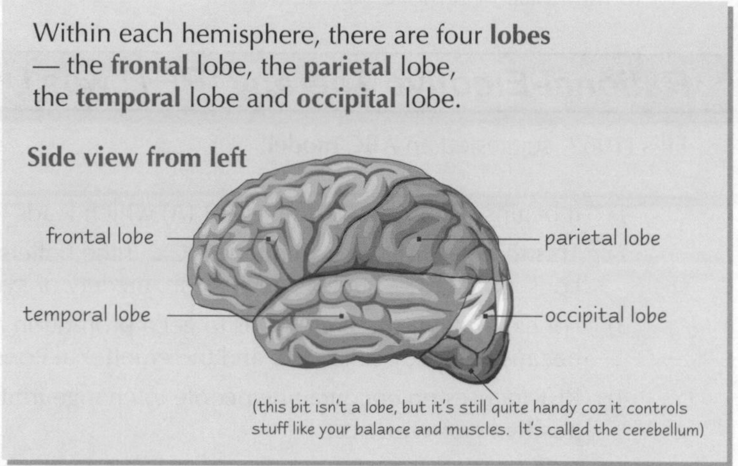

In most people, the **left** hemisphere handles the bulk of the **language** functions, **analysis and problem solving**, and **cognitive capacity**. The **right** hemisphere is more concerned with things like **spatial** comprehension, **emotions** and **face recognition**.

The **lobes** are named after their nearest **cranial** (skull) **bones** — each one is responsible for loads of specialised **functions** so they're generally not named after their function. (So, you wouldn't refer to, say, the memory lobe.)

Split-Brain Surgery Provides more Evidence for the Localisation of Function

Since you OCR dudes haven't had a **biology recap** since page 40, it's about time for another...

Information from the right visual field (that's the right half of what you see) goes to the left hemisphere.
Information from the left visual field goes to the right hemisphere (see the diagram below).
Information passes through the **corpus callosum** to whichever side of the brain needs to deal with it.

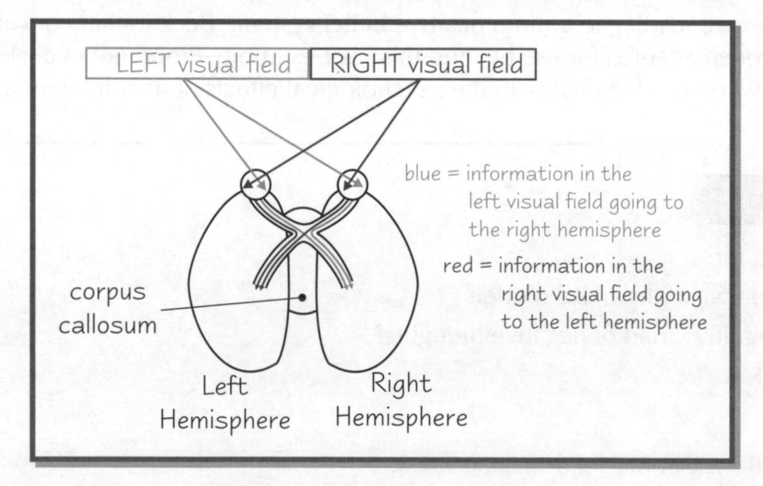

The effect of split-brain surgery:

1) In very severe cases of **epilepsy**, the only treatment available is to sever the corpus callosum. This stops information and seizures spreading across the brain.
2) But a side effect of splitting the hemispheres is that information can no longer move between them.
3) Scientists have used split-brain surgery patients to study the different roles of the two hemispheres — take a look at Sperry's study on the next page.

Localisation of Function

Sperry (1968) *Studied* ***Split-Brain Patients***

OCR Core Study

	Sperry (1968) studied individuals after split-brain surgery.
Method:	The study involved a combination of **case studies** and **experiments**. The 11 participants had undergone split-brain surgery as a result of epilepsy that couldn't be controlled by medication. A control group was used who had no hemisphere disconnection. In one of the experiments, participants covered one eye and looked at a fixed point on a projection screen. Pictures were projected onto the **right** or **left** of the screen at high speeds so that there was no time for eye movement.
Results:	If the picture was shown in the right visual field, all of the participants could say or write what it was without a problem. But if the image was flashed onto the left the split-brain participants couldn't say or write what they'd seen. They could select a corresponding object with their left hand, which represented what had been shown to their left eye (right hemisphere), even though they didn't know why they had selected this object.
Conclusion:	This shows that different areas of the brain specialise in different functions. The left hemisphere (which receives visual information from the right visual field) can convert sight into spoken and written language. Usually information entering the right hemisphere can cross over to be processed in the left. As the results show, this can't happen in split brains, so the information going to the right hemisphere can't be converted into language at all. But this doesn't mean that the right hemisphere is unaware.
Comment:	Using case studies as well as experiments meant that Sperry obtained both **qualitative** and **quantitative** data. Also, using both method types meant that the **reliability** and the **validity** of the study were increased. However, the study only used 11 participants, which is a very **small sample** size for being able to generalise the results to others. But, it would have been difficult to find a large number of split-brain patients to study. Epilepsy is usually caused by **brain damage** and the patients had also been on **medication** which may have affected their brains. Therefore, it is hard to conclude that the ways they processed information would be the same as for people **without** epilepsy or split-brain treatment. The study has also been criticised in terms of **ecological validity** — the experimental situation was artificial, so it's difficult to **generalise** the results to real-life situations.

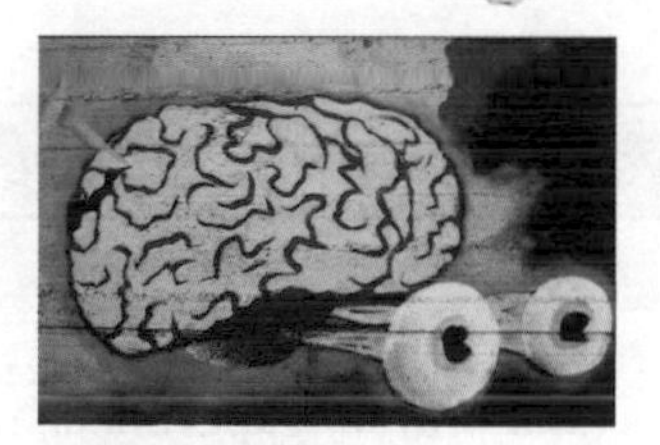

Practice Questions

Q1 What is meant by 'localisation of function'?

Q2 Where does information from the right visual field go to?

Q3 What is split-brain surgery?

Q4 Which two research methods did Sperry's study use?

Exam Questions

Q1 Outline why split-brain patients are used when studying localisation of function. [6 marks]

Q2 Describe and evaluate a study investigating localisation of brain function. [12 marks]

Brings a whole new perspective to being in two minds about things...

I heard a story about a man who got attacked with a machete. Very nasty story — read no further if you're at all squeamish. Anyway, someone chopped right through the middle of his head with the machete. Blood everywhere, but the guy was absolutely fine. It'd gone right between the two hemispheres and not touched a single brain cell. Lucky man eh?

Brain Structure and Behaviour

These pages are for OCR and Edexcel. *Biological psychologists reckon that behaviour is determined by brain structure. They use scanning techniques to look at people's brains and try to link structures and activity to various behaviours.*

Brain Scans Can Help Examine Patterns of Brain Activity and Anatomy

There are five basic techniques used:

1) **PET scans** (positron emission tomography — not what happens in the vets) show which parts of the brain are **active** during different tasks. They show average activity over a 60 second period, not moment by moment.
2) **CAT scans** detect **damaged** parts of the brain, tumours and blood clots. Brain **structure** is shown, not function.
3) **MRI scans** detect small tumours and provide **detailed** information about **structure**.
4) **Functional MRI scans** are **3D** scans providing **structural** and **functional** information.
5) **SQUID magnetometry** produces accurate images of brain **activity** by measuring the magnetic fields generated when neurones are activated. However, outside sources of magnetism can affect measurements.

*Raine et al (1997) used PET Scans to Study **Murderers' Brains***

Raine et al used PET scans to investigate the differences in **brain activity** of a sample of **violent** offenders:

Raine et al (1997) studied murderers' brains

Method:	A laboratory experiment compared 41 murderers (39 men, 2 women) with 41 control subjects who had been matched for age, gender and diagnosis of schizophrenia. The murderers had all pleaded 'not guilty by reason of insanity' (NGRI). **PET scans** were conducted on all 82 participants after completing a recognition task.
Results:	Murderers pleading NGRI were found to have different brain functioning compared to the control subjects. They found that they had **reduced** activity in the **prefrontal cortex** and **increased** activity in **subcortical** regions of the right hemisphere, such as the **thalamus**.
Conclusion:	The differences may mean that brain structure predisposes some people to be more aggressive than others.

*This study has several **strengths** and **weaknesses***

Strengths:

1) The study was a **laboratory experiment**, meaning that variables could be strictly **controlled**. This type of study provides **reliable** results.
2) By matching the participants, Raine et al were very careful to **control** for other variables, including mental health problems. As an additional control, the participants were told not to take their usual medication for two weeks prior to the study.

Weaknesses:

1) Although it seems likely that violent offenders have differently active brains, the results can't claim that violence is **solely** due to biology or that people claiming NGRI didn't know what they were doing.
2) We need to be careful about assuming **causality** between the brain activity and criminal behaviour. It could be that irregular brain activity is the result of criminal behaviour, rather than the cause of it.
3) The **sample** was only made up of **murderers**. This means that results cannot be **generalised** to those who commit other types of crime. Also, there may have been differences in the level of violence used by the individual murderers.
4) The study only measured the participants' brain activity after one type of task — a recognition task. This has an effect on the study's **internal validity**, as different types of task could have produced different brain activity.

Brain Structure and Behaviour

PET Scans *Show* ***Activity*** *in the Brain During Specific* ***Behaviours***

PET scans show that some areas of the brain are more **active** when specific **demands** are made of them. By studying PET scans, we can link certain areas of the brain with particular **functions**. They also allow us to see where the brain is most active when we are **thinking** about certain things.

There's also evidence from ***MRI*** *scans to show* ***changes*** *in brain structure*

OCR Core Study

Maguire et al (2000) studied taxi drivers' brains

Method: In a **natural experiment**, MRI scans from 16 licensed male London taxi drivers were compared with a control group who had never driven taxis. All of the participants were in good general, neurological and psychiatric health, and had an average age of 44. All of the taxi drivers had been working for at least 18 months.

Results: The average size of the right posterior hippocampus was **significantly larger** in the taxi driver group compared to the control group. Additionally, the increased size was relative to the length of time the taxi driver had been working — the **longer** they'd been working, the **larger** their right posterior hippocampus.

Conclusion: The hippocampus is responsible for storing a spatial representation of the environment — it seems that the specific navigational demands on the taxi drivers have resulted in physical change.

Evaluation: The findings of the study could be used to help those with brain injuries as it shows that the size of structures within the brain can be influenced through cognitive activity. This means **rehabilitation** could be tailored to the specific needs of individuals and their injuries. The study had a good level of **control** and could be **replicated**, which increases its **reliability**. The **sample size** is small though, and the results can only be **generalised** to male taxi drivers in London. Also, the results can't be generalised to **other areas** of the brain.

Practice Questions

Q1 What are PET scans used for?

Q2 Who were the experimental group in the Raine et al (1997) study?

Q3 How many taxi drivers were used in the Maguire et al (2000) study?

Q4 Identify a practical application of the Maguire et al (2000) study.

Exam Questions

Q1 Outline the method and results of the Raine et al (1997) study. [8 marks]

Q2 Evaluate the strengths and weaknesses of the Maguire et al (2000) study. [8 marks]

Grrrrrrrrrrrrrrrrrrrrrrrrrrrrrrrrrrrrrrrrrrrrrrrrrrrrrrrrrrrrrrrr...

Well, what an interesting page. Seeing as all our decisions come from the brain, I wouldn't be at all surprised if there were differences in brain activity between murderers and non-violent people. Although I doubt we'll find them properly any time soon. I mean, brains are pretty darned complicated things. Imagine actually finding the violent bits. Brain surgery time...

Sleep and Dreaming

Just OCR this time. The others can go to sleep... *We've all got biological rhythms that affect our behaviour. They regulate things like eating and blood pressure, but the big daddy of body rhythms is the daily sleep/wake cycle.*

The Sleep/Wake Cycle Takes Place Once a Day

Circadian rhythms are **biological rhythms** that take place **once a day**. The sleep/wake example is the most studied — we have a strong need for sleep each day. Several reasons have been put forward for the function of sleep:

Evolutionary theory says that sleep has **survival value**. For humans, it would have been an advantage to be still and quiet during the night to prevent being seen or eaten by predators with better night vision.

Restoration theory says that sleep allows the body to **restore** itself after a tiring day of biological processes. This explains why babies sleep much more than adults — they experience a big surge of development in a short space of time.

Memory consolidation theory says that sleep allows the brain to consolidate all the information it's absorbed during the day, and prevents any new information from **interfering** with this process.

Sounds like too much thinking and not enough sleeping.

Sleep Can Be Split into Stages of Different Brain Activity

Electroencephalograms (EEGs) measure electrical activity in the brain, and are used to record the stages of sleep.

Stage	EEG
Stage 1	
Stage 2	
Stage 3	
Stage 4	
REM Sleep (active sleep)	

1) Adults pass through the stages about five times a night, with each cycle lasting about 90 minutes. Who'd have thought we were so busy...
2) As you fall into deeper sleep from stages 1 to 4, the activity becomes **higher voltage** and **lower frequency**.
   - **Stage 1** is a bit like deep relaxation, with lowered heart rate, muscle tension and temperature. It's quite easy to wake people up.
   - **Stage 2** has slower and larger EEG waves, with some quick bursts of high frequency waves called **sleep spindles**.
   - **Stage 3** has even larger, slower waves.
   - **Stage 4** has the largest, slowest waves of all, because it's the deepest stage of sleep. Metabolic activity is pretty low in general, and the sleeper is very hard to wake.
3) After stage 4, the cycle reverses and goes back through stages 3 and 2. Then instead of stage 1, a period of '**active sleep**' occurs.
4) During the active stage, metabolic activity increases, and the body appears almost paralysed except for **rapid eye movement (REM)**. The EEG pattern is almost like when you're awake.

Several Methodologies and Techniques are Used in Sleep Research

The following equipment and techniques are often used in **sleep laboratories**... Zzzzzzz... Hmmm, what..? Oh... yes. Variables, such as noise and distraction, are **controlled** to increase the **reliability** of the research. However, they're **artificial environments**, which may affect the participants' sleep patterns — reducing **validity**.

1) **Equipment** such as EEGs provide quantitative reports which can easily be compared to others. They have high reliability and changes in sleep stages can be easily identified. Other equipment used includes EOGs (electrooculograms) which measure the electrical activity of the eyes, and EMGs (electromyograms) which measure the electrical activity in muscles.
2) **Self reports** involve participants keeping a record of their dreams or estimating their length. They're useful for gaining information which couldn't be collected in any other way, but they're limited by the accuracy of recall.
3) **Observations** of patterns and directions of **eye movements** can be recorded and related to sleep stages.

Sleep and Dreaming

Physiological Research Has Also Attempted to Understand **Dreaming**

There are several theories about the function of dreaming:

1) **Winson (1993)** suggested that REM sleep evolved so humans could dream about important information that they needed for **survival** — for example, for hunting and hiding from predators. This information is integrated with **past experiences** and provides a **plan** for future behaviour. Today, we'd dream about current problems like money, jobs and relationships.

2) The **activation-synthesis model** by **Hobson and McCarley (1977)** suggests that **random neural activity** is muddled up with **existing knowledge** and memories, and expressed in the form of a **dream**. Hobson later suggested that dreaming is a **by-product** of the brain sorting out what to keep and forget. This explains why dreams are often about recent events.

3) **Webb and Cartwright (1978)** suggest dreams are used to **problem-solve** issues and help us deal with and resolve problems that have arisen during the day.

Dement and Kleitman (1957) Investigated **Eye Movements** During Dreams

OCR Core Study

Dement and Kleitman (1957) — eye movements during dreams

Method: 9 participants were monitored in a sleep laboratory. Their brain activity was recorded using an EEG. They were woken several times and asked to comment on the content and duration of any dreams.

Results: It was seen that:

- Dreaming took place mostly during REM sleep.
- There was a positive correlation between the amount of time spent in REM and the person's estimate of how long they'd been dreaming.
- There was an association between the content of dreams and the pattern of eye movement. E.g. vertical eye movements when dreaming about looking up and down ladders.

Conclusion: The findings suggest that there is a relationship between REM and dreaming.

Evaluation: The study was designed to **control** for variables — amount of sleep, use of stimulants which could affect sleep, and the location of sleep. The **sample size** was small, making it difficult to **generalise** the results — they might only be applicable to this small group. In addition, these findings are not supported by later studies. The study lacks **ecological validity**, as sleep took place in a very artificial situation.

Practice Questions

Q1 What are EEGs used for?

Q2 Give two techniques used in sleep research.

Q3 What does the activation-synthesis model propose?

Exam Questions

Q1 Outline the different stages of sleep. [8 marks]

Q2 Kate can often remember her dreams when she wakes up.
Outline two theories which could explain the purpose of Kate's dreams. [6 marks]

*Zzzzzzzzzzz... *snort* — Wha? Oh... yeah, sleeping... nice... Zzzzzzzzzz...*

Last night I dreamt I was back at school, but school was also my house, and a bit like my old house and my new house, and my sister was there, then I can't remember what happened, but then we had some scampi but I don't know why cos I don't really like it. Then I woke up. Weird how your own dreams are always so much more interesting than other people's isn't it...

Gender Development — The Biological Approach

Just Edexcel. *There are loads of different theories flying around out there about why we behave like we do. There's the psychodynamic model and the social learning theory, but here you're going to learn about the biological approach.*

The Biological Approach looks at Physiology

First of all, let's get one thing clear — **gender** and **sex** aren't the same thing. Your **gender** is the way you **act** and identify yourself — the behavioural characteristics that you have that make you **masculine** or **feminine**. On the other hand, **sex** is determined **physiologically**. The biological approach explains differences in **behaviour** in terms of **physiology**. Some biological explanations focus on **genes** or **hormones**, and others focus on overall **brain** or **body structure**.

Genes Determine Your Sex

1) **Females** have **two X** sex chromosomes — XX. **Males** have **one X** chromosome and **one Y** chromosome — XY. It's the **Y chromosome** that leads to **male development**.
2) Some humans are born with **variations** in the standard sex chromosome pattern. Studies of people with such variations have indicated that **gender differences** can be caused by **different sex chromosomes** in males and females.

For example, in **Klinefelter's syndrome** males are born with **XXY sex chromosomes** — they have an **extra X chromosome**. Males with this syndrome are **sterile** and tend to be **less muscular** and have **less facial and body hair**. They can have problems using **language** to express themselves and may have trouble with **social interaction**.

Hormones Can Influence Gender

The major male and female hormones are **androgens** and **oestrogens**. Both types of hormone are present in males and females, but in very **different amounts**. Men produce much more testosterone (an androgen) each day than females, and females produce much more oestrogens than males.

However, some humans produce **smaller** or **larger** quantities of these hormones than normal.

For example, sometimes people are born with much more **testosterone** than normal — a syndrome called **CAH**.

1) Males with CAH aren't that much different.
2) The **behaviour** of **girls** with CAH tends to be **masculinised** — they have a preference for playing with boys' toys and enjoy 'tomboyish' activities.
3) **Physically**, girls with CAH tend to look more **masculine**. Their **growth** is fast and **puberty** can happen early.

Case studies of conditions like this suggest that the effect of **testosterone** on the **developing brain** is responsible for the **differences in gender behaviour**.

Young et al (1964) conducted an experiment on monkeys to see if **females** exposed to **testosterone** **behaved differently** from normal female monkeys. You might notice that it's not exactly that ethical...

	Young et al (1964) investigated testosterone in monkeys.
Method:	Pregnant female monkeys were injected with testosterone so that the foetus would develop with exposure to testosterone. The researchers assessed the behaviour of the offspring.
Results:	Male offspring were born with little difference to their behaviour. Female monkeys were born **'masculinised'** — they behaved like male monkeys, especially in terms of aggression.
Conclusion:	Testosterone causes male behaviour.
Evaluation:	This study only investigates testosterone — **other hormones** could be involved in gender behaviour. Also, this study has **ethical issues** — some people would consider it unethical to inject monkeys with extra hormones so that they develop in an unnatural way.

Gender Development — The Biological Approach

Brain Structure Links to Behaviour

Males and females differ in the ways that they **process language** and **information** and in their **emotional behaviour**. For instance, women tend to be a bit better than men at **human interaction** and **emotional expression**, whereas men are often better than women at **mathematical** and **spatial skills**. Some scientists have put these differences down to **brain structure**, and believe that it is this that causes people to behave in a typically male or female way.

Male and female **brains** differ in many ways. For instance, the **size** of certain parts of the brain vary depending on gender. For example, one part of the **hypothalamus** is over **two times larger in men** than in women. This difference is noticeable after about 4 years of age.

De Bellis et al (2001) — brain structure in males and females.

Method: De Bellis et al used **MRI scans** of 118 children and adolescents (6-17 years) of both sexes to see if there were any differences in brain structure between males and females.

Results: They found that different areas of the brain were **different sizes** in males and females depending on **age**.

Conclusion: Male and female brains mature differently with age and are physically different at equivalent age-related stages. These **structural differences** could be responsible for the **differences in gender behaviour**.

Evaluation: The **large sample size** used in the study increases its reliability. However, there could be **other factors** apart from brain structure that cause differences in gender behaviour. For example, behaviour could be due to an interaction involving both hormones and brain structure. Nurture could also play a part — girls and boys are often brought up differently, which could cause differences in behaviour.

The Evidence from the Biological Approach has Pros and Cons

There's plenty of convincing evidence out there to support the biological approach — from human **case studies** to **animal experiments**. Much of the evidence comes from **laboratory experiments**, which tend to be **reliable** as it's possible to have a lot of **control** over the variables. However, before you think it's all perfect, read on...

1) The downside to lab experiments is that they **lack ecological validity** — they lack the natural conditions that exist in the real world.
2) Also, the biological approach doesn't explain why there is so much difference in behaviour **within** a gender — not all males behave in the same way, even though they're biologically very similar.
3) The biological approach also doesn't take any **other factors** into account, such as the **environment**. For example, **Smith and Lloyd** (1978) provided evidence for **environmental** factors. It was seen that women treat babies differently if they know the baby's **gender**. This could affect the way that they are brought up, in turn affecting behaviour.
4) Lastly, there are many **problems** with using the results of **animal experiments** (see the next page).

Practice Questions

Q1 Give three physical factors that the biological approach focuses on.

Q2 Which hormone might be responsible for male behaviour?

Exam Question

Q1 Outline one experiment into the biological cause of gender behaviour.
Evaluate the strengths and weaknesses of the study. [8 marks]

Jeans determine sex — what about those emo boys wearing girls' jeans...

So, we've covered three features that the biological approach focuses on — genes, hormones and brain structure. You need to know what they are, and for each, make sure you can give an example of a study or a condition that supports the theory. And I probably don't even need to remind you of one key word — evaluation, evaluation, evaluation...

Gender Development — The Biological Approach

Just Edexcel again...

So, you've learnt that some evidence comes from experimenting on animals.
There are plenty of problems with doing that — and not just ethical ones.

The Biological Approach Uses Many Research Methods

Ethics play a large part in the types of study used in the biological approach. It would be simple if we could just, for example, take all the testosterone from a man and see if he started behaving like a woman. But... that's hardly ethical. So, other methods have to be used.

1) Biologists can study naturally occurring **sex anomalies** in humans. This is where people have been born with, or acquired, unusual sexual biology (e.g. people with Klinefelter's syndrome or CAH).
2) **Post-mortem studies** can be carried out to compare and examine the brains of males and females.
3) **Functional imaging** can be used to produce 2D and 3D images of the brain. This can be done when the participant is carrying out a task (e.g. reading or doing a maths problem) to allow the scientist to study which parts are activated. Male and female brains can be compared to see if there are any **gender differences** in **brain activation**.
4) Biologists experiment on **animals** by changing some aspect of their **biology** (e.g. altering the level of a hormone) and seeing if it affects their **behaviour**. However, some people would say that this isn't really that ethical...

There are Problems with Experimenting on Animals

Although there are many pros, there are also plenty of cons to do with experimenting on animals.
You could do with knowing both sides of the story for your exam.

On the Plus Side

1) Animal experiments allow researchers to study biological changes that would be **unethical** to study in humans.
2) Much of the **body chemistry** between animals and humans is **similar** — some **generalisations** can be made from animals to humans.
3) A large amount of **control over variables** can take place in laboratory conditions, so you're likely to get the same results each time — the results are likely to be **reliable**.

Bob didn't want them to generalise his behaviour to humans — he just wanted a banana.

On the Down Side

1) Humans are different from animals in that they tend to **think** and **analyse** situations. For example, several animal experiments involving memory have used mazes. Humans put into a maze would probably behave very differently to rats put into a maze. Humans might sit down and wonder why they're in a maze. They might try to reach the end of the maze, or they might try to escape.
2) Whilst we're pretty similar to animals in some ways, we still have many **genetic** and **physical differences**. Just because a male rat behaves like a female when a certain part of its brain is removed doesn't mean that the same will apply to humans. So, you've got to be careful when you make **generalisations** from animal research to humans.
3) Animals are not affected by as many kinds of **environmental influences** as humans are. It could be partly these influences that cause gender differences in behaviour.
4) It might be considered **unethical** to experiment on animals, especially if the research isn't essential (say, not designed to come up with a treatment to save lives). Sometimes, the animals may suffer **pain** or stress, and it's not like they can give **consent**.
5) Laboratory experiments aren't the same as real-world situations. People and animals might behave differently in lab conditions than in the real world, meaning that these experiments would **lack ecological validity**.

Gender Development — The Biological Approach

There are *Alternative Explanations*

Don't forget about the difference between sex and gender. Sex is physiological and gender is about identity.

As you've seen, there's plenty of convincing evidence to suggest that gender behaviour is caused by biological factors. However, there are **alternative explanations** out there.

1) There's a big **nature/nurture debate** about the cause of gender behaviour.
2) The nurture debate is supported by **social learning theorists**, who believe that we are born **gender neutral** and that it's our **surroundings** and **environment** that cause us to become girls and boys.
3) One way to test this would be to get identical **twin boys** and bring one up as a **girl**. If biology is responsible for behaviour, the twin will still act like a boy. Not exactly **ethical** though...
4) **Money** was a **social learning theorist** who believed that a boy who was brought up as a girl would behave as a girl and be happy. It seems that he was very wrong...

Money (1975) suggested that a boy could be brought up as a girl.

Method: Money suggested that a boy could be brought up as a girl. He carried out a case study into a boy, Bruce Reimer, who had accidently had his penis burnt off during a circumcision in infancy. Money advised Bruce's parents that the boy could be surgically changed into a girl and brought up as a female. This was what was done, and Bruce was brought up as a girl from the age of 18 months. He was renamed Brenda.

Results: According to Money, for the first part of her life, Brenda seemed to act more like a girl than a boy. However, as she grew up, she preferred to play with boys' toys, became 'tomboyish' and felt socially isolated from other girls. Eventually, at the age of 14, Brenda learned about her past and chose to return to living as a male. He called himself 'David', and lived the life of a male for some years after. However, David later became deeply unhappy and committed suicide.

Conclusion: Bringing up a boy as a girl doesn't work — especially when the boy has been exposed to normal amounts of testosterone during development.

Evaluation: All seemed to go well at first, and people were surprised by the idea that people might be born gender-neutral. However, many allegations were made that Money **did not reveal the true events** and that Brenda was **never happy** as a girl. Also, this case study does not rule out the possibility that a boy with an **abnormality in testosterone** levels might provide **different results**. If it was testosterone that caused Brenda to remain psychologically male, then having a lack of testosterone could mean that a boy could feasibly be brought up as a girl. 'David' was brought up as a boy for the first **year and a half** of his life. This could have had a significant impact on his **later feelings** about his gender. Perhaps if he had been brought up as a girl from a younger age the results would have been different. This study also has **ethical issues** — it's been suggested that Money encouraged the parents to consider a sex change for their son for the **benefit of his own research** into social learning theory.

Some big issues on this page. If gender behaviour really is down to biology, then it'd be impossible to bring up a boy as a girl, and vice versa. Being told you're a girl and later finding out you're not can't be the nicest thing in the world.

Practice Questions

Q1 Give two research methods used in the biological approach.

Q2 Name one alternative theory to the biological approach.

Exam Questions

Q1 Evaluate the strengths and weaknesses of using animal experiments to investigate the effects of biology on behaviour. [8 marks]

Q2 Does Money's (1975) case study support the biological approach to behaviour? Explain your answer. [6 marks]

No amount of Money can change you from a boy to a girl...

Now that you've learnt about the biological approach to gender development, I'd better warn you that you're gonna need to know about two other approaches — the social learning approach (p.116-117) and the psychodynamic approach (p.122-123). Not quite yet though... However, in the exam, be prepared to be asked to compare the three approaches.

Biological Psychology in the Real World

The final pages of this section are also just for Edexcel. *Believe it or not, the stuff you're learning about is relevant to issues in today's society. You need to know about one of these issues — so here are two just to keep you going.*

Autism is a **Developmental Disorder** That Appears Before the Age of **Three**

See page 22 for a description of some of the symptoms of autism.

1) **Kanner** first wrote about autism in 1943. Before this, individuals with the symptoms would have been classed as 'mentally retarded' or emotionally disturbed.
2) He suggested that autism was caused by **brain abnormalities** that were present before birth. Without firm evidence, this explanation went out of the window.
3) For a time, **parenting style** was seen as the cause. Emotional coldness in parents, especially the mother, was blamed for preventing children from developing their social and emotional skills properly. Again, because of a lack of evidence, this explanation was dismissed in the mid-1960s.

Baron-Cohen (1996) Proposed the **Extreme Male Brain** Theory

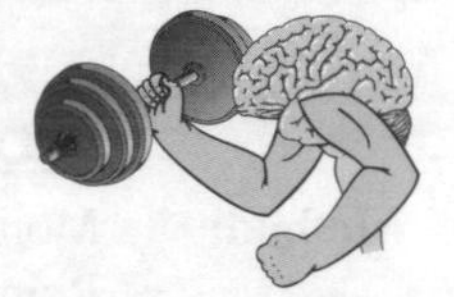

Baron-Cohen suggested that there are **two dimensions** that illustrate human sex differences — **empathising** and **systemising**.

1) **Empathising** means being able to understand other people's **thoughts** and **emotions** and then responding to them in an appropriate way. This allows us to care for people and make predictions about their behaviour.

2) **Systemising** means understanding how the **variables**, **rules** and **processes** within systems work. The brain analyses the inputs and outputs of systems, makes predictions about their behaviour and sometimes tries to control them. Examples of systems include mathematics and computer systems.

1) Baron-Cohen (2002) looked at over 30 studies that investigated gender differences and concluded that the **female** brain is stronger at **empathising**, and the **male** brain is stronger at **systemising**.
2) Because the symptoms of autism can include a poor understanding of other's **emotions** alongside ritualistic, **systematic** behaviour, Baron-Cohen suggests that autism can be described as an **extreme male brain condition**. This is because autistic symptoms mirror an **extreme form of systemising**.
3) Later, Baron-Cohen (2005) developed the theory to suggest a **cause** for the extreme male brain condition. He thought that **parents** who both have a **strong systemising dimension** are genetically more likely to produce children with a strong systemising dimension. In **extreme cases** this presents itself as autism.

The Theory Has **Strengths** and **Weaknesses**

Strengths

1) Autism has a strong **male bias**, which supports the idea that it's linked to having an extreme male brain.
2) Baron-Cohen provides **evidence** to support the idea that females have stronger empathising dimensions. **Hoffman (1977)** found that females are more **comforting** and more likely to share emotional distress. Baron-Cohen also provided evidence that males have stronger **systemising** dimensions — e.g. **Kimura (1999)** found boys had better **construction skills** with 2D and 3D models, even as young as 3 years old.

Weaknesses

1) There is a problem in that comparing genders may mean that **generalisations** are made about the gender groups. Baron-Cohen acknowledges this and emphasises that the evidence does show wide **variations** within gender groups. Therefore, it's better to assume that **more males** than females have a stronger **systemising** dimension, but that there are **some females** with strengths in this dimension. Likewise, it's better to assume that **more females** than males have a stronger **empathising** dimension, but that **some males** are also strong in this dimension.
2) It's a purely biological explanation for autism — it doesn't allow for **social** or **environmental** explanations.

Biological Psychology in the Real World

Money and Ehrhardt (1972) Proposed a **Biosocial** Theory of **Gender**

1) They suggested that a mixture of **biological** and **social** factors influence gender identity and development.
2) Firstly gender is identified at birth through **observation** of the genitals and the **label** of 'male' or 'female' is made — this is the **biological** aspect.
3) The **social** aspect is influential because people treat the baby as it grows in a way that fits in with the **social role** of 'male' or 'female'. The child **learns gender appropriate behaviour** in this way and develops an understanding of what it means to be a male or female.

They looked at case studies of individuals who had undergone **transgender operations** as children and were experiencing **unusual gender development**. For example, the participants had undergone surgery and had been raised as females, but tended to display tomboyish behaviour and preferred typically male activities.

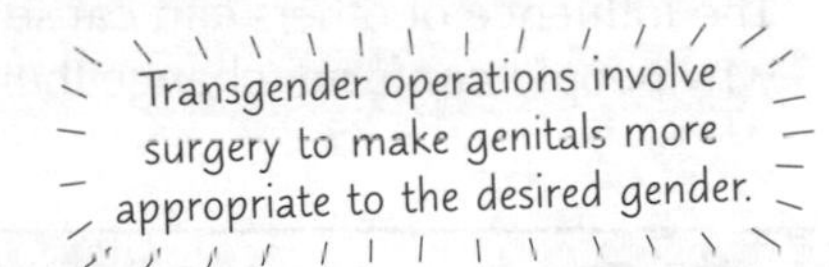

1) One example is the 1975 study of **David Reimer** (see page 67 for more on this).
2) Other participants were people with **biological disorders** that result in ambiguous genitalia which aren't clearly either male or female.

Transgender Operations Raise **Ethical Issues**

1) Money and Ehrhardt identified a **sensitive period** lasting until around the third year of life. During this time change in gender will not cause any psychological harm. After this age there is much more likelihood of **distress** and **psychological damage**. This suggestion has been criticised because the small number of case studies used may not be **representative** of everybody in these circumstances.
2) Surgery at a young age requires **permission** from parents who may give consent believing that it's the best for their child. If surgery is left as an **option** for the individual to choose themselves as adults, they may make a different decision.

I wouldn't have said that — he's in his sensitive period at the moment.

Practice Questions

Q1 What did Baron-Cohen mean by an empathising dimension?

Q2 What did Baron-Cohen mean by a systemising dimension?

Q3 Is autism more common in males or females?

Q4 How long did Money and Ehrhardt think that the sensitive period lasted?

Exam Questions

Q1 Outline the extreme male brain theory of autism. [8 marks]

Q2 Discuss the ethical issues associated with transgender operations. [6 marks]

Football and fast cars — the stuff of the extreme male brain...

So, you can see how all the theoretical stuff can be applied to problems in the real world. Psychologists have a part to play in some of the questions facing many people in society today — like whether it's right to perform transgender operations on children just because their anatomy isn't quite right. Pretty interesting. Better than those endless abstract theories.

The Social Approach

These pages are for y'all. Yes ma'am. *Social psychology is about how we influence each other. Our behaviour is affected by the social situation we're in — so it might be normal to be naked in the bath, but it's not normal to be naked on the bus. To be fair, not all of the research is about being naked, but at least it's got your attention...*

Social Psychology Looks at How **People Affect Each Other**

1) **Social behaviour** occurs when two or more people interact. People interact differently depending on the situation — so you may act differently with a parent, a friend, a stranger, or when you're in a group.
2) Social psychology also considers how we **think** about **other people**. This is **social cognition**, which can involve things like **stereotyping** and **prejudice**.
3) The influence of others can cause individuals to change their behaviour. Social psychologists have studied why people **conform** (change their behaviour to fit in with a group), and why they **obey** authority figures.

Social Psychologists Use Loads of Different **Research Methods**

Fortunately they're all methods that are used in some of the other approaches too. There's more general stuff on research methods on pages 126-127. And more on ethical issues on pages 136-137.

Laboratory experiments

Advantages
- They're **highly controlled**, so the effect of the independent variable can be measured.
- This also means that it's possible to establish **cause and effect**, and to **replicate** the method.
- Participants in different conditions can act as comparisons.

Disadvantages
- They create an **artificial environment**, so studies have **low ecological validity** — most social interactions don't normally take place in labs. Unless you're a rat.
- This means there are problems with **generalising** the results.

Field experiments

are conducted in **real-life settings** — e.g. hospitals (see Hofling et al's study on page 83).

Advantages
- The variables are still highly controlled, so it should be possible to establish **cause and effect**.
- Studies take place in the participants' natural environments, so they're more likely to capture natural social behaviour. This means they have **higher ecological validity** than lab experiments.
- **Demand characteristics** are reduced if the participants don't know they're being studied.

Disadvantages
- It's very difficult to control all the variables in a natural environment, so the results can still be affected by **confounding variables**.
- Lots of field experiments involve using **deception** (e.g. Piliavinet et al's study on page 88). This has **ethical implications** — you can't get **informed consent**, and it can be difficult to **debrief** participants.

Natural experiments

look at **naturally occurring situations** — the independent variable isn't manipulated.

Advantages
- Studies take place in the participants' natural environments, and nothing is manipulated, so they're likely to capture natural social behaviour. This means they have **high ecological validity**.
- Researchers can investigate variables that it would be **unethical** to manipulate.

Disadvantages
- Because none of the variables are controlled, experiments tend to have **low internal validity**. It's really hard to tell what actually caused the results. This means it's difficult to establish **cause and effect**.
- Natural experiments often involve **deception**, which raises ethical issues.

The Social Approach

Naturalistic observation

Naturalistic observation is when the experimenter just **observes** behaviour, without manipulating any variables.

Advantages

- Participants are in a natural environment, and are often unaware they're being observed. This means that studies should have **high ecological validity**.
- Results from observations can be used to **develop theories**, which can then be tested in experiments.

Disadvantages

- Not controlling the independent variable means it's very difficult to establish **cause and effect**.
- The results are **subjective** — observers can be biased about what they record.
- Observation can involve **deception**, which brings up problems of gaining **informed consent** and **debriefing** participants. Ethically it's OK to observe people in places where they might expect to be observed by strangers — so you can watch them in the street, but you can't train a telescopic lens on their bedroom.

Surveys are used a lot

Surveys can include **questionnaires** and **interviews**. They can be really useful, but the problem is that there's no way of knowing whether people are telling the truth. Unless you rig them up to a lie detector like on Jeremy Kyle.

Questionnaires can include **closed** or **open-ended questions**. Closed questions have a limited set of answers e.g. yes or no. Open questions don't have a restricted set of answers — e.g. 'what do you think of Jeremy Kyle?'
Interviews can be **structured** or **unstructured**. Structured interviews use pre-decided questions that are the same for all of the participants. In unstructured interviews the interviewers give the participant more freedom, although they might still guide the conversation to cover certain topics.

Advantages

- With questionnaires you can gather lots of data quickly and cheaply. This means you can have a large sample, making the results more reliable.
- Closed questions and structured interviews produce **quantitative data**, which is really easy to analyse.
- Open questions and unstructured interviews produce **qualitative data**, which is really detailed.

Disadvantages

- Questionnaires and interviews rely on self-reporting. This means people can lie in order to show themselves in a good light — **social desirability bias.**
- Interviews can be very time-consuming.
- It's easy to write bad questions. Researchers have to avoid **leading questions** (ones that lead the participants towards certain answers), or questions that can mean different things to different people.

Practice Questions

Q1 What sorts of behaviour is social psychology concerned with?

Q2 Outline the experimental methods on these pages that involve manipulating the independent variable.

Q3 In terms of ethics, where can observational studies be conducted?

Q4 What's the difference between structured and unstructured interviews?

Exam Questions

Q1 Some social psychologists are investigating obedience. They design a questionnaire to ask students under what sort of conditions they would disobey their teachers.

a) Outline one disadvantage of using this method. [2 marks]

b) Explain one strength of quantitative data. [2 marks]

Q2 Outline one advantage and one disadvantage of field experiments. [4 marks]

Remember — social psychology is all about how people affect each other...

Phew, it's all gone a bit research methodsy round here. Not sure how that happened. Still, it's good really cos this stuff turns up all over the shop, so learn it now and you'll be laughing all the way to the exam hall. I can just picture you now, having a whale of a time. Just remember to cool it to a gentle giggle once you're in there though, else you might get hiccups.

Types of Conformity

Ignore the next 2 pages if you're doing Edexcel.
***Conformity** is when the behaviour of an individual or small group is **influenced** by a larger or dominant group.*

There's **More Than One Type** of **Conformity**

Compliance is **Going Along** with Things Even if You **Disagree** with Them

1) **Compliance** is where you go along with the majority, even if you don't share their views.
2) You do this just to appear '**normal**' — going against the majority might lead to exclusion or rejection from the group. This is called **normative social influence**.

Internalisation Means Accepting the **Majority's** Views as **Your Own**

1) **Internalisation** is following along with the majority and **believing** in their views — you've accepted and **internalised** them so they're now your own too.
2) This might happen if you're in an unfamiliar situation, where you don't know what the 'correct' way to behave is. In this situation, you'd look to others for **information** about how to behave. This is called **informational social influence**.

Asch (1951) Looked at **Normative Social Influence**

Asch designed an experiment to see whether people would conform to a majority's incorrect answer in an **unambiguous task** (one where the answer is obvious).

Asch (1951) — conformity on an unambiguous task

Method: Asch carried out a **laboratory experiment** with an **independent groups** design. In groups of 8, participants judged line lengths (shown below) by saying out loud which comparison line (1, 2 or 3) matched the standard line. Each group contained only one real participant — the others were confederates (who acted like real participants but were really helping the experimenter). The real participant always went last or last but one, so that they heard the others' answers before giving theirs. Each participant did 18 trials.
On 12 of these (the **critical trials**) the confederates all gave the same wrong answer.
There was also a **control group**, where the participants judged the line lengths in isolation.

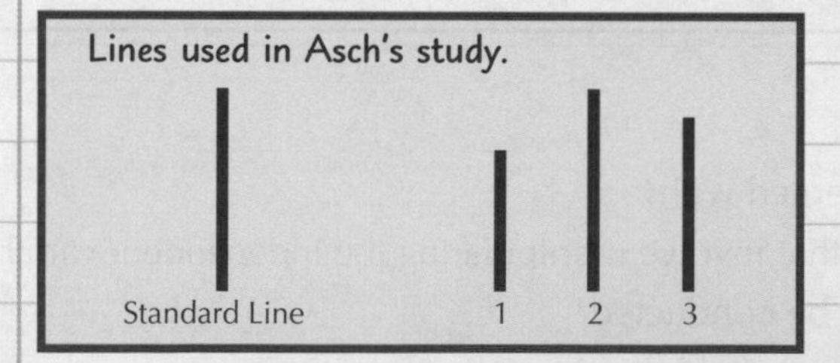

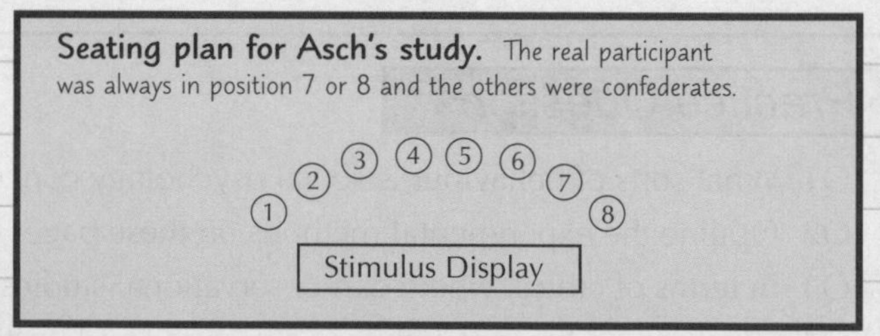

Results: In the control trials, participants gave the wrong answer **0.7%** of the time. In the critical trials, participants **conformed** to the majority (gave the same wrong answer) **37%** of the time. **75%** conformed at least once. Afterwards, some participants said they didn't really believe their answers, but didn't want to look different.

Conclusion: The control condition showed that the task was easy to get right. However, 37% were wrong on the critical trials. They conformed to the majority — this was **normative social influence**.

Evaluation: This was a **laboratory experiment**, so there was **good control** of the variables. This minimises the effects of **extraneous variables**. Strict control of the variables also means that you could easily **repeat** the study to see if you get the same results. However, because the participants weren't in a **natural situation**, the study lacks **ecological validity**. Whether they were right or wrong didn't really matter to the participants — they might have been less likely to conform if their answer had had real-life consequences. In terms of **ethics**, the participants were **deceived** and might have been embarrassed when they found out the true nature of the study.

Types of Conformity

Sherif (1935) Tested the Effects of *Informational Influence*

Sherif researched whether people are influenced by others when they're doing an **ambiguous task** (one where the answer isn't clear).

Sherif (1935) — conformity and the autokinetic effect

Method:	This was a **laboratory experiment** with a **repeated measures** design. Sherif used a visual illusion called the **autokinetic effect**, where a stationary spot of light, viewed in a dark room, appears to move. Participants were falsely told that the experimenter would move the light. They had to estimate how far it had moved. In the first phase, individual participants made repeated estimates. They were then put into groups of 3 people, where they each made their estimate with the others present. Finally, they were retested individually.
Results:	When they were alone, participants developed their own stable estimates (**personal norms**), which varied widely between participants. Once the participants were in a group, the estimates tended to **converge** and become more alike. When the participants were then retested on their own, their estimates were more like the **group estimates** than their original guesses.
Conclusion:	Participants were influenced by the estimates of other people, and a **group norm** developed. Estimates converged because participants used information from others to help them — they were affected by **informational social influence**.
Evaluation:	This was a **laboratory experiment**, so there was strict control of the variables. This means that the results are unlikely to have been affected by a third variable, so it should be possible to establish **cause and effect**. It also means that the method could be **replicated**. The **repeated measures** design meant that **participant variables** that could have affected the results were kept constant. However, the method is flawed because the participants were being asked to judge the movement of a light that wasn't moving — this rarely happens in real life. This study is less successful than Asch's in demonstrating the effects of conformity — the answer was obvious, so the only reason Asch's participants conformed was to avoid standing out. This experiment created an **artificial situation**, so the study lacks **ecological validity**. As well as this, the **sample** used was quite limited — all of the participants were male, so the results can't be **generalised** to everyone. An **ethical problem** with this study was **deception** — the participants were told the light was moving when it wasn't.

Zimbardo et al (1973) Studied *Conformity* to *Assigned Roles*

Zimbardo et al set up a mock prison to see if people would conform to the **assigned roles** of prisoner or guard.

Zimbardo et al (1973) — Stanford Prison Experiment

Method:	Male students were recruited to act as either guards or prisoners in a mock prison. They were randomly given the roles of prisoner or guard, and their behaviour was observed. The prisoners were 'arrested' at home, taken to 'prison' and given uniforms and numbers. The guards also wore uniforms and mirrored sunglasses.
Results:	Initially, the guards tried to assert their authority and the prisoners resisted by sticking together. The prisoners then became more passive and obedient, while the guards invented nastier punishments. The experiment was abandoned early because some prisoners became very distressed.
Conclusion:	Guards and prisoners adopted their social roles quickly. Zimbardo claims this shows that our **social role can influence our behaviour** — seemingly well-balanced men became unpleasant and aggressive in the role of guard.
Evaluation:	This was a **controlled observation**, so there was **good control** of variables. However, because it was an artificial environment, the results can't really be **generalised** to real life situations. In terms of **ethics**, some participants found the experience very distressing. There's also a problem with **observer bias**, as Zimbardo ran the prison himself, and later admitted that he became too personally involved in the situation. This experiment doesn't take **individual differences** into account — not all of the participants behaved according to their new roles.

Types of Conformity

This page is for everyone. But if you're doing Edexel you can ignore the top bit and just learn the study underneath.

Reicher and Haslam (2006) Developed the Ideas in Zimbardo's Study

1) In the **Holocaust** during World War Two, approximately 6 million Jews were horrifically murdered by the Nazis.
2) Psychologists had different theories about the soldiers who'd carried out the killings. Some thought they must be 'evil' individuals, but others thought they were 'normal' people who'd committed atrocities because of the social role they were in.
3) **Zimbardo's** (1973) study showed that normal people will shape their behaviour in order to fit into a social role, even if it's only been randomly assigned.
4) It seemed that the participants' behaviour was **situational** (due to the social situation they were in), rather than **dispositional** (due to their internal characteristics).
5) **Reicher and Haslam** (2006) recreated a similar situation to Zimbardo's experiment, but they were particularly interested to see how the group dynamics changed over time.

OCR Core Study

Reicher and Haslam (2006) — the BBC Prison Study

Method: This was a **controlled observation** in a mock prison, which was filmed for television. The participants were 15 male volunteers who had responded to an advert. They were randomly assigned to 2 groups of 5 guards and 10 prisoners. They had daily tests to measure levels of depression, compliance with rules, and stress. The prisoners knew that one of them, chosen **at random**, would become a guard after 3 days. An independent **ethics committee** had the power to stop the experiment at any time in order to protect the participants.

Results: The guards failed to form a united group and identify with their role. They didn't always exercise their power and said they felt uncomfortable with the inequality of the situation. In the first 3 days, the prisoners tried to act in a way that would get them promoted to guard status. After one was promoted, they became a much **stronger group** because they knew there were no more chances of promotion. The unequal system collapsed due to the **unwillingness of the guards** and the **strength of the prisoner group**. On Day 6 the prisoners rebelled and the participants decided to live in a democracy, but this also collapsed due to tensions within the group. Some of the former prisoners then wanted to set up a stricter regime with them as leaders. The study was **abandoned** early on the advice of the ethics committee, as the participants showed signs of stress.

Conclusion: The participants didn't fit into their expected social roles, suggesting that these roles are **flexible**.

Evaluation: In contrast to Zimbardo's findings, Reicher and Haslam's prisoners were a strong group, and the guards were weak. However, it's possible that this was because Reicher and Haslam's guards were not as empowered as Zimbardo's, who were actively encouraged to maintain order. This study has been criticised for being made for TV — many people (including Zimbardo) argued that elements of it were staged and the participants played up to the cameras. Because this was an artificial situation, the results can't be **generalised** to real life. The **ethics** of this study were good — the participants were not **deceived**, so they were able to give **informed consent**. The participants were **protected** by the ethics committee and the study was abandoned as soon as they appeared to be becoming stressed. They were also **debriefed** and offered counselling afterwards.

Practice Questions

Q1 What is normative social influence?

Q2 Outline the strengths and weaknesses of the method in Asch's study.

Q3 What's the difference between situational and dispositional behaviour?

Exam Questions

Q1 Outline two types of conformity. [6 marks]

Q2 Outline and evaluate Reicher and Haslam's (2006) 'BBC Prison Study'. [12 marks]

Oh doobee doo, I wanna be like you-oo-oo...

Conformity's handy because it means you don't have to make any decisions for yourself... It's all about wanting to fit in with a group, even if you think it's actually a bit rubbish. Personally I reckon joining a group that involves being arrested and put in a fake prison isn't really ideal. I'd probably just say thanks but I'm washing my hair that week.

Independent Behaviour and Social Change

This next bit is a 3-page stunner, just for AQA A...
Sometimes we're influenced by others and conform. But at other times we resist these influences and behave ***independently****. There are various factors that affect whether we resist the pressure to conform.*

Asch's Participants were Influenced by Situational Factors

1) **Group Size**

You might expect that the **bigger** the majority is, the more **influential** it will be. If that was the case, it would be easier to resist conforming when there were fewer people to influence you. To test this, **Asch (1956)** conducted his conformity experiment with different numbers of confederates as the majority.

With only **two confederates**, the real participant **conformed on only 14%** of the critical trials. With **three confederates**, conformity rose to **32%**. There was **little change** to conformity rates after that — no matter how big the majority group got. So, very small majorities are easier to resist than larger ones. But influence doesn't keep increasing with the size of majority.

2) **Social Support**

Asch absolutely loved doing his conformity experiment, so he ran yet another version of it to test the effect of having a **supporter** in the group. When one of the confederates **agreed** with the **participant** rather than with the other confederates, the rate of conformity **fell** to **5.5%**.

A fellow **dissenter** (someone who disagrees with the majority) made it easier for the participant to **resist** the pressure to conform.

Confidence and Expertise Might Affect Conformity

When Asch **debriefed** his participants, he found a common factor of **confidence** in the people who hadn't conformed. If someone felt confident in their judgements, they were more able to **resist** group pressure.

1) **Wiesenthal et al (1976)** found that if people felt **competent** in a task, they were **less likely** to conform.
2) **Perrin and Spencer (1980)** replicated Asch's study with participants who were engineering students. Conformity levels were much **lower**. This could have been due to the fact that engineers had **confidence** in their skills in making accurate observations.

Gender Might Also be a Factor

Until the mid-1970s the dominant view was that **females conform more than males**.
Then **Eagly and Carli** did a load of research that suggests it might not be as simple as all that...

Eagly (1987) argued that men and women's **different social roles** are responsible for the difference in conformity rates — women are more concerned with **group harmony** and **relationships**, so they're more likely to agree with the opinions of others. **Assertiveness** and **independence** are valued male attributes, so maintaining your own opinion under pressure fits with the perceived male social role.

This ties in with **Becker's (1986)** findings that women conform more than men in **public** settings, but not when their opinions are **private**.

Eagly and Carli (1981) did a **meta-analysis** of conformity research, where they re-analysed data from a number of studies. They did find some sex differences in conformity, but the differences were **inconsistent**. The clearest difference between men and women was in **Asch**-like studies where there was **group pressure** from an **audience**.

Eagly and Carli (1981) also pointed out that male researchers are more likely than female researchers to find female participants higher on conformity. This could be because **male researchers** use tasks that are more familiar to men (so they don't need to look to others as much for help). This is an example of **gender bias**.

Independent Behaviour and Social Change

How likely someone is to conform could all be down to something called their 'locus of control'. In a nutshell it comes down to the old question — do you believe you're in control of your destiny, or do you believe in fate?

Aspects of **Personality** may Influence **Independent Behaviour**

Rotter (1966) developed a **questionnaire** to measure a personality characteristic called **locus of control.** It indicates how much **personal control** people believe they have over events in their lives. The questionnaire involved choosing between **paired statements** like these ones:

1) Misfortune is usually brought about by people's own actions.
2) Things that make us unhappy are largely due to bad luck.

If you agree with the first statement, you have an **internal locus of control**. This is categorised by a belief that what happens in your life results from **your own behaviour or actions**.

E.g. if you did well in a test you might put it down to how much work you did for it.

If you agree with the second statement, you have an **external locus of control**. This is a belief that events are caused by external factors, like **luck** or the **actions of others**.

E.g. if you did well in a test you might put it down to good questions coming up, or a lenient examiner.

People with an **internal locus of control** feel a stronger sense of control over their lives than people with an **external locus of control**. This means that they're more likely to exhibit **independent behaviour**. People with an **external locus of control** may be more likely to conform.

Minority Influence can be Quite **Powerful**

1) Obviously people don't always go along with the majority — if they did, nothing would ever change.
2) Sometimes **small minorities** and even **individuals** gain influence and change the way the majority thinks.
3) In **minority influence**, it seems that a form of **internalisation** (see page 72) is taking place. Members of the majority actually take on the beliefs and views of a **consistent minority** — rather than just complying.

Moscovici et al (1969) did some research into **minority influence** that compared **inconsistent** minorities with **consistent** minorities.

Moscovici et al (1969) — Minority influence

Method: This was a laboratory experiment into **minority influence** using 192 women. In groups of 6 at a time, participants judged the colour of 36 slides. All of the slides were blue, but the brightness of the blue varied. Two of the six participants in each group were **confederates**. In one condition the confederates called all 36 slides 'green' (consistent) and in another condition they called 24 of the slides 'green' and 12 of the slides 'blue' (inconsistent). A control group was also used which contained no confederates.

Results: In the **control group** the participants called the slides 'green' **0.25%** of the time. In the **consistent** condition **8.4%** of the time participants adopted the minority position and called the slides 'green'. In fact, **32%** of the participants called the slides 'green' at least once. In the **inconsistent** condition the participants moved to the minority position of calling the slides 'green' only **1.25%** of the time.

Conclusion: The confederates were in the **minority** but their views appear to have influenced the real participants. The use of the two conditions illustrated that the minority **had more influence when they were consistent** in calling the slides 'green'.

Evaluation: This study was a laboratory experiment so it **lacked ecological validity** because the task was artificial. The participants may have felt that judging the colour of the slide was a **trivial** exercise. They might have acted differently if their principles were involved. Also, the study was only carried out on women so doesn't allow for **gender** differences and the results can't be generalised to men. However, owing to the use of a **control** group, we know that the participants were actually influenced by the minority rather than being independently unsure of the colour of the slides. In a similar experiment, participants were asked to **write down** the colour rather than saying it out loud. In this condition, even more people agreed with the minority, which provides **more support** for minority influence.

Independent Behaviour and Social Change

It's easy to see why you might go along with the majority. But minorities sometimes shake things right up...

Minorities can Cause Social Change

There are many examples in history of things changing because the ideas of a few have taken hold. Try these for starters:

The Suffragettes

1) In the early 1900s in Britain, a small minority began to campaign for women to be allowed to **vote**. This was called the **suffragette movement**.
2) Suffragettes **chained** themselves to railings outside Downing Street and Buckingham Palace.
3) The suffragettes' campaign involved **violent** methods such as assault and arson.
4) In 1913 a suffragette threw herself under the feet of the King's horse. She **died** from her injuries.
5) Eventually **the majority was influenced** by the suffragettes' point of view and in 1928 women were finally given the right to vote on the same terms as men.

Suzie was confident that it was only a matter of time before everyone started dressing like her.

Martin Luther King

1) In the 1950s in America, black people did not have the same **rights** as white people. For example, in parts of America, buses were **segregated** and black people had to give up their seats to white people.
2) **Reverend Martin Luther King** challenged the views of the majority to bring about **political and social rights** for black people. He and other activists used **peaceful** protests like marches and sit-ins. This was known as the **Civil Rights Movement**. His ideas were so unpopular that during this time his home was bombed by activists, he was subjected to personal abuse, and he was **arrested**.
3) In the end though, the actions of civil rights activists influenced the **majority**. Nowadays there are **laws** that ensure people are given equal rights regardless of racial origin, and in 1964 Martin Luther King was awarded the **Nobel Peace Prize**.

Gay Rights Movements

1) Homosexuality used to be **illegal** in the UK. It was **decriminalised** in England and Wales in 1967 — but the age of consent was 21 (higher than for heterosexual people) and homosexuals were still treated **negatively**.
2) Over the last decade, there have been moves towards equality as a result of **Gay Rights Movements**. These **minorities** have successfully **changed attitudes**. For example, the Equality Act (Sexual Orientation) 2007 made it **illegal to discriminate** against gay men and women in the provision of goods and services.

Practice Questions

Q1 What situational factors did Asch identify that affected conformity levels?

Q2 Why might social roles be responsible for gender differences in conformity?

Q3 What's the difference between an internal and an external locus of control?

Q4 According to Moscivici et al's (1969) study, how does consistency affect minority influence?

Exam Questions

Q1 Outline and evaluate one study into minority influence. [8 marks]

Q2 Outline two examples of social change caused by minority influence. [6 marks]

The times they are a-changing...

So minority influence can be a big deal. Here's an example: I think you should learn the stuff on this page — most people probably don't agree — but you will won't you? I've really got under your skin haven't I? Power to the minority. Woo!

Obedience to Authority

These pages are for everyone — hooray. *Obedience means acting in response to a direct order (usually from authority). It's mostly not a bad thing, and in some situations it's really important. But it can also cause problems...*

Milgram (1963) did a Famous Study of Obedience

OCR Core Study

	Milgram (1963) — the original 'remote learner' experiment
Method:	Milgram conducted **laboratory experiments** to test factors thought to affect obedience. This 'remote learner' condition tested whether people would obey orders to shock someone in a separate room. It took place at the prestigious Yale University. **40 men** took part, responding to newspaper adverts seeking **volunteers** for a study on 'learning and memory'. They received payment for attending, which didn't depend on them proceeding with the experiment. The experimenter wore a grey technician's coat. Each participant was introduced to a **confederate** (acting like a participant, but who was really part of the experimental set-up). They drew lots to see who would act as 'teacher' and 'learner', but this was fixed so the participant was always the teacher. The participant witnessed the confederate being strapped into a chair and connected up to a shock generator in the next room. It didn't actually give electric shocks, but the participants thought it was real. The switches ranged from 15 volts (labelled 'Slight Shock') to 450 volts (labelled 'XXX'). The participant taught the learner word-pairs over an intercom. When the learner answered incorrectly, the participant had to administer an **increasing level of shock**. As the shocks increased, the learner started to scream and ask to be let out. After the 330 V shock, he made no further noise. If participants hesitated, the experimenter told them to continue. **Debriefing** included an interview, questionnaires and being reunited with the 'learner'.
Results:	**26 participants (65%)** administered **450 V** and **none stopped before 300 V** (when the learner started protesting). Most showed obvious signs of stress during the experiment, like sweating, groaning and trembling.
Conclusion:	**Ordinary people** will **obey orders** to hurt someone else, even if it means acting against their consciences.

Milgram did lots of Variations on his Experiment

Ooh look, a table. That must say something good. Milgram carried out his experiment in loads of slightly different ways to investigate the effect that certain conditions would have on the results.

Some of Milgram's variations on this experiment	Percentage administering 450 volts
Male participants	65%
Female participants	65%
Learner's protests can be heard	62.5%
Experiment run in seedy offices	48%
Learner in same room as participant	40%
Authority (experimenter) in another room, communicating by phone	23%
Other teachers (confederates) refuse to give shock	10%
Other participant (a confederate) gives shock instead	92.5%

Milgram's Experiment had Good and Bad Points

1) **Experimental (internal) validity**: It's possible that participants didn't really believe they were inflicting electric shocks — they were just going along with the **experimenter's expectations** (showing **demand characteristics**). But Milgram claimed participants' **stressed reactions** showed they believed the experiment was real.
2) **Ecological (external) validity**: Milgram's participants did a task that they were unlikely to encounter in real life (shocking someone). So the study **lacks ecological validity**. However, because it was a **laboratory experiment** there was good control of the variables, so it's possible to establish **cause and effect**.
3) **Ethical issues**: The participants were **deceived** as to the true nature of the study. This means they couldn't give **informed consent**. They weren't informed of their **right to withdraw** from the experiment. In fact, they were prompted to continue when they wanted to stop. The participants showed signs of stress during the experiment, so they weren't **protected**. However, they were extensively **debriefed** and 84% of them said they were pleased to have taken part. As well as this, at the time of the experiment there weren't any formal ethical guidelines in place, so technically Milgram didn't breach any. There's more general stuff on ethics on pages 136-137.

Obedience to Authority

Milgram Identified **Factors** that **Affected Obedience**

1) **Presence of allies**: When there were 3 teachers (1 participant and 2 confederates), the real participant was less likely to obey if the other two refused to obey. Having allies can make it easier to resist orders than when you're on your own.
2) **Proximity of the victim**: Milgram's results suggest an important factor was the **proximity (closeness)** of the **learner**. In the 'remote learner' condition, 65% gave the maximum shock. This dropped to 40% with the learner in the same room, and 30% when the participant had to put the learner's hand onto the shock plate. Proximity made the learner's suffering harder to ignore.
3) **Proximity of the authority**: When the authority figure gave prompts by phone from another room, obedience rates dropped to 23%. When the authority figure wasn't close by, orders were easier to resist.

Milgram's **Agency Theory (1973)** Explains **Obedience**

1) When people behave on behalf of an **external authority** (do as they're told), they're said to be in an **agentic state**.
2) This means they act as someone's **agent**, rather than taking personal responsibility for their actions.
3) The opposite of this is behaving **autonomously** — not following orders.
4) Milgram claimed that there were some **binding factors** that might have kept his participants in the **agentic state**:

> **Reluctance** to **disrupt the experiment** — participants had already been paid, so may have felt **obliged** to continue.
>
> The **pressure** of the **surroundings** — the experiment took place in a prestigious university. This made the experimenter seem like a **legitimate authority**.
>
> The **insistence** of the **authority figure** — if participants hesitated they were told that they **had** to continue the experiment.

Before his study, Milgram believed that people were **autonomous** and could **choose** to resist authority.
His **agency theory** shows Milgram's findings changed his mind about how much impact legitimate authority figures have.

> **Evaluation of Agency Theory**
>
> 1) There's lots of **experimental evidence** to support agency theory — Milgram's participants often claimed they wouldn't have gone as far by themselves, but they were just following orders.
> 2) Sometimes people **resist** the pressure to obey authority. This can be because of the situation, or because of individual differences (see page 81). Agency theory doesn't explain why some people are more likely to exhibit **independent behaviour** than others.

Practice Questions

Q1 Outline the method of Milgram's (1963) experiment.

Q2 In Milgram's original ('remote learner') experiment, what percentage of participants gave the maximum shock?

Q3 Why was the experimental validity of Milgram's study criticised?

Q4 What is meant by 'proximity' and why is it a factor in obedience?

Exam Questions

Q1 In social psychology, there are many ethical issues to be considered when involving human participants in research. Evaluate Milgram's (1963) study of obedience in terms of ethical issues. [6 marks]

Q2 Outline two factors that might affect obedience levels. [4 marks]

Pretty shocking results, don't you think?

Milgram crops up all the time, so you need to learn this stuff well. You've got to admit it's pretty incredible that people would give someone a 450 V shock just because they were told to. Everyone always thinks that they wouldn't have done it if they were one of the participants, but really it's impossible to know. I definitely would have done though. I love electricity.

Obedience to Authority

These pages are for everyone — except for Edexcel. So not everyone then.
There are different factors that make people more or less likely to obey authority...

*Milgram's Findings Tell Us About **Why** People **Obey***

*An **Agentic State** is When You Act for Someone Else*

1) Milgram's **Agency Theory** (page 79) stated that when we feel we're acting out the wishes of another person (being their agent), we feel **less responsible** for our actions.
2) This effect is seen in Milgram's studies. Some participants were concerned for the **welfare** of the learner and asked who would take **responsibility** if he were harmed. When the experimenter (authority) took responsibility, often the participant would continue.
3) This **agentic state** was also in the experiment's set-up. The participants voluntarily entered a **social contract** (an obligation) with the experimenter to take part and follow the procedure of the study.
4) People can start off acting in an **autonomous** way (thinking for themselves), but then become obedient. This is known as an **agentic shift**. When Milgram's participants arrived for the experiment they were in an **autonomous state**, but as soon as they started following orders they underwent an **agentic shift**, and entered an **agentic state**.

***Gradual Commitment** Can Make Us More Obedient*

1) Gradual commitment means agreeing to something gradually — in **small steps**. It makes it **harder to refuse** the next request. In Milgram's study, participants were asked to deliver only a 15 volt shock at the start. This was gradually built up to very large shocks.
2) Participants might have been more **reluctant** to obey if they'd been asked to deliver the 450 volt shock at the start. They obeyed at the lower levels, so it was harder for them to justify disobeying the later requests.
3) Gradual commitment is also known as the **'foot-in-the-door'** effect. Once you've gone along with a minor request, the request could be gradually increased until you're doing something you might never have agreed to in the first place.

*We See Some People as **Justified Authorities***

Boris's authority may not have been justified, but he was the best damn cop in Düsseldorf.

1) We're socialised to recognise the authority of people like **parents**, **police officers**, **doctors**, **teachers** etc.
2) These kinds of people are **justified authorities** — they're given the **right** to **tell us what to do**. This means we're more likely to obey them.
3) When Milgram re-ran his study in some **run-down offices**, obedience rates were lower than when the study was run in the university.
4) He argued that the experimenter's authority was higher in the university situation because of the **status** of the university.
5) **Bickman (1974)** conducted a field experiment where researchers ordered passers-by to do something like pick up a bit of litter. They were dressed either in a guard's uniform, as a milkman, or just in smart clothes. People were much more likely to obey the person in a guard's uniform. This was because he seemed to be the most **legitimate authority figure**.

*Some Things Can Act as **Buffers***

1) **Buffers** are things that **protect us** — in this case **from the consequences of our actions.**
2) Milgram's participants were **more obedient** in conditions where they **could not see or hear** the victim receiving the shocks. When they were in the same room as the learner, there wasn't any buffer.
3) So... losing the buffer made it harder for Milgram's participants to act against their conscience and go along with someone's unjust orders to hurt the learner.

Obedience to Authority

Sometimes People Resist the Pressure to Obey Authority

The Situation Can Make People More Resistant

1) More of Milgram's participants resisted orders if there were **other participants present** who refused to obey (see page 79). This suggests that people find it easier to stand up to authority if they have support from others, because they no longer have to take full responsibility for rebelling.

> **Gamson et al (1982)** found that support can help people resist authority, particularly if the request is unreasonable or unjust. They studied a **group** of participants **who felt they were being manipulated**. Participants rebelled against the unjust authority figure. This happened through a process of **minority influence** — with one or two people resisting the authority's requests at first. This rebellion then spread to the whole group.
> **Conclusion**: The presence of **allies** and **collective action** seemed to help the participants in their resistance.

2) This ties in with Asch's research on conformity. He found that participants were more likely to resist the pressure to conform if one of the confederates agreed with them (page 75). It seems that people are more likely to display independent behaviour if they've got support from others.
3) It doesn't really make sense to call this behaviour **independent**, seeing as it depends on having someone else there to agree with you... But just go with it...

Resistance to Authority can be Explained by Individual Differences

1) If an individual has a high level of **moral reasoning** (thinking about right and wrong) they may be more able to resist an order that goes against their conscience.
2) One of Milgram's participants had experienced a Second World War concentration camp. She **refused** to administer any level of shock, because she didn't want to inflict pain on another person.
3) Those who resisted may have still felt personally responsible — they **weren't** in an **agentic state**.

> **Rotter (1966)** claimed that people could be categorised as having an **internal** or **external locus of control** (page 76). People with an **internal locus of control** take responsibility for their actions more than people with an **external locus of control**. This means that they're more likely to exhibit **independent behaviour** — they're less likely to conform, or be obedient, than people with an **external locus of control**.

> Sometimes people feel that they're being pushed too far or a rule restricts them too much. In this situation they might react by doing the **opposite** of what they're told. This is known as the **'boomerang effect'**.

Practice Questions

Q1 Why might obedience rates have dropped when Milgram's study took place in run-down offices?

Q2 Give an example of a buffer that reduced obedience rates in one of Milgram's studies.

Q3 What did Gamson et al (1982) conclude from their research on independent behaviour?

Q4 How do individual differences influence independent behaviour?

Exam Questions

Q1 Rosie was approached by a man at the bus stop, who told her to go and stand somewhere else.
Outline two factors that might make Rosie more likely to obey his authority. [4 marks]

Q2 Outline two factors that may help people resist authority. [4 marks]

I can never resist a man in uniform...

The good thing about this obedience stuff is that it's mostly quite obvious. Everyone knows some people are more likely to obey authority than others. And the only explanation anyone can come up with for why this happens is that they just are, and that's that. So it shouldn't be too difficult to learn. And buffers is a pretty funny word too, which always helps...

Obedience to Authority

These pages are just for you cheeky scamps doing Edexcel and OCR. *You might have thought it was only Milgram who did obedience research... Oh, no, no, no. Once Milgram had done his study everyone wanted a piece of the action...*

Cross-Cultural Studies Tell Us About *Obedience* in Different *Societies*

Milgram's research took place in the **USA**, so it only tells us about levels of obedience in that culture. Further research was needed in order to find out about obedience in other cultures.

Meeus and Raaijmakers (1986)

Method: Meeus and Raaijmakers carried out their study in **The Netherlands**. They felt that Milgram's work lacked ecological validity, because people aren't often asked to give electric shocks to strangers in real life. So they wanted to test a more subtle form of obedience. They conducted a **laboratory experiment** with volunteers who had responded to an advert about research into stress and performance. Participants were asked to conduct interviews to test job applicants' reactions to stress. The job applicants were really trained confederates. The participants believed that if applicants failed the test, they wouldn't get the job and would remain unemployed. During the interview, the participants were prompted to deliver 15 **'stress remarks'** — criticisms of the job applicant. The remarks were designed to inflict increasing levels of psychological harm. The strongest remarks included telling the applicant, 'this job is too difficult for you'. The confederates acted confidently at first, but then broke down as the stress remarks were delivered, eventually begging the interviewer to stop. If the participants hesitated when asking the questions, they were prompted by the experimenter to continue.

Results: Despite recognising the distress of the applicant, 22 of the 24 participants delivered all 15 stress remarks.

Conclusion: A high percentage were prepared to inflict psychological harm in this realistic, face-to-face situation.

Evaluation: **Ecological validity** was higher than in Milgram's research, because the interview is more of a real-life setting than being asked to give someone electric shocks. 96% of participants believed that the test situation was real, indicating that **experimental validity** was also high. **Ethical issues** include the use of **deception**. Because the participants were deceived they couldn't give **informed consent**. However, you could argue that this was scientifically justified — participants had to believe the setting was real for the experimenters to observe genuine behaviour. Another issue was **protection**, as the participants found the situation stressful. Another criticism of the study is that it's debatable how bad the participants really thought the 'stress remarks' were. There are loads of worse things to say than 'this job is too difficult for you'. How about 'you're ugly and your mum's fat' for starters?

We Can Draw *Cross-Cultural Conclusions* from This *Research*

1) Meeus and Raaijmakers' study was designed to improve on Milgram's study. It tested whether people would follow orders to inflict **psychological** harm, which is much more likely to happen in real life.
2) Their study was also very culturally relevant — The Netherlands was going through an unemployment crisis at the time, so job interviews were really important.
3) The fact that participants were still prepared to cause distress to people in a job interview suggests that obedience is a universal human characteristic. It provides extra evidence for Milgram's **agency theory** (page 79).

However, there are **problems** with comparing these studies. The methods are different because Meeus and Raaijmakers wanted to improve on Milgram's study (and ethical guidelines meant they wouldn't have been allowed to replicate it anyway). But because the methods measure obedience in **different situations**, it's difficult to **generalise** the results and say that Dutch people are just as likely to be obedient as Americans. They were tested on different things, so we can't really know for sure.

The other problem with comparing these studies is that they were done at **different times** (Milgram's was in the 1960s, Meeus and Raaijmakers' was in the 1980s). Societies can change a lot in 20 years — we can't know for sure whether Milgram's study would have got the same results in America in the 1980s. The results are **products** of **different times**, as well as different cultures. So trying to draw cross-cultural conclusions from them is a bit of a nightmare really.

Obedience to Authority

Hofling et al (1966) Studied Obedience Amongst Nurses

Hofling et al investigated whether nurses would obey a doctor if it meant breaking hospital rules:

Hofling et al (1966) — obedience in nurses

Method: Hofling et al carried out a **field experiment** in hospitals in the USA. The participants were 22 staff nurses, who were phoned by a researcher posing as an unknown doctor. He instructed them to administer a drug to a patient before he arrived on the ward. He said he'd sign the paperwork when he got there.
If the nurses obeyed they'd be breaking a number of rules, including:
Taking instructions from a stranger, who might not be a doctor,
Taking instructions over the phone without the necessary paperwork,
Administering a drug at twice the maximum dose indicated on its label.

Results: 21 out of the 22 nurses obeyed the doctor and prepared the medication. They said they were often given telephone instructions and doctors got annoyed if they refused.

Conclusion: In this real-life setting, levels of obedience to authority were high.

Evaluation: The nurses didn't know they were in an experiment, meaning the study has high **experimental validity**. Obeying doctors' requests is part of a nurse's normal role. This was a realistic position for the nurses to be in, so the study also has high **ecological validity**. The results provide support for Milgram's **agency theory** — the nurses acted on behalf of what they thought was a legitimate authority, so they didn't have a sense of personal responsibility for their actions. In terms of **ethics**, the study used **deception**, meaning that it wasn't possible to get **informed consent** from the participants. There is also the issue of **protection**, as the nurses may have been distressed when they were confronted with the fact that they were willing to break the rules.

Well that was nice. Trouble is there's a whole big space left here that needs to be filled with something. How about some pictures of hospitals to remind you of Hofling...

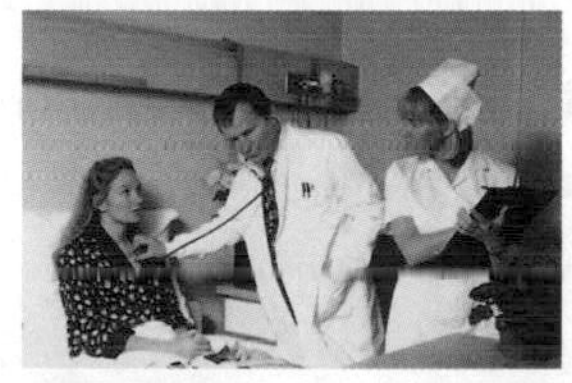

Look at this nurse being all obedient like Hofling's nurses.

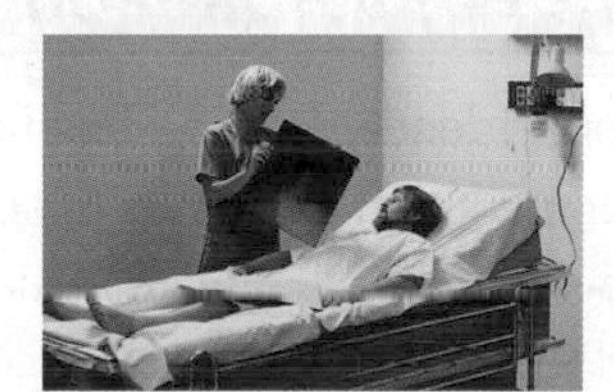

Look at this man being eaten by his mattress.

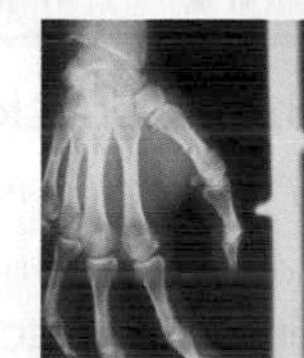

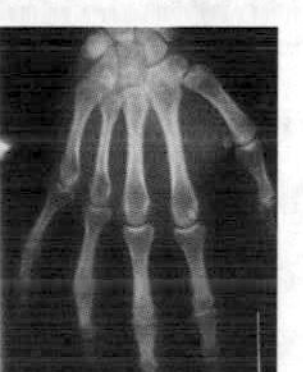

Look at these scary hands. Wooooh...

Practice Questions

Q1 Outline the method of Meeus and Raaijmakers' (1986) study.

Q2 Why were Meeus and Raaijmakers' findings more ecologically valid that Milgram's?

Q3 Why are there problems with making cross-cultural comparisons between Milgram's study and Meeus and Raaijmakers' study?

Q4 How many of the nurses in Hofling et al's study obeyed the 'doctor'?

Exam Questions

Q1 a) Outline the findings of one study of obedience conducted in a country other than Milgram's (USA). [6 marks]

b) Evaluate this study in terms of issues of ethics and validity. [4 marks]

Q2 Outline the procedure used by Hofling et al (1966) in their study testing obedience. [4 marks]

Milgram was angry with the Dutch — he'd drawn a cross cultural conclusion

It's a bit of a shame for old Meeus and Raaijmakers really, everyone remembers Milgram and ignores them. Never mind, lads — there's more to life than getting people to make job applicants cry anyway. You should take a leaf out of Hofling's book — invent a study about obedience in hospitals, then you'd get to spend your time giving orders to naughty nurses. Ooh saucy...

Research into Conformity and Obedience

These pages are for everyone. And it's a good thing too cos it would be terrible if some of you had to miss out. Look at all those lovely words just waiting to be read. This bit's about the implications of research into conformity and obedience for social change — basically, what we can learn from people like Milgram.

Milgram's (1963) Findings Were Revolutionary

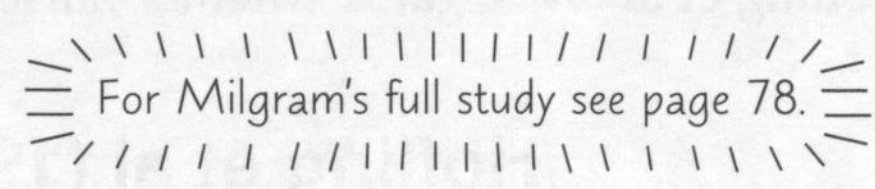

1) Before the study Milgram asked different experts on human behaviour (e.g. psychiatrists) to predict the results. They thought the maximum average shock that participants would go up to was 130 V, and that only someone with a **psychopathic personality disorder** would administer a 450 V shock.
2) He actually found that 65% of participants went up to 450 V, even when they clearly didn't want to.

Milgram's study completely changed what people thought about obedience, and it's had a huge impact ever since.

It showed that his participants **deferred responsibility** for their actions onto the authority figure. Milgram found the highest rate of obedience when the experiment took place in a university and he wore a lab coat. This exposed the huge amount of trust that people have in **justified authorities**. **Hofling et al (1966)** also showed this when they got nurses to break hospital rules because they thought they were following a doctor's orders.

Application to real life

We often have no choice but to place our trust in experts, but with this comes the potential for abuse of power. A contemporary example of this is the case of **Harold Shipman** — a doctor who murdered patients by injecting them with huge overdoses. He was able to do this because his patients **trusted** him, and he got away with killing over 200 of them before anybody became suspicious.

Zimbardo Looked at the Effect of Deindividuation

Deindividuation is when people lose their personal identity (stop feeling like **individuals**), and identify with a group.

1) **Zimbardo (1970)** replicated Milgram's experiment and examined the effect of different conditions.
2) He compared participants who wore their own clothes and were treated as individuals, to ones who wore **hoods** covering their faces and were spoken to as a group.
3) He found that the average level of electric shock **doubled** when the participants were wearing a hood.

When the participants were **deindividuated**, they became more **obedient** and more **antisocial**. Zimbardo later demonstrated this in the **Stanford Prison Experiment (1973)** (page 73). The prison guards wore **uniforms** and **sunglasses**, and they quickly became aggressive towards the prisoners. It seems that they stopped taking **personal responsibility** for their actions, and changed their behaviour to fit into their social role.

Deindividuation Also Happens in Large Crowds

Mann's (1981) study looked at newspaper coverage of suicide attempts. It focused on the crowds that gathered below when someone was threatening to jump off a tall building or a bridge. The newspaper reports showed that people in large crowds were likely to start jeering and telling the person to jump. This was even more common when it was dark. Mann concluded that the **anonymity** you get in a big group can lead to more extreme behaviour, because the sense of personal responsibility is **shifted onto the group**.

Application to real life

These studies help explain problems like police brutality and rioting behaviour. Zimbardo's research suggests there are ways of combating the negative effects of deindividuation — he found that when participants wore name tags instead of hoods, they gave less severe electric shocks. This has implications for social change — e.g. hoodies are banned in some public places. It could be that wearing hoodies makes people more likely to behave in an antisocial way. Or it could be that people find hoodies threatening because the people wearing them can't be identified. Or it could just be a load of rubbish.

Research into Conformity and Obedience

People in Groups Feel Pressure to Conform

1) **Sherif (1935)** and **Asch (1956)** (pages 72-73) showed that participants' responses to tasks changed when they were in a group.
2) In Sherif's study this was because they were in an **unfamiliar situation**, so they looked to other people for information on how to behave. Asch's participants felt pressure from the group to give the wrong answer, just so they would **fit in.**
3) These findings have wider implications for society, as we rely on groups to make important decisions — e.g. governments and juries.

Chris wasn't sure why the players had to be naked, but he wanted to fit in.

Janis (1972) found that groups having to make important decisions can be guilty of **Groupthink**. This happens especially in very **cohesive** groups, which are isolated from other influences, and have very **powerful leaders** — e.g. governments. Janis saw that members of the group converge their thinking so that it falls in line with what they imagine the general view of the group is. This leads to a unanimous decision that doesn't actually reflect what everyone in the group wants. It happens because individuals want to preserve the unity of the group. **Groupthink** is most common in situations where there's lots of **pressure** to make a quick, important decision.

Janis proposed ways of combating Groupthink:

1) Initially, group leaders shouldn't express their opinions, so other members won't feel **pressured** to agree with them.
2) One member should be given the role of **devil's advocate** (always expressing the opposite argument) to make sure that all possibilities are explored.
3) **Objective people** outside of the group should be consulted.

Research into Conformity and Obedience has Ethical Implications

There are loads of ethical issues surrounding studies like Milgram's and Hofling's. The participants were deceived and put under stress. However, it's important with every study to do a **cost / benefit analysis** — consider whether the cost to the participants was worth the benefit of the findings to society.

1) Despite feeling pressured during the studies, a high proportion of Milgram's and Hofling's participants said they were **pleased to have taken part**. This was because they felt they'd learned valuable lessons about themselves.
2) Research into conformity and obedience can lead to **social change**. Studies like Milgram's **raised awareness** of the possible negative outcomes of blind obedience. Janis's ideas on **Groupthink** showed that some conflict within a group is necessary, not destructive. His ideas have been taken on board by group leaders to help ensure they make the best decisions.

Practice Questions

Q1 What is deindividuation?

Q2 When is Groupthink most likely to occur?

Exam Question

Q1 Apply findings from the social approach to explain a real-life instance of conformity or obedience. [6 marks]

Now all repeat after me — conformity is bad...

The trouble with a lot of this research is that it forgets about all the good things that come from obedience and conformity. If you weren't so obedient and conformist then you wouldn't be sitting here revising right now, and that would be a crying shame. And anyway, a bit of good old-fashioned discipline never hurt anyone. Although a 450 volt shock might have done...

Group Identity and Prejudice

These pages are just for Edexcel people. *Whether we like it or not, we're lumped into groups. Some we choose, like doing Edexcel so we can learn about being lumped into groups. And some we don't, like gender. Social psychologists have done loads of studies to see how prejudice can develop between different groups.*

Prejudice and Discrimination are Easily Confused

Prejudice and **discrimination** are kind of the same but different, so it's no wonder lots of people get them mixed up...

1) **Prejudice** is a **preconceived** opinion of a person or a group, that isn't based on experience or reason. An example of prejudice is **disliking** someone because of their race or religion.
2) **Discrimination** is the **unfair treatment** that results from prejudice — e.g. an employer might not give someone a job because of their race or religion.
3) So, **prejudice** is an **attitude**, **discrimination** is **acting on it**.

Tajfel Explained Prejudice with Social Identity Theory

Tajfel's (1978) Social Identity Theory suggests that our personal identities are partly made up by membership of social groups (our social identities).

1) Examples of social groups are sports teams, colleges, workplaces, peer groups and families.
2) Once you're in a group, you **identify** with other members of the group. This could include things like sharing the same views or wearing the same clothes.
3) The group you're in is the **in-group**, so any other group is an **out-group**.
4) People will **compare** their in-group with any out-group. They emphasise their group's strengths and the other group's weaknesses to boost their self-esteem. This is because they feel that the success of their group reflects on them as individuals.
5) This then leads to **prejudice** against the out-group.

"Ha! Look at those losers — they haven't even got any cheese."

Strengths

Tajfel's theory can help explain real-life examples of prejudice, such as rival football fans disliking each other (see page 90). It's also backed up by experimental evidence — e.g. the **minimal group** experiment on the next page.

Weaknesses

A weakness of this theory is that the supporting evidence is mainly from **laboratory experiments**. They create artificial situations, so the results lack **ecological validity**. This means there are problems with applying the findings to real-life situations.

Sherif Explained Prejudice with Realistic Group Conflict Theory

1) **Sherif's (1966) Realistic Group Conflict Theory** suggests that prejudice occurs because of **competition.**
2) If two groups have to compete for **scarce resources** then they'll form negative attitudes towards each other, causing conflict.

Strengths

Sherif's theory helps to explain real-life examples of prejudice — rival football fans have to compete for scarce resources, like a trophy (see page 90). There's also experimental evidence to support it — e.g. the **Robber's Cave** experiment on the next page.

Weaknesses

The theory has been criticised because prejudice often occurs in situations where there **isn't** any apparent competition for resources.

Group Identity and Prejudice

*You need to know **two** studies really well. Everyone has to learn **Hofling et al (1966)** on page 83, but then you can choose the other. It's either **Sherif** or **Tajfel** below, or **Reicher and Haslam (2006)** on page 74. Fun fun fun...*

Sherif et al (1961) Tested *Realistic Conflict Theory*

Sherif et al (1961) — Robber's Cave experiment

Method: This was a **field experiment** to test whether **competition** leads to **prejudice**. A further aim was to see whether the prejudice could then be **reduced**. 22 boys went to the Robber's Cave summer camp in the USA. They were split into two groups — the Rattlers and the Eagles. When competitions were organised, hostility grew between the groups — they picked fights and tried to steal from each other. In the next phase of the experiment, the researchers tried to reduce prejudice by **desegregating** the groups. Boys from different groups had to sit with each other at dinner, but they just ended up having a food fight. The researchers then created problems (like breaking the water supply), which could only be overcome if the groups cooperated.

Results: Conflict and competition led to prejudice between the groups. This led to discrimination. Prejudice was then reduced when the groups had to work together to achieve a common goal. By the end of the study, prejudice between the groups was reduced considerably. Boys from different groups sat together on the bus home.

Conclusion: 'Realistic conflict' leads to prejudice — groups become hostile towards each other if they're in competition. Desegregation alone doesn't reduce prejudice — the introduction of common goals works better.

Evaluation: This was a **field experiment**, so it has **high ecological validity**. It suggests ways of reducing prejudice, so the findings can be applied to **real life**. However, the **sample** was small and only made up of white, middle-class boys, so you can't **generalise** the results. The groups were hostile towards each other **before** formal competitions began, so Sherif's 'realistic conflict' explanation for prejudice might not be accurate.

Sherif's study is quite a nice one, but here's Tajfel's anyway. It's a bit less interesting, but the choice is yours...

Tajfel (1970) Tested *Social Identity Theory*

Tajfel (1970) — minimal group experiment

Method: This was a **laboratory experiment**. 64 boys aged 14-15 were assigned to random groups (they didn't know who any of the other group members were). They were given pairs of numbers to choose from — the top number went to a member of one group, the other number went to a member of the other group. The points would be converted into money, but the participants wouldn't actually receive any of it. This meant that there was **nothing to gain** from awarding more points to your own group.

Results: Participants gave more points to members of their own group than members of the other group. They awarded the points which gave the greatest **difference** between the two groups.

Conclusion: Participants favoured their own group and discriminated against the other group.

Evaluation: This supports Tajfel's social identity theory — once the participants were in an in-group, they were prejudiced against the out-group. The variables were strictly controlled, making it possible to establish **cause and effect**. However, the study lacks **ecological validity** because it created an artificial situation. The **sample** was only made up of adolescent boys, so it's difficult to **generalise** the results to other groups.

Practice Questions

Q1 What is meant by the terms 'prejudice' and 'discrimination'?

Exam Questions

Q1 Outline one theory that explains prejudice. [2 marks]

Q2 Outline and evaluate one study of group identity and prejudice. [8 marks]

Sherif, this town ain't big enough for the both of us...

Here's a clever little way for you to remember what prejudice is — it looks a bit like pre-judge. And why does it look like pre-judge, I hear you cry... Well, it's because that's what it means. Ah, the English language is a wonderful thing. It never ceases to amaze me with its letters and words and that. It doesn't mean that prejudice is a wonderful thing though. Oh no.

Situational Variables (Bystander Behaviour)

These pages are just for OCR people. *But if anyone else wants to give them a read too then please feel free. You never know — you might like them. They're all about how we behave as bystanders, especially when someone needs help. Whether we act to help them, or ignore what's happening, can depend on the situation we're in.*

The Murder of ***Kitty Genovese*** *Led to Research into* ***Bystander Behaviour***

Kitty Genovese was **murdered** outside her apartment block in 1964.

1) After the attack it was revealed that **38 people** had either seen or heard the attack, which lasted 35 minutes.
2) They reported hearing Kitty pleading for help, shouting that she had been stabbed and she was dying.
3) None of the witnesses called the police until 20 minutes after the attack.
4) Reasons given by the witnesses for not acting to help her included thinking it was a lovers' argument, being afraid, being tired, and not wanting to get involved.

The case prompted **Darley and Latané (1968)** to do a study into **bystander behaviour**. They felt that the witnesses might not have acted to help Kitty Genovese because there were **so many** of them:

Darley and Latané (1968)

Participants were told they were taking part in a discussion using intercoms with at least one other person, who was actually a confederate. They were all in separate rooms so that they couldn't see anyone. The confederate then starting making sounds like he was having a seizure and started begging for help.

When participants believed they were the only person available, **85%** reported the problem within 2 minutes. When they thought they were in a six-person group, only **31%** did.

This demonstrates a **diffusion of responsibility**. Although all participants considered the situation to be an emergency, they were less likely to help if there were more people involved who also didn't help.

Piliavin et al (1969) *Studied* ***Bystander Behaviour***

OCR Core Study

Piliavin et al (1969) — bystander behaviour on the subway

Method: This was a **field experiment** to test bystander behaviour on a subway train. A man pretended to collapse on a train and the researchers observed to see if other passengers would help him. He was either white, black, drunk or carrying a cane in the different conditions of the study.

Results: The participant with a **cane** was helped **95%** of the time. On average he was helped within **5 seconds** of collapsing. The participant who appeared **drunk** was helped **50%** of the time. The participant who was black and appeared drunk was less likely to receive help than any of the others. **90%** of 'first helpers' were male. The more passengers there were in the immediate vicinity of the victim, the more likely people were to help.

Conclusion: Bystanders on subway trains are very likely to help others if they collapse, unless they appear to be drunk. Men are more likely to offer help than women.

Evaluation: People were generally much more helpful than previous laboratory-based studies have shown. This study goes against Darley and Latané's findings for the diffusion of responsibility effect — passengers were actually **more likely** to help when there were more of them around. This was a **field experiment**, so it has good **ecological validity** as it took place in a **naturalistic** setting. This means it's possible to **generalise** the results. However, it also means that the results could have been caused by an **extraneous variable**, so it's difficult to establish **cause and effect**. There are **ethical problems** with this study — participants couldn't give **informed consent**, they might have experienced **stress**, and they weren't **debriefed**.

Situational Variables (Bystander Behaviour)

Piliavin et al's Findings can be Explained Using **Cost-Benefit Theory**

After their study **Piliavin et al (1981)** developed cost-benefit theory. Well, not straight after. In fact it took them about ten years to get round to it. But whatever. You might also know it as the arousal-cost-reward theory or model. It proposes that we go through **three stages** when we're deciding whether or not to help someone:

1 **Physiological Arousal**
Witnessing an emergency causes physiological arousal, like an increased heart rate.
Doing something to help can **reduce** this feeling.

2 **Labelling**
This is how we **interpret** the physiological arousal.
We're more likely to help if we label the arousal as **personal distress** — helping will make us feel better.

3 **Cost-Benefit Analysis**
We then weigh up the **pros** and **cons** of getting involved. **Costs** are things like putting yourself at risk, and the time it might take if you stop to help. **Benefits** are things like gaining social approval, and feeling good about yourself for helping. The **lower** the **costs** and the **higher** the **benefits**, the **more likely** you are to help.

This model can be used to explain the results of **Piliavin et al's (1969)** study. Bystanders were much more likely to help the victim with the cane than the one who was drunk:

1) The **cost** of helping the drunk victim was higher than helping the one with a cane. His behaviour could have been unpredictable, so people could have felt they were putting themselves at risk by helping him.
2) The **benefits** of helping the drunk victim were lower. Bystanders could have felt that the drunk victim was partly responsible for what happened to him, so they felt less disapproval from other people for not helping.

Men were more likely to help than women:

1) The **cost** of helping may be higher for women than for men, in terms of putting themselves in personal danger.
2) The **benefit** for helping may be higher for men than for women — men might be expected to help more, and so feel more disapproval from others if they don't.

Practice Questions

Q1 What was it about Kitty Genovese's murder that interested psychologists?
Q2 What were the findings of Darley and Latané's (1968) study into diffusion of responsibility?
Q3 What research method was used in Piliavin et al's (1969) study?
Q4 What were the findings of Piliavin et al's (1969) study?
Q5 What are the three stages outlined in Piliavin et al's (1981) cost-benefit theory?

Exam Questions

Q1 Evaluate Piliavin et al's (1969) study [6 marks]

Q2 Briefly describe the cost-benefit theory suggested by Piliavin et al to explain how people behave when deciding whether to help a victim. [4 marks]

It's no good looking away and assuming someone will learn this for you...

Spare a thought for the people who made Piliavin's study possible — they spent weeks pretending to fall over on trains, just so you could have the pleasure of studying what happened to them. It might sound like fun for a couple of hours, but I reckon it would wear pretty thin after a while. Black / white / drunk man with/without cane, we salute you...

Contemporary Issues in Social Psychology

Just Edexcel. *Concepts from the social approach can be used to explain issues that are relevant to today's society. We've laid out a smorgasbord of contemporary issues for your delectation — you just need to pick* ***one*** *of the three and learn it good. That's right,* ***just one of them****... It's worth having a look at the studies on these pages — even if you're not familiar with them — they can be really useful for backing up your answer.*

1) **Social Psychology** Can Be Used to Explain **Football Violence**

1) Football teams identify themselves by wearing **distinctive strips**. (That's just a little reminder in case you get an examiner who doesn't know what football is...)
2) There have been lots of instances of aggression and violence between fans of different teams — e.g. England and Germany fans at the Euro 2000 tournament.
3) This is a problem, as large groups of people can cause lots of damage and injuries. It also requires a large police presence, so it's a big drain on resources.

Crowds can be very intimidating.

There are different theories to explain why this might happen:

Tajfel's (1978) Social Identity Theory (see page 86) states that we all want to belong to an **in-group**. We will categorise others as being the **out-group**, and compare our group to them. So England supporters think that they're in the best group, and become prejudiced against the Germany supporters. Fans identify themselves as part of their group by wearing the same shirts.

Sherif's (1961) Realistic Group Conflict Theory (page 86) states that competition for **scarce resources** leads to prejudice. He demonstrated this in his **Robber's Cave** experiment (page 87). It can be applied to football supporters because only one team can win. However, **Tajfel's (1970)** study of **minimal groups** (page 87) showed that simply being categorised into different groups will lead to competition, even if the groups have nothing to compete over.

Crowds tend to **deindividuate** people (stop them feeling that they have individual responsibility for their actions). This is because people have anonymity in a crowd, so they can form a **collective mind** and just go along with everyone else. The effect is heightened when people are in **uniform** — in this case, a football strip.

2) The **Mi Lai Massacre** is an Example of **Obedience** to **Authority**

1) In the **Vietnam War**, American troops fought guerrilla fighters called the **Viet Cong**. (A guerrilla army is an irregular armed force that fights a stronger force by small-scale raids and ambushes. The soldiers can sometimes be difficult to identify from civilians.)
2) After being told that there was a suspected Viet Cong presence in the village of **Mi Lai**, American soldiers attacked the village and killed hundreds of people, including many women and children, and even animals. But no weapons were ever found there.
3) Some of the soldiers seemed reluctant to carry out the attack, but still did. Later in court the lieutenant in charge of the unit said that he was just **following the orders** of his commanding officer.

In **Milgram's (1963)** study of **obedience** (page 78) 65% of participants obeyed orders to give someone electric shocks that they thought were extremely dangerous. Milgram explained these results with his **agency theory** (page 79). Just like Milgram's participants, the soldiers who carried out the Mi Lai massacre did something that they didn't necessarily think was right, because they'd been told to by an **authority figure**. They acted as **agents**, so they felt less individual responsibility for their actions.

Zimbardo (1973) (page 73) found that when 'well-balanced' people were given the role of prison guards, and a uniform, they behaved brutally. He concluded that this was because they were fitting into the role they'd been given. It suggests that the soldiers who carried out the Mi Lai massacre were responding to the **role** and **situation** they were in, rather than being inherently violent or 'evil' individuals.

Contemporary Issues in Social Psychology

3) Social Psychology Could Explain the **Abuse** at **Abu Ghraib**

1) In 2004 reports came out that American soldiers had been **abusing** Iraqi detainees in **Abu Ghraib** prison.
2) The guards took photos of each other posing and smiling while they tortured prisoners.
3) The American government condemned the guards' behaviour, and some of them were given prison sentences.
4) However, it was revealed that soldiers had been told to 'take the gloves off' when they interrogated prisoners. It seemed that they'd interpreted this as giving them absolute power to treat the prisoners however they wanted.

Zimbardo et al (1973) (page 73) conducted a study where people were randomly assigned the role of prisoner or guard. It was found that the guards started to act aggressively and cruelly, and the prisoners displayed 'learned helplessness'. These findings are mirrored in the real-life situation at Abu Ghraib. Like the American soldiers, Zimbardo's guards were given **absolute power** over the prisoners. It appears that they adapted their behaviour to fit into their social role. This was heightened by the fact that they wore uniforms, which **deindividuate** people, meaning that they feel less personal responsibility for their actions.

Reicher and Haslam (2006) (page 74) carried out a prison experiment, but didn't explicitly tell the guards how much power they had over the prisoners. In their study the guards were much more reluctant to display their authority over the prisoners than in Zimbardo's. This suggests that the behaviour of the guards at Abu Ghraib can be explained by the fact that they felt they were **given authority** to treat the prisoners with **unrestricted cruelty**.

1) **Sherif's (1935)** study of **informational influence** (page 73) showed that people will look to each other for information on how to behave in an unfamiliar situation. One of the criticisms of the American army was that some of the soldiers were inexperienced. It could be that the guards at Abu Ghraib were following each other because they were unsure about how to behave.
2) **Asch's (1956)** study of **normative influence** (page 72) showed that people will **conform** towards a group norm so they don't stand out, even when they think what the group's doing is wrong. They could have been going along with everyone else because they didn't want to seem different.
3) These two types of conformity then lead to a situation where people feel even less individual responsibility, because they're just doing what everyone else is doing. This could be why the guards took photos of the abuse — in the environment they'd created, they began to think of it as normal and acceptable.
4) On the other hand, all Sherif and Asch's participants had to do was give an opinion about a spot of light or the length of a line. It's difficult to see how that's the same as torture. This means there are problems with **generalising** the results of these experiments to real life.

Practice Questions

Q1 How does social identity theory explain football violence?

Q2 How do Milgram's findings explain the Mi Lai massacre?

Q3 What is the effect of wearing a uniform?

Q4 What happened at Abu Ghraib?

Q5 How do Zimbardo's findings explain brutality?

Exam Questions

Q1 Outline a key issue from the social approach. [6 marks]

Q2 Apply concepts and ideas from the social approach to explain a key issue you have studied. [12 marks]

Don't go learning all of these — you only need to know one of them...

Not a particularly nice section to end on, but that's the social approach done anyway. Just remember the whole point of the social stuff is that it's about people doing things because they're influenced by those around them, even if that ultimately means doing something wrong. Well, I guess it's time for you to move on to pastures new — fly, my pretties, fly...

The Individual Differences Approach

These 2 pages are just for AQA and OCR. *This section's all about individual differences — basically the fact that everyone is different. And an individual. Mind-blowing stuff. What psychologists want to know is how, and why...*

Individuals **Differ** in Their Psychological Characteristics

The **individual differences approach** studies how psychological characteristics, like aggression and memory span, differ from person to person.

Psychologists argued for ages about whether an individual's personality is influenced by **nature** (inherited factors) or **nurture** (environmental factors). This is known as the **nature-nurture debate**. It's now thought most likely that **both** have an effect and interact with one another, so there shouldn't be much more debate over which one is solely to blame.

There are Lots of Different **Perspectives** Within the Approach

These will be covered in more detail further on in the section, but for now, here's a brief overview...

The Biological Approach (see pages 100-101)

This approach explains behaviour in terms of **physiological** or **genetic** factors. It focuses on physical treatments for psychological disorders, e.g. using **drugs** or **electroconvulsive therapy**.

The Psychodynamic Approach (see pages 102-103)

The psychodynamic approach puts abnormal behaviour down to underlying **psychological problems**, often caused by past events and experiences. Treatment comes in the form of **psychoanalysis**, where the therapist tries to find and sort out these underlying problems.

The Behavioural Approach (see pages 104-105)

The behavioural approach claims that all behaviour, including abnormal behaviour, is **learned**. It's believed that old behaviours can be **'unlearned'** — treatment of abnormal behaviour is based on this.

The Cognitive Approach (see pages 106-107)

This approach puts abnormality down to **irrational and negative thoughts**. So, as you can probably guess, treatment focuses on changing the way a person thinks about things.

Several Different **Methods** are Used in the Individual Differences Approach

1) Case Studies (see page 121 and 127)

In a **case study** you use **interviews** and **observation** to collect **information** about an individual or group. You can study behaviour over a **long period of time** — this means you could observe some behaviours that might not be seen in another type of study. Also, it's often possible to observe behaviour in a **natural setting**. However, in a natural setting it's harder to control all **variables**, and it's mighty tricky to **replicate** the study.

2) Meta-analysis

This is where you analyse the results from loads of different studies and come up with some **general conclusions**. They're a good way of **bringing together data** (which is a general aim of the scientific process), and by doing this they reduce the problem of **sample size**. However, one problem is that there are loads of **conflicting results** out there, which obviously makes doing a meta-analysis a bit tricky...

3) Correlational Studies (see page 127)

These use **statistics** to compare two **variables**. For instance, you might give a questionnaire to all participants to measure their stress levels on a scale. They'd then do another task, e.g. a memory test, for which they'd also get a score. A correlation would **compare** the scores to see if there is a **relationship** between stress and memory. But you couldn't use this to show that one **causes** the other.

4) Physiological Studies

These include methods such as **brain scanning**, which can produce a detailed picture showing up any **structural abnormalities**. This means psychologists can make links between **structures** in the brain and **behavioural abnormalities**. However, scanning is a pretty **expensive process**, so it's not always possible.

The Individual Differences Approach

Psychologists Try to **Classify** People

The **DSM** is the American Psychiatric Association's Diagnostic and Statistical Manual of Mental Disorders. It contains all known mental health disorders, and offers a new **method of classification** — a **multiaxial classification**:

1) Individuals can be rated on **multiple axes/dimensions**. Diagnostic categories are used, for example organic mental disorders, personality disorders etc.
2) The DSM made diagnosis more **concrete and descriptive** than it had been.
3) Classifications are useful to acquire new information about a disorder. This can help in the development of new **treatments** and medication.
4) This type of classification has been criticised for **stigmatising** people and ignoring their 'uniqueness' by putting them in **artificial groups**.

Rosenhan (1973) — psychiatric classification can be inaccurate.

OCR Core Study

Method 1: In a field study, eight 'normal' people tried to be admitted to 12 different psychiatric hospitals around the USA, with only one symptom — claiming they heard voices, saying 'empty', 'hollow' and 'thud'.

Results 1: Seven were diagnosed with **schizophrenia** and all eight were **admitted** to psychiatric hospital. On admission, they said they were sane and had faked symptoms to get admitted, but this was seen as a symptom itself. It took, on average, 19 days before they were released, usually with a diagnosis of 'schizophrenia in remission'. Other, real patients could tell that these people were not mentally ill.

Method 2: Rosenhan later told staff at a psychiatric hospital that one or more **pseudopatients** (normal people pretending to have schizophrenia) were trying to be admitted to the hospital.

Results 2: No pseudopatients appeared, but 41 genuine patients were judged to be pseudopatients by staff.

Conclusion: Medical staff could not distinguish the sane from the insane (although many of the real patients could).

Evaluation: Being a field study, it wouldn't have been possible to control all variables, and so the results lose some of their **reliability**. Staff would probably not **expect** 'normal' people to try to gain admission to a psychiatric hospital, and so this might explain why the participants were initially admitted. 'Schizophrenia in remission' is a diagnosis that is **rarely** used, which suggests the psychiatrists concerned may not have believed they were really suffering from schizophrenia. There are **ethical** considerations in this study — people had their freedom taken away, mentally healthy people may have received treatments, professionals were deceived, and the study risked genuine patients not being treated.

Remember — it's the medical staff here who are the sample being studied, not the pseudopatients.

Practice Questions

Q1 What does the individual differences approach study?

Q2 List the four different perspectives within the individual differences approach.

Q3 What is meant by multiaxial classification?

Q4 Who were the sample in Rosenhan's (1973) study?

Exam Questions

Q1 Explain one strength and one weakness of using case studies in individual differences research. [4 marks]

Q2 Outline and evaluate Rosenhan's (1973) study of psychiatric hospital admission. [12 marks]

Get me out of here, I'm not crazy — I'm as sane as any other rabbit...

The first pages of a new section. Isn't it exciting... Anyway, before you get too excited and rush onto the next pages, make sure you've got to grips with the basics here first. Oh, and all you OCR people — there's one of your core studies here.

Psychometric Tests

Two more pages to skip if you're doing Edexcel.
Psychometric tests are pretty fun to do. I love nothing better than a good hard psychometric test when I get home of an evening. Then I like to have my tea and watch the Simpsons. Just so you know...

***Psychometric Tests** Measure Psychological Factors*

The idea with **psychometric tests** is that if things like personality or intelligence (psychological factors) exist, then we should be able to **measure** them. The **questions** are whether these things really do exist, and whether it's possible to measure them if they do.

Traits are aspects of personality — like punctuality, liveliness or laziness. Psychometric tests try to measure traits — the idea is that with enough information about specific traits, you can describe someone's **personality**.

***Psychometric theorists** developed **standardised tests**:*

1) Standardised tests provide information about how certain **groups** of people generally perform. The scores of an **individual** can then be compared to the scores of these groups. This is called... wait for it... wait for it... **standardisation**.
2) In these tests, everyone has the **same** set of instructions and the **same** task to do. This makes sure that differences in results are not due to differences in the test.
3) There are detailed **instructions** for administrators and people scoring the tests.
4) The tests, in theory, allow us to make **objective, statistically based judgements** on things like:

a) people's **capacities** and **potentials** to act or behave in certain ways.
b) the **severity** of psychological problems.
c) the likelihood that someone will **cope** with a training course.
d) someone's potential aptitude for certain types of **job**.

Clive had the capacity to behave in a normal way — he just didn't.

*Designing a Psychometric Test **Isn't Easy**...*

...unless you're as great as me. When mere mortals are **designing** a psychometric test, there are plenty of things they have to think about:

1) It's important to carefully choose questions that are **relevant** to what you hope to measure. So in a test of motivation, for example, don't ask questions about bowls and dictionaries. Instead, think about centring them around themes like drive, energy and goals.
2) You've also got to think about:

a) **scope** (who the test is for, e.g. children, adults or both)
b) **accuracy** (how well the test measures the factor)
c) **fairness** (whether everyone it's designed for will be able to use it equally easily)
d) **practicality** (how easy it is to use, in general)

3) Sometimes the thing you want to measure will turn out to be made up of a number of **factors**, and so won't be so easy to measure. D'oh.
4) For example, **intelligence** may not be just a single trait, but be made up of variations such as problem solving, lateral thinking, social intelligence, spatial reasoning, memory, imagination and many others.
5) However, **correlations** exist between different types of intelligence. This suggests that although intelligence can be split up into different traits, they're not as independent as was first thought.

Psychometric Tests

Psychometric Tests *Aren't Perfect*

Never mind not perfect — often they're a bit shoddy. Learn why:

1) Tests are designed to measure what the person developing the test thinks they should measure. If there aren't **agreed definitions** of what is actually being measured, there can be difficulties.
2) There is also the difficulty of whether personality traits are **stable attributes**. It's difficult to know whether an individual will perform the same on a test on different days.
3) Many factors from age to ethnicity can affect test performance, so **fairness** should be considered carefully.

Reliability and *Validity* are Important

Reliability and **validity** are pretty damn important in psychometric test design. There's no point in using a test if it's not reliable and valid:

Reliability

A **reliable** test is one that measures a trait **consistently**. To **test** reliability, you could give the same person the same test **twice** to see how the scores **correlate** (i.e. if they're the same).

When a test doesn't measure **consistently**, it could be because someone administered or scored it differently, for example.

Sometimes being the reliable one got too much for Jim.

Validity

A **valid** test is one that really measures what it's **claimed** to measure. It's hard to say whether many psychometric tests are valid as there might be no agreed **definition** for the trait anyway.

Practice Questions

Q1 What are psychometric tests designed to measure?
Q2 What is meant by standardisation?
Q3 What is reliability?
Q4 What is validity?

Exam Questions

Q1 Outline the potential weaknesses of psychometric tests. [6 marks]

Q2 Discuss the issues which need to be considered when constructing psychometric tests. [12 marks]

The only thing this is testing is my patience...

If psychology's going to keep claiming it's a science, I guess it needs to have some good, dry tests to keep all the geeks happy. None of them are perfect though, so you don't have to believe the results if you don't want to. Like if you take an IQ test and it turns out your score's the lowest out of everyone you know, it probably means there's something wrong with the test...

Defining Abnormality

Only AQA people need to look at these pages.
Defining what's abnormal is easy — it's just what's not normal. But what's normal...?

*Abnormality Can be Described as **Deviation from Social Norms***

1) All societies have their **standards** of behaviour and attitudes. Deviating from these can be seen as abnormal.
2) But **cultures vary**, so there isn't one universal set of social 'rules'.
3) One problem with defining abnormality as deviation from social norms is that it can be used to **justify** the removal of 'unwanted' people from a society. For example, people opposing a particular political regime could be said to be abnormal.

The concept of deviation from the majority can be expressed statistically in terms of the **normal distribution**:

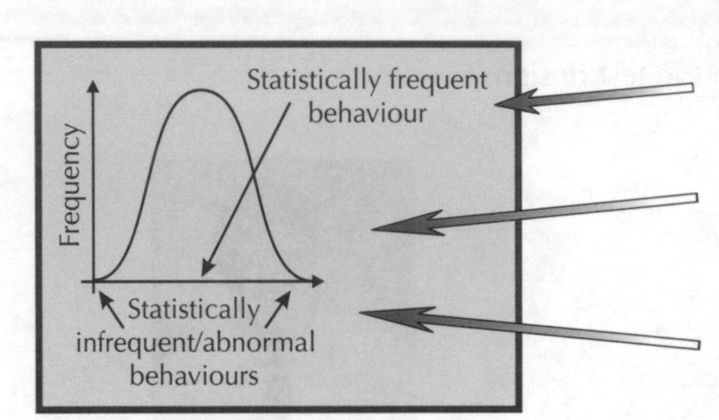

People who behave in the average way make up the middle of the bell-shaped curve.

Those people who behave 'abnormally' make up the tail ends of the bell curve — this behaviour is rare (statistically infrequent).

This axis shows a numerical measure of the behaviour, e.g. the number of hand washes per week.

Not all traits show a normal distribution.

However, there are **problems** with defining abnormality simply in terms of statistical infrequency:

1) It doesn't take account of the **desirability of behaviour**, just its frequency. For example, a very high IQ is abnormal, as is a very low one, but having a high IQ is desirable whereas having a low IQ is undesirable.
2) There's **no distinction** between **rare**, **slightly odd** behaviour and **rare, psychologically abnormal** behaviour.
3) There's **no definite cut-off point** where normal behaviour becomes abnormal behaviour.
4) Some behaviours that are considered psychologically abnormal are quite common, e.g. mild depression. **Hassett and White (1989)** argue that you cannot use statistical infrequency to define abnormality because of this. Using the statistical infrequency idea, some disorders would not be classed as anything unusual.

Interestingly, as recently as 1974, homosexuality was classified in the DSM as a **disorder**. However, the diagnosis was dropped because it was found that homosexuality **wasn't as infrequent** as previously thought, and that homosexuals don't differ from heterosexuals in terms of **psychological well-being**.

Failure to Function Adequately** is Another Definition of **Abnormality

You can't function adequately if you can't cope with the demands of day-to-day life.
Various **criteria** are used for diagnosis, including:

1) **Dysfunctional behaviour** — behaviour which goes against the accepted standards of behaviour.
2) **Observer discomfort** — behaviour that causes other individuals to become uncomfortable.
3) **Unpredictable behaviour** — impulsive behaviour that seems to be uncontrollable.
4) **Irrational behaviour** — behaviour that's unreasonable and illogical.
5) **Personal distress** — being affected by emotion to an excessive degree.

If you can tick the box for **more than one** of the criteria above, the person's behaviour is considered to be **abnormal**. It does seem a bit unfair though — we've probably all done stuff that could fit under these categories at some point. People are always uncomfortable around me, but that could be because I've got fleas.

Defining Abnormality

Jahoda (1958) Identified **Six Conditions** Associated with **Good Mental Health**

Jahoda's six conditions were:

1) Positive self-attitude
2) Self-actualisation (realising your potential, being fulfilled)
3) Resistance to stress
4) Personal autonomy (making your own decisions, being in control)
5) Accurate perception of reality
6) Adaptation to the environment

As far as Doug was concerned, he was in control of everything he needed in life.

However, it can be **hard to meet** all the standards set in this list, and they're **subjective** (ideas of what is required for each will differ from person to person).
Also, a violent offender, for example, may have a positive self attitude and be resistant to stress etc. — yet society wouldn't consider them to be in good mental health.

The Idea of Ideal Mental Health **Varies** Across **Time** and Between **Cultures**

What's considered mentally 'healthy' at one time, wouldn't necessarily be at another.
For example, in some cultures today, it's considered **abnormal** for women to **enjoy sex** — they may be forced to have their clitoris surgically removed to prevent their enjoyment. In Victorian times here, women who enjoyed sex were deemed abnormal and hence Freud coined the term '**nymphomania**'. There's still influence from this today — there are still **double standards** about male and female sexual activity.
But the idea of 'ideal' mental health can be a useful one because it moves away from focusing on mental 'illness'.

Some **Symptoms** are Associated with Mental Illness

The Department of Health provides a guide to assess symptoms associated with mental illness.
To be classified as a mental illness, there should be **one or more** of the following (**not temporary**) symptoms:

1) Impairment of **intellectual functions**, such as memory and comprehension.
2) Alterations to **mood** that lead to **delusional appraisals** of the past or future, or lack of any appraisal.
3) Delusional **beliefs**, such as of persecution or jealousy.
4) Disordered **thinking** — the person may be unable to appraise their situation or communicate with others.

Practice Questions

Q1 Define abnormality using the deviation from social norms explanation.
Q2 What does Jahoda (1958) say are the six conditions associated with mental health?
Q3 Give three of the symptoms that the Department of Health uses to classify mental illness.
Q4 If someone's forgotten their trousers, should they be allowed on the bus?

Exam Questions

Q1 Outline the problems with defining abnormality in terms of deviation from social norms. [6 marks]

Q2 Outline the key features of the idea of abnormality as the failure to function adequately. [6 marks]

I'm not abnormal — I'm just a little socially deviant...

Ah, wouldn't it be easier to just be a fish... Nobody minds if you're abnormal when you're under the sea — you can swim around any way you like. You could befriend a manatee and have an adventure. The kindly sea cow — he'd never judge you for your dysfunctional and unpredictable behaviour. Yes, life is much better down where it's wetter, take it from me...

Defining Abnormality

Just for AQA — no need to bother with these two pages if you're doing OCR or Edexcel. *Maybe trying to define abnormality is just wrong altogether. I mean, calling someone 'abnormal' isn't exactly very nice. I got called abnormal the other day and it cut me pretty deep. Mothers can be so cruel...*

*The Concept of Abnormality **Varies** from One **Culture** and **Time** to Another*

1) **Cultural relativism** means that judgements made about abnormality are relative to individual cultures. That's because what's normal in one culture is sometimes considered to be abnormal in another. So definitions of abnormality are **limited** because they're **culturally specific**.
2) It's important to work out whether an abnormality is **absolute**, **universal**, or **culturally relative**.

    a) **Absolute** — occurring in the same way and frequency across cultures.
    b) **Universal** — present in all cultures, but not necessarily with the same frequency.
    c) **Culturally relative** — unique to a particular culture.

3) Many **physical** conditions are **absolute**. The same goes for some mental conditions. However, **social norms** vary from one culture to another. This can affect how these conditions are **perceived**. For example, in some **cultures** it's considered normal to experience **hallucinations**, but in the western world it can be seen as a **symptom** of **schizophrenia**.
4) Some abnormal behaviours are **universal**, e.g. **depression** occurs in all cultures, but is more common in women and in industrial societies.
5) Some abnormal behaviours are **culturally relative** — these are known as **culture-bound syndromes**.

'Witiko' is an example of culturally relative behaviour. It is a culture-bound syndrome, suffered by native Canadians, who **lose their appetite** for ordinary food, feel **depressed** and believe they are **possessed by the Witiko**, who is a **giant man-eating monster**. This can result in cannibalism, murder or pleas for death from the sufferer. It is thought to be an extreme form of **starvation anxiety**.

*Attempts to **Define** Abnormality May Be **Biased***

There are often problems when it comes to defining abnormality — these often relate to **stereotypes**.

Gender...

Factors such as **biological** or **hormonal** differences, and the different ways that men and women are **brought up**, could lead to gender differences in the frequencies of disorders.

However, the **gender stereotype** can lead people to believe that women are generally moodier, and men generally more violent and antisocial. This could be a factor in clinicians tending to diagnose more **mood** disorders in women and more **antisocial** disorders in men — the clinicians **expect** to find them.

Race...

Several studies have found that very large numbers of **black people** in Britain are being diagnosed with **schizophrenia**. Surveys of inpatients by **Bagley (1971)** and **Cochrane (1977)** found that **immigrant groups** in Britain are more likely to be diagnosed as schizophrenic than native-born people. This is particularly so for people originating in Africa, the Caribbean and Asia. It was first thought that this could be explained in terms of **genetic** or **biological** factors, except that the same rates of occurrence were **not found** in the **countries of origin**.

Therefore, possible reasons include **racial stereotypes** in diagnosis and **greater stress**. Stress could be due to poorer living conditions, prejudice, or the general stress of living in a new culture.

Even if stereotypes alone are to blame for a diagnosis, the person could 'develop' the disorder. Once a person is **labelled** with a mental disorder, they may begin to behave in the expected way due to the label. The diagnosis then becomes a **self-fulfilling prophecy**.

Defining Abnormality

Classification Systems **Pigeon-Hole** People

A major **problem** with systems for classifying abnormality is that they can lead to pigeon-holing people into **certain categories**. This leads to **practical**, **theoretical** and **ethical considerations**, which **you need to know** about.

1) **Diagnosis** — when people report how they feel 'psychologically', these are **subjective** feelings. One person's "I'm extremely depressed" may mean the same as someone else's, "I'm fed up". A more **idiographic approach** would be useful — that is, focusing on each unique case and viewing patients on their merits.
2) There are many **different theories** of abnormality — psychodynamic, learning, cognitive, etc. They all have their own definitions and ideas of what causes abnormality.
3) There's little evidence of **validity** — how much any of the classification systems measure what they're supposed to. It's hard to find a central cause **(aetiology)** for most disorders. And, if patients have more than one disorder it can be difficult to spot symptoms of one disorder.
4) Psychiatrists may not always agree from category to category, so classification systems may not always be **reliable**.
5) **Treatment** — grouping patients can be useful for prescribing treatments, but treatment often depends on diagnosis. Therefore, if the diagnosis is subjective initially, the treatment may not be correct.
6) **Labelling theory (Scheff, 1966)** argues that if people are treated as mentally ill, their behaviour will change and become more like that expected from their diagnosis.
7) **Szasz (1974)** said that psychiatric labels were **meaningless**. He said illness was a bodily problem, so 'mental' illness could not exist. He believed the term was used to exclude non-conformists from society.
8) Finally, it's hard to say where normality ends and abnormality starts anyway.

Just so you know, there's a difference between psychologists and psychiatrists. Psychiatry is a part of medicine that deals with the prevention, diagnosis and treatment of mental disorders. So, a psychiatrist is trained in medicine as well as psychology.

In some cultures marrying your horse is perfectly normal.

Practice Questions

Q1 What is cultural relativism?

Q2 What is meant by a universal abnormality?

Q3 What are culture-bound syndromes?

Q4 What is meant by an idiographic approach to abnormality?

Q5 What did Scheff (1966) propose in his labelling theory?

Exam Questions

Q1 Outline how stereotypes can cause problems in defining abnormality. [8 marks]

Q2 Evaluate the use of classification systems for defining abnormality. [10 marks]

In the seventies people thought men with huge perms were normal...

You've got to know all the stuff on these pages if you're going to answer a 'defining abnormality' question in the exam. I reckon the best way is to read the pages and make a list of all the main points in note form. Then cover the pages up, and try to write them out again from the notes you've just made. This process is known as 'learning' or 'revision'...

The Biological Model of Abnormality

These pages are just for AQA and Edexcel. *There are many different models of abnormality that describe symptoms and treatments differently. You need to know about the biological model, including its strengths and weaknesses.*

*The Biological Model Assumes Psychological Disorders are **Physical Illnesses***

The **biological (or medical or somatic) model** assumes that psychological disorders are **physical illnesses** with physical causes. In principle they're no different from physical illnesses like flu, except they have major psychological symptoms. When the same symptoms frequently occur together, they represent a reliable **syndrome** or **disorder**. The cause or '**aetiology**' may be one or more of the following:

1) **Genetics** — Faulty genes are known to cause some diseases that have psychological effects, e.g. Huntington's disease that leads to a deterioration of mental abilities.
2) **Neurotransmitters** (see page 40) — Too much or too little of a particular neurotransmitter may produce psychological disorders, e.g. an increased level of **dopamine** is linked to schizophrenia — **drugs** like cocaine, which increase dopamine levels, can lead to schizophrenia-like symptoms.
3) **Infection** — Disorders may be caused by infection. **General paresis** is a condition involving delusions and mood swings, leading to paralysis and death. It is caused by **syphilis**, and can now be treated.
4) **Brain injury** — Accidental brain damage may produce psychological disorders. E.g. in 1848 an explosion sent an iron rod through **Phineas Gage's** head, destroying parts of his frontal lobes. He survived, but he became more impulsive and disorganised, couldn't plan for the future and had a strangely different personality.

*Research Has Been Done into the **Genetic Basis** of **Schizophrenia***

Twin Studies

Identical twins share **100%** of their genes. So in theory, if schizophrenia has a purely **genetic basis**, if one twin suffers from schizophrenia then the other twin will too. **Non-identical twins** share **50%** of their genes, so the risk of both suffering should be lower.

	Gottesman (1991) conducted a meta-analysis of twin studies
Method:	Gottesman carried out a meta-analysis of approximately 40 twin studies.
Results:	It was found that having an **identical twin** with schizophrenia gave you a **48%** chance of developing the condition. This reduced to **17%** in **non-identical twins**.
Conclusion:	Schizophrenia has a strong **genetic basis**.
Evaluation:	The meta-analysis was carried out on field studies, giving the research **high ecological validity**. Because identical twins share 100% of their genes, it might be expected that both twins would always suffer from the same conditions. The fact that both twins had developed schizophrenia in only about half of the cases means that **another factor** must also be involved. Identical twins tend to be treated more similarly than non-identical twins, and so the **family environment** might play a large role.

Adoption Studies

Adoption studies have also provided evidence for a **genetic basis** of schizophrenia.

	Heston (1966) conducted an adoption study
Method:	47 adopted children whose biological mothers had schizophrenia were studied. The control group consisted of 50 adopted children whose biological mothers didn't suffer from schizophrenia. The children were followed up as adults and were interviewed and given intelligence and personality tests.
Results:	Of the experimental group, 5 of the 47 became schizophrenic, compared to 0 in the control group. Another 4 of the experimental group were classified as borderline schizophrenic by the raters.
Conclusion:	The study supports the view that schizophrenia has a **genetic basis**.
Evaluation:	Interview data can be unreliable and affected by **social desirability bias**. However, interviews are a good way of getting data in a **naturalistic way**. The adopted children whose mothers didn't suffer from any conditions might have not shown any symptoms of schizophrenia **yet** — it can't be completely ruled out.

The Biological Model of Abnormality

Biological Disorders Can Be **Treated** with Biological Therapies

The biological model says that once the physical cause of a psychological disorder has been identified, a physical (biological) therapy is needed to treat the physical problem. One or more of the following may be used:

1) **Drugs** — Drugs can be used to change **neurotransmitter levels** in the brain. For example, **phenothiazines** reduce levels of dopamine and can therefore relieve symptoms of schizophrenia.
2) **Psychosurgery** — Psychosurgery is brain surgery involving destruction or separation of parts of the brain. **Moniz** developed the '**frontal lobotomy**' in the 1930s to separate parts of the frontal lobes from the rest of the brain. This reduced aggression and generally made people more placid. However, it's **not a cure**, but a change — the **irreversible** changes to personality may have just made patients easier to manage. Psychosurgery is now only a last resort treatment for some disorders, e.g. very serious depression.
3) **Electroconvulsive therapy (ECT)** — During ECT, an electric shock of around 225 volts is given to a person's brain. This can help to relieve depression, but can also produce memory loss. Although quite commonly used in the past, it's now only used as a last resort therapy.

The **Biological Model** Has **Strengths** and **Weaknesses**

Strengths:

1) It has a **scientific** basis in biology and a lot of evidence shows that biological causes **can** produce psychological symptoms.
2) It can be seen as **ethical** because people are **not blamed** for their disorders. They just have an illness.
3) Biological **therapies** have helped relieve conditions (e.g. schizophrenia) that could not be treated very well previously.

Weaknesses:

1) Biological therapies raise **ethical** concerns. Drugs can produce addiction and may only suppress symptoms rather than cure the disorder. The effects of psychosurgery are irreversible.
2) Psychological disorders may not be linked to any physical problem. **Psychological therapies** can be just as effective as biological treatments, without any interference to biological structures.

Practice Questions

Q1 Give two possible causes of psychological disorders according to the biological model.

Q2 What type of studies have been used to investigate the genetic basis of schizophrenia?

Q3 What is psychosurgery?

Q4 What is electroconvulsive therapy?

Q5 Give one strength and one weakness of the biological model.

Exam Questions

Q1 Outline the key features of the biological model relating to the causes of abnormality. [6 marks]

Q2 Outline and evaluate a piece of research conducted into the genetic basis of schizophrenia. [8 marks]

Biological, medical, somatic — it just needs to make up its mind...

That's the first of many models of abnormality. Make sure you know this one thoroughly before you look at the next one. And that means the key features, the studies, the treatments and the strengths and weaknesses. Phew. You don't want to start getting all the details mixed up with the other models. So, when you're ready, on to the psychodynamic model...

The Psychodynamic Model of Abnormality

You only need these pages if you're doing AQA or Edexcel.
If you're doing Edexcel, you need to learn a load more about this topic — see pages 120 and 121.
You've probably forgotten what you read about the psychodynamic approach back on page 92. So, luckily for you, here it is again. And even better, it's in more detail. What more could you possibly want...

The Psychodynamic Model is Based on **Conflict in Development**

1) The model is based on **Freud's** division of personality into the **id**, **ego** and **superego**.
2) It also uses his **stages of development** — the oral, anal, phallic, latency and genital stages.
3) The model suggests that **conflict** and **anxiety** may occur during childhood because the **ego** is not yet **developed** enough to deal with the id's desires, understand real-world issues or cope with the superego's moral demands (e.g. knowing right from wrong).
4) Psychological disorders may also come from **conflict** or **anxiety** which happens in a certain **stage** of development. For example, during the anal stage, conflict may occur during potty training.
5) Anxiety from the conflicts is repressed into the **unconscious mind**. **Stress** or **trauma** in adulthood may 'trigger' the repressed conflicts, leading to **psychological disorders**.

Read the first half of p.27 if any of this isn't too clear.

Psychoanalysis is Used as a **Treatment** in the Psychodynamic Model

1) Freud introduced **psychoanalysis** as a treatment in the early twentieth century.
2) Its aim was to allow the patient to **access** repressed thoughts and unconscious conflicts — Freud called this **'insight'**.
3) Patients were then encouraged to **deal** with the conflicts.
4) Freud recognised that this process would be painful and cause anxiety, and that people would be **resistant** at first. However, patients were encouraged to focus on the **feelings** that the repressed thoughts brought about.

Freud used three psychoanalytic techniques to uncover his patients' repressed thoughts:

For more on psychoanalytic therapies, see page 125.

Hypnosis

Hypnosis is an **altered mental state**, involving deep relaxation. Freud believed that people could access repressed thoughts whilst in this state. He gradually lost interest in the technique for two main reasons — he found it **difficult** to hypnotise people, and also found that people become very **suggestible** when hypnotised.

Free Association

In free association, the patient is given a **cue word** and is asked to say any **ideas** or **memories** that come into their mind. Freud believed that by doing this repressed thoughts would eventually **emerge**, giving an **insight** into the unconscious problems causing abnormal behaviour.

Dream Analysis

Dream analysis was also used by Freud. It was thought that a certain part of the mind keeps repressed thoughts in the **unconscious** and that this part is **less active** during **sleep**. Therefore, Freud believed that repressed thoughts are likely to appear in **dreams**.

So, your dream of a cow eating corn. Had any corned beef lately...?

The Psychodynamic Model of Abnormality

*The **Psychodynamic Model** Also Has **Strengths** and **Weaknesses***

Strengths:

1) It's quite a unique approach to abnormality, suggesting that disorders may be linked to **unresolved conflicts** related to **biological needs**.
2) It offers methods of **therapy** which may also uncover unconscious conflicts. The client can then **understand** the causes of their problems and so **resolve** them and release their anxieties (see also pages 120-121).
3) It was the first theory to focus on **psychological causes** of disorders. Before this, the focus had been on **physical causes** or things like possession by **evil spirits**.

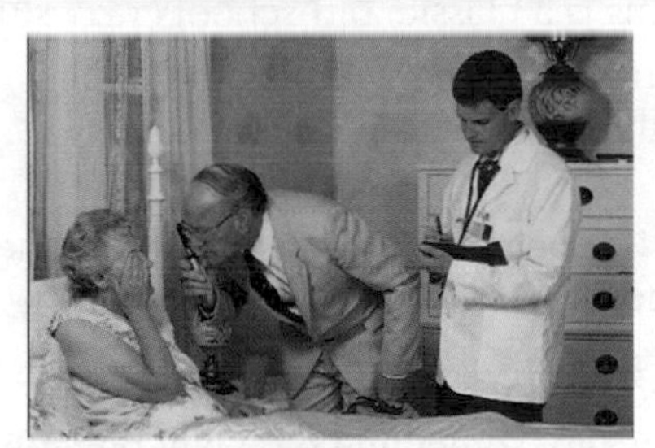

So... hearing voices. Ever get pushed out of the sand pit at school...?

Weaknesses:

1) Freud's claims are based on his subjective interpretations of his patients' dreams, etc. Therefore they're hard to **scientifically test** and so can't be proved right or wrong.
2) **Psychoanalysis** may take a long time and so be very expensive. The childhood conflicts that are 'uncovered' may be emotionally distressing and possibly inaccurate, depending on the reliability of the patient's memory, the techniques used to uncover them and the analyst's interpretations.
3) The focus is on the patient's **past**, rather than on the problems that they are **currently suffering**.

Practice Questions

Q1 Who introduced psychoanalysis as a treatment?

Q2 According to the psychodynamic model, what might lead to psychological disorders?

Q3 What did Freud mean by 'insight'?

Q4 Why might people be resistant to psychoanalysis at first?

Q5 What is 'free association'?

Q6 Tell me about your mother...

Exam Questions

Q1 Outline the assumptions of the psychodynamic model relating to the treatment of abnormality. [6 marks]

Q2 Evaluate the strengths and weaknesses of the psychodynamic model. [8 marks]

We all experience conflict during childhood — that's what siblings are for...

My sister once pinned me down and spat on my face. I wouldn't mind, but I was 21 at the time and it seemed a little undignified. Still, at least it didn't happen before my ego was properly developed, else it might have messed me up good and proper. Isn't that right, Freud? Freud? Sigmund? He's not answering — how rude. His silence speaks volumes...

The Behavioural Model of Abnormality

You need to know this stuff if you're doing AQA or Edexcel. But by the way, if you're doing Edexcel, you need to know even more stuff about this — the fun continues on pages 118 and 119.

*The Behavioural Model of Abnormality says **Behaviours** are all **Learnt***

Behaviourists argue that abnormal behaviours are learnt in the same way that all behaviours are learnt — through **classical** and **operant conditioning**. This page is all about their take on the matter.

(1) Behaviourists reckon that classical conditioning can be used to explain the development of many abnormal behaviours, including **phobias** and **taste aversions**.

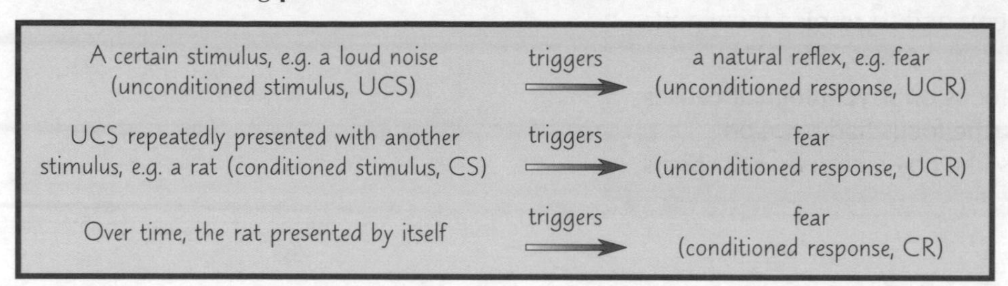

Phobias can be created when the natural fear response is associated with a particular stimulus.

1) **Watson and Rayner (1920)** experimented with an 11-month-old boy, **'Little Albert'**, producing fear of a white rat by associating it with a loud, scary noise (see page 113). This is a classic, old-school crazy study.
2) **Taste aversions** are often created if you're ill after a certain food or drink. Its taste will become a CS, producing a CR of nausea. So, if you were ill after eating a curry with bad meat, the taste of curry might always make you feel ill.
3) **Extinction** is where the conditioned response **disappears** when a CS is repeatedly presented without the UCS. If the CR suddenly **reappears**, this is known as **spontaneous recovery**.

(2) **Operant conditioning** is learning from the **consequences** of actions. Actions which have a good outcome through **positive reinforcement** (reward) or **negative reinforcement** (removal of something bad) will be repeated. Actions which have a bad outcome (**punishment**) will not be repeated. Some examples include:

a) Maintaining **phobias** — we get anxious around phobic stimuli (heights, spiders etc.) and avoid them. This prevents the anxiety, which acts as negative reinforcement.
b) **Bulimics** feel guilt and disgust, so make themselves sick. The removal of these feelings is negative reinforcement.
c) **Anorexics** desire to lose weight, or to have more control of their life, so not eating is positive reinforcement.

Reinforcement can be **primary** or **secondary**. Primary reinforcement involves something that's **naturally satisfying**, such as **food** or **drink**. You **don't** need to learn to value the reward. On the other hand, secondary reinforcement is when you have to **learn to value** the reward through positive experience. For example, you have to learn how to use **money** to buy things like food and drink before you will value money.

*Behavioural Therapies are Based on **Changes** Through **Conditioning***

Behaviourists try to identify what **reinforces** unwanted behaviours and try to change them through conditioning.

1) **Operant conditioning therapies** are often used in psychiatric hospitals. They control abnormal behaviour by removing the reinforcements which maintain the behaviour, and giving new reinforcements for better behaviour. For example, psychiatric patients might receive **tokens** for behaving 'normally'. These can be exchanged for **reinforcements**, such as sweets or being able to watch TV. This is called a **token economy** — see page 118.
2) Behavioural therapies can also use **classical conditioning** to change behaviour, for example...

1) Aversion Therapy

This removes an undesired behaviour by associating it with **unpleasant feelings**. For example, alcoholics are given alcohol at the same time as a drug that naturally produces nausea. Nausea becomes a conditioned response to alcohol, so they should then feel no urge to drink, but instead feel sick at the idea of it.

The Behavioural Model of Abnormality

2) Systematic Desensitisation

This is a treatment for **phobias**.

1) First, the phobic person makes a **'fear hierarchy'**. This is a list of feared events, showing what they fear least (e.g. seeing a picture of a spider) through to their most feared event (e.g. holding a spider).
2) When put in the situation of their least feared event, they're **anxious**.
3) Then they're encouraged to use a **relaxation** technique.
4) Relaxation and anxiety can't happen at the same time, so when they become relaxed and calm, they're no longer scared.
5) This is repeated until the feared event is only linked with relaxation.
6) This whole process is repeated for each stage of the fear hierarchy until they are **calm** through their **most feared** event.

Margaret was still anxious around beards, but she'd learnt to grin and bear it.

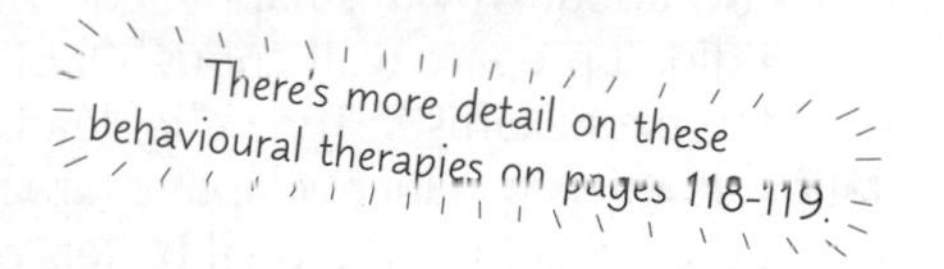

The Behavioural Model Has Strengths and Weaknesses

Strengths:

1) It's a **scientific** approach — it has clear **testable** concepts, which have been supported in many experiments.
2) Behavioural **therapies** can be very **effective** for treating phobias, eating disorders, obsessions and compulsions.

Weaknesses:

1) It cannot explain all behaviours because it neglects:
   a) The influence of **genetics** and **biology** — for example, how brain functioning affects behaviour.
   b) The influence of **cognitions** — how thought processes contribute to disorders (see pages 106-107).
2) Behavioural therapies are **not effective** for **all** disorders, e.g. conditioning doesn't cure schizophrenia.
3) The procedures sometimes raise **ethical** issues, e.g. aversion therapy may be quite distressing.
4) It only treats the behaviour, so it doesn't address any underlying causes for it.

Practice Questions

Q1 How might classical conditioning explain abnormal behaviour?

Q2 Give an example of how operant conditioning could explain behaviour.

Q3 What is meant by extinction in classical conditioning?

Q4 Give an example of a primary reinforcer.

Q5 What is meant by secondary reinforcement in operant conditioning?

Exam Questions

Q1 Explain an assumption of the behavioural approach to abnormality and give a criticism of this approach. [6 marks]

Q2 Outline the process of systematic desensitisation. [4 marks]

So, you're scared of spiders — oooh, look what I have here...

Hmmm... you wouldn't be able to use the excuse of 'phobia of revision' if your teacher was a behaviourist. So I guess you'd better just get on with it just in case. Doing well in your exam will be a positive reinforcement — or something... Anyway, it's just the usual stuff — features of the approach, treatments, and the good old strengths and weaknesses.

The Cognitive Model of Abnormality

Another two pages of fun that all you OCR types unfortunately have to miss out on.
Guess what... Another model you've got to learn. And if more models are right, that means they're all a bit wrong...

*The Cognitive Model of Abnormality Concentrates on **Thoughts** and **Beliefs***

The cognitive model assumes that behaviours are controlled by thoughts and beliefs. So, irrational thoughts and beliefs cause abnormal behaviours. A few different versions of the model have been suggested:

Ellis (1962) — The '**ABC model**' claims that disorders begin with an **activating event (A)** (e.g. a failed exam), leading to a **belief (B)** about why this happened. This may be rational (e.g. 'I didn't prepare well enough'), or irrational (e.g. 'I'm too stupid to pass exams'). The belief leads to a **consequence (C)**. Rational beliefs produce adaptive (appropriate) consequences (e.g. more revision). Irrational beliefs produce maladaptive (bad and inappropriate) consequences (e.g. getting depressed).

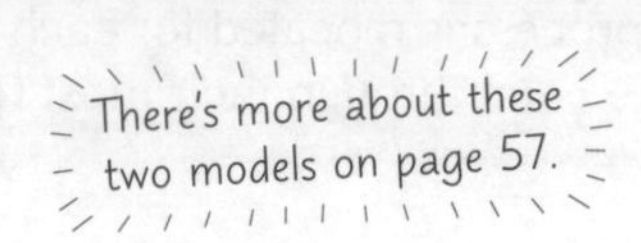
There's more about these two models on page 57.

Young Arthur grasped the ABC model at a very young age.

Beck (1963) — Beck identified a '**cognitive triad**' of negative, automatic thoughts linked to **depression**: negative views about **themselves** (e.g. that they can't succeed at anything), about the **world** (e.g. that they must be successful to be a good person) and about the **future** (e.g. that nothing will change).

*Cognitive Therapies Try to Change **Faulty Cognitions***

Cognitive therapies assume that we can treat psychological disorders by **eliminating** or **changing** the original faulty thoughts and beliefs. They're used to treat a wide range of conditions, and can be particularly helpful with problems such as **depression** and **anxiety**. They've also been shown to be as effective as **medication** for some conditions.
This is generally what happens during cognitive behavioural therapy:

1) The therapist and client **identify** the client's faulty **cognitions** (thoughts and beliefs).
2) The therapist then tries to show that the cognitions aren't true, e.g. that the client doesn't always fail at what they do.
3) Together, they then set **goals** to think in more positive or adaptive ways, e.g. focusing on things the client has succeeded at and trying to build on them.
4) Although the client may occasionally need to look back to past experiences, the treatment mainly focuses on the **present situation**.
5) Therapists sometimes encourage their clients to keep a **diary** — they can record their thought patterns, feelings and actions.

Examples of cognitive therapies are **Hardiness Training** and Meichenbaum's **Stress Inoculation Training (SIT)**, which, as you can probably guess, was developed to reduce stress (see page 56).

The Cognitive Model of Abnormality

The Cognitive Model, Surprise Surprise, Has **Strengths** and **Weaknesses**

Strengths:

1) The cognitive model offers a **useful** approach to disorders like depression and anorexia. This is because it considers the role of **thoughts** and **beliefs**, which are greatly involved in problems like depression.
2) Cognitive therapies have often **successfully treated** depression, anxiety, stress and eating disorders.
3) It allows a person to **take control** and make a positive change to their behaviour.

Strengths — looks good in pink. Weaknesses — only has half a pair of trousers.

Weaknesses:

1) Faulty cognitions may simply be the **consequence** of a disorder rather than its cause. For example, depression may be caused by a chemical imbalance in the brain, which causes people to think very negatively.
2) Cognitive therapies may take a long **time** and be **costly**. They may be more effective when **combined** with other approaches, e.g. cognitive-behavioural methods.
3) The treatments work **better** with some conditions than others.
4) The person could begin to feel like he or she is to **blame** for their problems.

So, you're probably getting the point by now. All these different models and approaches are great in some ways, but are actually kinda dodgy in other ways. It makes it tricky to see which model best explains abnormality, or whether they're all partially right.

Practice Questions

Q1 Outline the ABC model of abnormality.

Q2 What three factors make up Beck's 'cognitive triad'?

Q3 What are the main features of cognitive therapy?

Q4 For which conditions are cognitive therapies particularly effective?

Q5 Give two examples of cognitive therapies.

Exam Questions

Q1 Outline the assumptions of the cognitive approach to the causes and treatment of abnormality. [6 marks]

Q2 Evaluate the strengths and weaknesses of the cognitive model of abnormality. [8 marks]

I think I'm mentally ill, therefore I am...

What's a bit confusing is that all these theories seem to make sense — you read them and think, 'So that's what it's all about. Get in. I must be well brainy.' The tricky thing is, they probably can't all be right... If I had to back one, I'd go with the cognitive people — I wouldn't want to mess with anyone who'd had 'hardiness training'. Those guys are built...

Multiple Personality Disorder

Right, these are for OCR only. Do what you want with them if you're doing AQA or Edexcel. *Go on, eat them. This is a scary topic. Imagine if one day you woke up with no memory of the previous night, but everyone said you were acting like a different person... and you'd not had a drop to drink...*

Multiple Personality Disorder (MPD) is Very Rare

1) **Multiple personality disorder**, or **dissociative identity disorder** (DID), is where a person develops different personalities.
2) These different personalities may have different memories, behaviours, attitudes and cognitive functioning, and may or may not be aware of each other.
3) There has been debate over whether such a condition actually **exists**. Having said that, people now generally believe that it does, and that it's a consequence of **extreme abuse** in childhood.
4) It's suggested that a **dissociation** (a lack of **connection**) from reality happens as a form of **mental escape** from trauma. This will produce changes in memory and perhaps, if this happens often, the person's whole sense of history and identity will change.

The **clinical characteristics** of MPD include:

1) The person is **unable to recall personal information** which would not normally be forgotten.
2) Two or more **distinct personalities** exist, each with their own perceptions of the environment and themselves.
3) These personalities take turns at **controlling** the behaviour of the person.
4) The disturbance is **not due** to other physiological effects, such as alcohol abuse or epilepsy.

Eve White Was the First Convincing Account of MPD

Yeah, I know this looks bad, but it's actually quite interesting. Actually, I don't know why I'm hyping it up — you've got to learn it whether it's as dull as James Blunt and David Gray all rolled into one, or not.

OCR Core Study

Thigpen and Cleckley (1954) — case study of Eve White

Eve White's real name was Christine Sizemore. She was a 25-year-old married woman, who after suffering from **headaches**, **blackouts** and **memory loss**, was referred to a psychiatrist.

Her psychiatrist received a letter with the final lines written in a different handwriting and tone. Eve White said she had started a letter but not finished it. In a therapy session, she asked if hearing voices was a sign of insanity. Then she put her hands to her head as if in pain — and another personality who called herself **'Eve Black'** appeared. Eve White was **not aware** of Eve Black until informed, but Eve Black was **aware** and critical of Eve White.

A number of Eve's **life events** suggested that she was suffering from **MPD**:
Eve White recalled being punished for things she didn't remember doing in childhood. Her parents confirmed this. Eve Black claimed responsibility for many childhood pranks. Additionally, Eve Black denied knowledge of Eve White's husband and of any relationship to her daughter. She claimed to have been married to someone else — a husband who Eve White claimed no knowledge of. A relative revealed that there had been a previous marriage, and later Eve Black admitted that this had been a time when she was in control, not Eve White.

Psychometric tests revealed the extent of the two personalities' differences: Eve White had a **slightly higher IQ** and **memory** function in tests. Eve White was found to be serious, anxious, conscientious and emotionally **repressed**. Eve Black, by comparison, was hedonistic, shallow, irresponsible and less anxious, lacked compassion and often **regressed** to childlike behaviour. Only Eve White could be hypnotised and was thought to be the **dominant** personality. 'Black' was Eve White's maiden name, which suggested that Eve Black was not a different personality as such, but the same personality at an earlier stage of life, perhaps brought about by a desire to return to this earlier, more irresponsible time of life.

During the progress of therapy, improvements seemed to occur. Eve White stopped having headaches and blackouts and hearing voices. Eve Black also caused less trouble, although still acted quite irresponsibly. Later, a third personality, **Jane**, appeared who was more mature, capable and interesting than Eve White, yet lacked Eve Black's faults. Jane was seen as a compromise between the two previous personalities. In the years after Thigpen and Cleckley's case study, over 20 different personalities appeared. The final one was **Christine Costner Sizemore** (her real name), who said she had **assimilated** her different selves.

Multiple Personality Disorder

There is Debate Over Whether Some MPD Cases are **Genuine**

1) At the time of Thigpen and Cleckley's case study, **very few** cases of MPD had been reported.
2) A rash of reported cases followed a popular book and film called **Sybil** about a case of MPD.
3) It has been suggested that this book and film led to an inadvertent trend among therapists to **diagnose** their patients with MPD.
4) People now sometimes use MPD as a **defence** for committing crimes, claiming they did not do the crimes and that another personality did. It would be easy to **fake** a case of MPD — little more than good acting skills would be required.
5) However, even if this trend in therapists once existed, and faking now occurs, these aren't reasons to dispute that the condition **does exist**.

Case Studies Can Be **Unreliable**

There are a number of weaknesses of the Eve White case study:

1) The case study was reliant on **interviews**, so we have lots of 'rich' information that wouldn't be available through any other method.

BUT

2) Only one individual was studied, so it can't tell us anything about general trends in people — only about one person's individual **quirks**.
3) Case studies are more likely to be **retrospective**, relying on personal accounts from memory, which can be **biased**.
4) Case studies also suffer the possibility of **biased** information through the individual trying to **impress** the therapist, or saying what they think he/she **wants to hear**. However, in the case of Eve White, the therapists did try to corroborate their information by also interviewing relatives.
5) Case studies can also become **biased** because of the **therapist** or interviewer (often inadvertently) — they might only record what they want to hear, miss out important information, or skew the information to fit with their diagnosis or expectations.

Since watching *Many Limbed Dancing People*, everyone wanted to get in on the action.

Watch *The Three Faces of Eve* about Eve White, and watch *Sybil*... but don't watch *Me, Myself and Irene* — it's rubbish.

Practice Questions

Q1 What are the clinical characteristics of MPD?

Q2 What does 'DID' stand for?

Q3 Who studied Eve White?

Q4 What was thought to have led to an increased diagnosis of MPD?

Q5 List four criticisms of case studies as a research method.

Exam Questions

Q1 Explain why Thigpen and Cleckley's 'Eve White' study of MPD has been criticised. [6 marks]

Q2 Evaluate the evidence for and against the existence of MPD. [12 marks]

The best thing about me is there are so many of me...

Thigpen and Cleckley don't really sound like psychologists. They sound like policemen in a children's book — Thigpen, Cleckley and Plod. PC Thigpen is tall and thin, and PC Cleckley is big and round. At the moment they're solving the big case of the missing sausages. I think the dog took them. There — wasn't that lovely, children? Now time for beddy-byes...

Cognitive Bias and Gambling

OCR only again. Another two pages all to yourselves. Don't you feel special...
Psychologists have even looked into the thought processes that go on when we're using fruit machines. Just an excuse to go to Las Vegas, I reckon... Oooh, look at all those pretty flashing lights....

Cognitive Biases **Distort Thinking**

Cognitive biases are **mental errors** or **distortions of thinking** that lead to **perspectives** and **judgements** that can be very different to **reality**.

1) These faulty judgements can come about because we often subconsciously **simplify things** and use **rules of thumb** when processing information and making decisions.
2) Cognitive biases can be like **optical illusions**. Even when you're aware of the mistaken thinking, it still seems right. Because of this, they can be pretty difficult to overcome.
3) Cognitive biases appear all over the place. Things like **demand characteristics**, where people change their behaviour during a study because they think it'll please the researcher, are an example of cognitive bias.

Single Pieces of Information Can Make Us Change Our Minds

One example of a cognitive bias is where you tend to take notice of a **single piece** of evidence even if it **goes against** statistically tested information.

1) For example, you might be thinking of buying a new car, and have a particular brand in mind.
2) The brand rates highly on tests of **reliability**, so you reckon it's a good choice.
3) However, one day, your friend who also drives this brand of car complains of a **breakdown**.
4) It's quite likely that you'll be inclined to go back on your decision.
5) It seems strange that we'd change our minds based on **one isolated incident** when we know of loads of **statistical information** proving otherwise, but it's pretty common.

Yeah mate, great cars. Just one minor electrical fault. I'd highly recommend 'em.

Cognitive Biases Can Exist in **Gambling**

Cognitive biases also appear in **gambling**. People often believe that the **probability** of a future event, such as tossing a coin, is dependent on **past events**. When you stop and think about it, it seems quite daft, but you'd be surprised at how common it is.

So, for example, if you're tossing a coin, and tails comes up four times in a row, you might expect heads to be more likely to come up next based on the fact that it's **about time** that it happened. However, as you probably know, this isn't the case. Each coin toss is an **independent event**, unaffected by the results of the previous tosses. Each time, heads and tails are equally likely.

Cognitive Bias and Gambling

Griffiths (1994) Investigated **Cognitive Bias** in **Gambling**

Griffiths compared regular gamblers with non-regular gamblers to see if there was any difference in the way that they make **judgements** and **perceive winning** whilst using fruit machines. Similar to the coin-tossing example, gambles on a fruit machine are all independent events.

Griffiths (1994) looked at cognitive bias using fruit machines

OCR Core Study

Method: 30 participants who had previously only **occasionally** used a fruit machine volunteered to take part in a **field study** along with 30 **regular gamblers**. The study took place at an amusement arcade. Each participant was given £3, which initially gave them 30 gambles on the fruit machine. Participants were asked to try to stay on the machine for at least 60 gambles. If they reached 60, they were given the choice of keeping any winnings or carrying on gambling. Participants were randomly assigned to one of two groups — **'thinking aloud'** or **'non-thinking aloud'**. Thinking aloud required the participants to say all their thoughts out loud during the task. The time that each participant was on the machine was recorded, along with the total number of gambles, the amount of winnings and the outcome of every gamble.

Results: Regular gamblers made **more gambles** than non-regular gamblers, and were found to play **more gambles per minute**. There was no difference in **total winnings** but there was a difference in the **number of wins** — regular gamblers had more. Some regular gamblers **objected** to gambling on the fruit machine chosen for the study. Regular gamblers also made **more irrational verbalisations** than non-regular gamblers, such as personifying and talking to the machine whilst gambling (e.g. "the machine likes me").

Conclusion: Griffiths' study provided evidence for the existence of a cognitive bias in gambling. Regular gamblers played faster so it was likely that they would have more wins than a non-regular gambler. This means that they can **claim** to win more, even though it's likely that they also have a greater number of losses. This shows that an **illusion** is created, which causes the gambler to believe that they are doing well. The fact that some gamblers opposed to using the fruit machine selected for the study indicates that an **illusion of control** exists, where they believe that if they are familiar with a machine they will win more. Also, the fact that many regular gamblers **talked to the machine** shows that their behaviour was not in line with **reality**.

Evaluation: The experiment took place in a natural setting, increasing its **ecological validity**. However, this also means that the results could have been affected by **extraneous variables**. Only one of the regular gamblers was **female**, so the results may not have been **representative** of the whole population. Also, thinking aloud might have an effect on the **cognitive processes** taking place, making the study **invalid**.

Practice Questions

Q1 What is cognitive bias?

Q2 What can cause cognitive bias?

Q3 Describe an example of cognitive bias.

Q4 Who studied cognitive bias in gambling using fruit machines?

Exam Questions

Q1 Describe the procedure of Griffiths' (1994) study of cognitive bias in gambling. [6 marks]

Q2 Identify one flaw in the design of Griffiths' (1994) study and suggest how this could have been overcome. [4 marks]

Fruit machines — the alternative to going to the grocer's...

That can't have been such a bad study to take part in — being given money to play on fruit machines. Although I might've been tempted to just go and play on the grabber machine instead. Even though they always pack the toys in so tightly that nobody wins. I guess that's another cognitive bias — even though you know you won't win, you still have about ten goes.

The Behaviourist Approach

This bit's just for Edexcel, so ignore it if you're not doing Edexcel. In fact, the next 14 pages are just for you.

As you'll remember from page 104, behaviourists believe that all our behaviours are learnt.

*Behaviourism is Also Known as '**Learning Theory**'*

1) Behaviourism ('**Learning Theory**') started in America in the early 1900s, mainly through the ideas of **John Watson**.
2) Watson felt that earlier psychological research wasn't as scientific as it should be.
3) For example, Wilhelm Wundt tried to study consciousness using **introspection**. This involves analysing your own experiences. However, there's no way of finding out whether what a person said is true or not, so introspection can never be properly scientific.
4) Watson came up with some assumptions on which to base a **scientific** approach to psychology.

*There are **Three** Main **Assumptions** of Behaviourism*

Remember — this is theory, not fact.

1) **Nearly all behaviour is learnt.**
The only exceptions are a few inborn **reflexes** (e.g. blinking when we get dirt in our eyes) and a few inborn **instincts** (e.g. instinctively running when in some types of danger).
However, evidence now shows that **genetics** can influence psychological features, e.g. genetics may contribute to the development of schizophrenia. Behaviourism still claims, though, that learning, and not genetics, is the cause of the **majority** of behaviours, even if some vague genetic causes can be found.

2) **Animals and humans learn in the same ways.**
Humans can do much more complex things than other animals, but the **principles** by which we learn are the **same**. So, we learn to drive a car through the same principles as a cat learns to use a cat-flap. This is based on the idea that we can form **stimulus-response associations** between stimuli and our actions. However, although we may both use conditioning, humans can be said to use other forms of learning as well, such as **social learning** (see pages 114-115).

3) **The 'mind' is irrelevant.**
We can't directly observe and measure a person's thinking.
So we can only obtain **testable scientific data** by studying behaviour.
However, although **cognitive abilities** cannot be directly, scientifically measured, they may give a more complete explanation of behaviour — as shown by **Social Learning Theory** (see pages 114-115).

'All learnt through stimulus-response associations'. Pretty impressive, but does beg the question 'why?'

*Behaviourists Use Their **Assumptions** to Design **Research Methods***

The research methods used by the behaviourists follow directly from their **assumptions**, as follows:

1 — Nearly all behaviour is learnt.
So, understanding the principles of **learning** is the main research goal.

2 — Animals and humans learn in the same ways.
Animals can be used as research subjects because what is true for them should also be true for humans.
Using animals has **practical advantages**, e.g. they are easy to keep, in many circumstances they don't know they are being studied and so behave 'naturally', and procedures can be used with them which would be illegal with humans (e.g. cutting out bits of their brains to see what happens).

3 — The 'mind' is irrelevant.
Behaviourists only observe **quantifiable behaviour** — e.g. how many times a lever is pressed, how long it takes to solve a puzzle. Typical research therefore involves **laboratory experiments** on animals, to see how they learn.

The Behaviourist Approach

Behaviourist Research Has Provided Great **Insights** into Learning

1) **Pavlov's research on classical conditioning.** Pavlov wasn't a behaviourist, but his work was useful to them. He showed how dogs could be **'conditioned'** to produce a reflexive response (e.g. salivation) to a stimulus that would not normally trigger that response (e.g. a bell). Pavlov **precisely measured** how much saliva his dogs produced and showed that it increased each time the bell was rung before feeding.
2) **Skinner's research on operant conditioning.** Hungry pigeons were placed in a box and fed once every 15 seconds. The pigeons began to show **unusual behaviours** such as walking in circles and stretching their neck just before being fed. Skinner reckoned that the pigeons had come to **associate** the strange behaviours with being fed — in other words, they believed that they had to walk in circles to get food.
3) **Human research**. Some experiments were done on humans, e.g. Watson and Rayner's experiment on **'Little Albert'**:

Watson and Rayner (1920) showed fear could be learned

Method:	The participant was an 11-month-old boy called 'Little Albert'. He showed no fear of white fluffy objects such as rats or rabbits. The researchers tried to create a conditioned response to these objects. A white rat was placed in front of Little Albert. As he reached out for it, a metal bar was struck loudly behind his head. This was repeated twice at first, then 5 more times a week later.
Results:	When Little Albert was shown a rat, he would start to cry. This also extended to other white fluffy objects, such as a white Santa Claus beard.
Conclusion:	A fear response to white fluffy objects had been **conditioned** in Little Albert, showing that abnormal behaviour can be **learned**.
Evaluation:	The experiment was extremely **unethical** — such an experiment couldn't be repeated today. Also, **not everyone** goes on to develop a fear or phobia after a negative situation, so learning theory can't be the full story.

Absolutely nothing to worry about, Mrs Albert — all within the guidelines.

Comment — Behaviourists are often criticised for focusing research on animals. Plenty of research has been done on humans, which has shown things like:

- our **genes** influence our behaviour
- we can **learn in ways other than conditioning**
- that **mental, cognitive processes are relevant** to understanding behaviour.

Practice Questions

Q1 Who pioneered behaviourism?

Q2 What did behaviourists think about the mind?

Q3 Give an advantage of studying animals in learning experiments.

Q4 Why may the assumptions of behaviourism be questioned?

Exam Questions

Q1 Outline two assumptions of behaviourism. [6 marks]

Q2 Outline one ethical issue relevant to Watson and Rayner's (1920) study of 'Little Albert'. [2 marks]

Learn like a dolphin — lob live fish in the air and catch them in your mouth...

The behaviourist assumption is that humans and animals learn in the same way. Still, I've never met an animal who was scared of Santa. Apart from the reindeer of course, they can't stand him. But that's because there's no pension scheme — once those reindeer can't fly any more, that's it. He sends them off to the glue factory. And uses their antlers as shoe horns.

Social Learning Theory

Edexcel only... *Social learning theory is a development of the behaviourist theory which can be used to explain abnormality. The main difference is that social learning theory also takes into account social factors (big surprise).*

Social Learning Theory (SLT) Takes Account of Cognitive Processes

1) SLT developed in America during the 1950s. Like behaviourism, it accepts that humans can learn by classical and operant conditioning, but SLT emphasises that humans learn a lot by **observation** and **imitation** of **role models** (models).
2) So, social learning isn't just stimulus-response learning — **cognitive processes** are involved too.
3) For example, someone must pay **attention** and **perceive** what their role model does, **think** about the purpose of the behaviour they observe, and **remember** it to accurately **reproduce** it later (although this doesn't necessarily happen at a conscious level).

Various Factors Influence Social Learning

We don't imitate **everything** we see, so there must be some factors helping us decide what to copy and what to ignore.

1) The consequences of the model's actions have an important influence on us — this is **vicarious conditioning**. So if someone in your class asked the teacher for doughnuts, and then got them, you'd be likely to do the same. **Vicarious reinforcement** is when the model's actions have a desirable consequence — we are more likely to imitate the action. **Vicarious punishment** is when there was an undesirable outcome — we are then less likely to imitate.
2) The **characteristics of the role model** are also important. We are more likely to imitate models who we see have **desirable qualities** (e.g. power, status, talent) and also who are **similar** to us in important ways (e.g. people of the same gender or cultural group).

SLT Can Explain the Learning of Aggression

The idea is that **aggression** may be learnt by direct **conditioning**, e.g. if we find through trial and error that aggression can get us what we want (so the aggression is reinforced). However, we may also learn particular actions by watching role models. This was shown by **Bandura, Ross and Ross** (also on page 29).

Bandura et al (1961) — imitation of aggressive models

Method: 36 girls and 36 boys with a mean age of 52 months took part in the study. The study had a **matched participants design** and had three conditions. Children were matched on ratings of aggressive behaviour shown at their nursery school. In the first condition, children observed **aggressive adult models** playing with a Bobo doll (a large inflatable self-righting doll designed to be hit). In the second, children observed **non-aggressive models** playing with other toys and ignoring the Bobo doll. The third condition was a **control condition** in which children had no exposure to the models. Half of the participants in each experimental condition observed **same-sex models** and the other half observed models of the **opposite sex**. The children's behaviour was then observed for 20 minutes in a room containing aggressive toys (e.g. a Bobo doll, a mallet) and non-aggressive toys (e.g. crayons).

Results: Children exposed to aggressive models imitated a lot of their aggressive behaviour. Children in the non-aggressive and control conditions showed barely any aggressive behaviour — aggressive behaviour was slightly higher in the control condition than in the non-aggressive condition. Boys were seen to be more aggressive than girls after observing an aggressive male model.

Conclusion: Aggressive behaviour is learned through **imitation** of others behaving aggressively.

Evaluation: There may be important **implications** from the study. Children may imitate aggression shown on TV if it is not seen to result in negative consequences. However, there are problems with the study's **internal validity** — it didn't distinguish between playfighting and real aggression. The results are likely to be **reliable**, as it was a **lab experiment** and so variables could be strictly controlled. The study encouraged aggression in children — this could be an **ethical problem**. As well as this, it's not known if there were any **long-lasting** effects from the learning, or whether it was only **short-term**.

Social Learning Theory

*Studies of **Aggression in the Home** should be More Ecologically Valid*

In Bandura et al's 1961 study (see previous page), the children only watched the model — so there wasn't any interaction. This may be relevant to children imitating violence on TV, but children may be more influenced by the models they interact with, such as their parents.
Patterson et al produced evidence showing that children may imitate aggression observed in the home:

	Patterson et al (1989) — aggression and home environment
Method:	Families with at least one **very aggressive child** were compared with families without such a child. They were matched for family size, socio-economic status and other factors. Observations were made in the home, and family members, peers and teachers were also surveyed.
Results:	Aggressive children were more likely to be from homes where **less affection** was shown, more **arguments** occurred and more **punishment** was used.
Conclusion:	The children may have become more aggressive by **imitating** the aggression of their parents.
Evaluation:	The evidence is only **correlational**, so doesn't **prove** that aggression is learnt by modelling. There may also be **genetic influences** that cause one child to be more aggressive than another. The children in the study may have **behaved differently** to the way that they normally do because they knew that they were being observed. If this was the case, then the results lose their **validity**. This study also has some **ethical issues** as it will have been their parents who gave informed consent for the research to take place. Related to this, the children may have behaved more aggressively than normal due to not wanting to take part.

*Social Learning Theory Has Been **Criticised***

1) SLT says that **reinforcement** is **not essential** for learning and that learning can happen just through observation. However, reinforcement is an important influence on whether or not we **perform** the behaviour. If we think we might be punished we are less likely to perform the behaviour. This means that the role of reinforcement is **underestimated** by SLT.
2) SLT neglects the influence of **genetics** and so supports the '**nurture**' side of the **nature-nurture debate**. But some behaviours may be more influenced by genes than learning. For example, in all cultures, aggression is more common in males than females. Males may have **evolved** to be more aggressive because this has helped them survive (e.g. by being better hunters or better at competing with other males).
3) There is **mixed evidence** that violence on TV will influence children.

Practice Questions

Q1 What type of learning is emphasised in SLT?

Q2 What is meant by 'vicarious conditioning'?

Q3 Outline the three conditions in Bandura et al's (1961) study.

Q4 What does the study by Patterson et al (1989) show?

Exam Questions

Q1 Briefly evaluate Bandura et al's (1961) study in terms of **one** ethical issue. [6 marks]

Q2 Outline one strength and one limitation of the social learning approach. [6 marks]

For some quality social learning, watch 'Itchy and Scratchy'...

Big, huge, massive debate, this — does watching violence on TV make kids more violent... Would kids who grew up watching 'Lethal, Gory, Alien Attack IV' grow up more violent than ones who just watched Blue Peter? They certainly wouldn't be as good at making things out of cardboard tubes and pipe cleaners. So it's swings and roundabouts really...

Gender Development — The Learning Approach

These pages are just for Edexcel. *Our environment has a huge impact on the way that we behave. Some psychologists reckon that it can even determine whether we act in a masculine or feminine way.*

Social Learning Explains Gender Differences in **Several Ways**

In psychology, the environment is anything that has an **outside influence** on us — such as our friends and family, TV, music, magazines, the internet and even computer games. The social learning approach proposes that these factors influence our gender development in the following ways:

1) Modelling

This is **imitating** or copying what we see (see page 114 for more information about this). For example, children might observe and imitate the behaviour of their older siblings or copy the behaviour of someone they've seen on TV.

2) Reinforcement (see page 104 for more about this)

This is a behaviourist term that's used when something in our environment **'rewards'** us for behaving in a certain way. For example, a father showing an interest in playing with his son's racing car will act as a reinforcer for that gender-specific behaviour. The child will be more likely to act like this in the future. In gender development, our family and friends play a big part in this process.

3) Shaping behaviour

This is a result of the previous processes. When modelling and reinforcement of a behaviour repeatedly occurs, the behaviour becomes more **long-term** and **predictable**. So, the boy will continue to play with more typically male toys.

Bandura Studied the Effects of **Modelling** on Young Children

Bandura did loads of experiments looking at how children copy the behaviour of adults and other children. You saw one of the experiments on page 114 — here's another:

Bandura (1965) — the effects of TV on children

Method: In a **controlled observation** with an **independent measures** design, children watched a video of a male or female model behaving aggressively towards a Bobo doll. The behaviour shown by the adults was distinctive — e.g. they used a hammer, threw the doll into the air or shouted particular things. The children either saw the model being told off (**punished**) for their aggressive behaviour or being rewarded with sweets (**reinforced**). In a **control condition**, the model was neither rewarded nor punished.

Results: Boys tended to imitate the male model more, and girls tended to imitate the female model more. Boys were more likely than girls to imitate the behaviour and girls were influenced more by the punishment. Children who had seen the model being rewarded and those in the control condition imitated more aggressive behaviours than those who saw the model being punished.

Conclusion: Children learn gender behaviour through observation and imitation.

Evaluation: The models used distinct actions that the children were unlikely to produce spontaneously. This meant that Bandura could be sure that imitation was taking place. However, the conditions were pretty artificial — children would be unlikely to see adults behaving aggressively towards toys in real life, so the study lacks **ecological validity**. The study also didn't consider the differences between playfighting and aggression towards other people. The **previous** behaviour of the children wasn't considered, and no **follow-up** was done to see if the imitated behaviour was long-term.

Gender Development — The Learning Approach

Williams Looked at the Effect of **TV** on **Gender Development**

Like Bandura, Williams believed that children are influenced by what they watch on TV. Rather than focusing on aggression observed in a lab, Williams conducted a **natural experiment** to see whether children learn gendered behaviour from the programmes they watch in real life.

	Williams (1986)
Method:	The behaviour of children in a small town in Canada without TV ('Notel') was observed. It was compared with a control town that did have TV. During the two-year study, 'Notel' gained access to one TV channel.
Results:	The children in the town that had TV displayed more stereotypical gender behaviour than children in 'Notel'. After the introduction of TV, sex-role stereotyping increased amongst children in 'Notel'.
Conclusion:	Children learn gender behaviour from TV probably because it depicts males and females in traditional roles.
Evaluation:	This was a **natural experiment**, so it has good **ecological validity** because none of the variables were manipulated. However, this means that the results could have been affected by a third variable, so it's difficult to establish **cause and effect**. The sample was relatively small, so it's difficult to **generalise** the results.

The Social Learning Approach has Some **Problems**

1) It doesn't explain where the stereotypical male and female behaviours **originally** came from.
2) If we all copied gender-typical behaviour then we'd all end up behaving in the **same way**. However, there are loads of different **variations** in behaviour within each gender.
3) It neglects **biology** — differences in behaviour could be down to genetics or different brain structure.
4) Children are able to observe both **same-gender** and **opposite-gender** behaviour. However, learning theory doesn't explain how children know which gender to focus their observations on.

This Isn't the **Only Approach** to Gender Development Though...

You need to be able to **compare** the learning approach with the biological approach (see pages 64-67), and also with the psychodynamic approach that you'll soon be meeting (see pages 122-123 for a sneak peek).

Contrast with the Psychodynamic Approach

Both theories pinpoint aspects of the **environment** which influence behaviour — both state that children can copy or identify with the behaviour of the same-sex parent. The psychodynamic perspective suggests that one of the driving forces for our gender behaviour is a **biologically inherited drive** — the id. However, the learning approach doesn't account for any built-in drives.

Contrast with the Biological Approach

The learning approach explains the more **subtle behaviours** — like having a preference for certain toys or clothes. However, the biological approach can explain why there are **universal consistencies** of gender behaviour, e.g. males being seen as more aggressive than females, and females being seen as more nurturing.

Practice Questions

Q1 What is meant by reinforcement?

Q2 Name one researcher who studied the effects of modelling on children.

Exam Questions

Q1 In an observational study of children's behaviour, it was seen that girls and boys chose to play with different toys. How would the learning approach explain this? [6 marks]

Q2 Outline and evaluate one experiment that looked at the environmental causes of gender behaviour. [12 marks]

The only effect of TV that I got told about was square eyes...

Don't forget that this theory isn't necessarily the whole story. There's also the biological and psychodynamic approaches out there too. You could be asked to compare two of them, or even all three, in the exam — aren't you so incredibly lucky that you're doing the Edexcel exam ? Poor AQA A and OCR types just don't know what fun they're missing out on

Behaviourist Therapy

Edexcel only again. *Behaviourists developed therapies based on the findings of their research. You've got to know it all.*

Learning Theory Assumes Behaviour is Shaped Through Conditioning

Learning theory assumes that virtually all behaviour is learnt, so the principles of conditioning should explain most things.

Skinner (1971) claimed that we are constantly being conditioned by the environment. So '**free will**' is an illusion — our behaviours are shaped by the desire to obtain reinforcement (eat the cake) and avoid punishment (dodge the stick). He reckoned our patterns of behaviour are completely due to our individual '**reinforcement histories**'.

Classical Conditioning Can Be Used in Therapy

The principles of classical conditioning (see pages 104-105) have been used in therapy to deliberately change behaviour. This can be done by:

Systematic desensitisation for **phobias**, involving relaxation techniques (see page 105)

or:

Aversion therapy to remove an undesired behaviour by associating it with **unpleasant feelings** (see page 104).

Operant Conditioning Can Be Used in Therapy

Parents and teachers use operant conditioning without realising it. Whenever a child is praised (**reinforcement**) or told off (**punishment**), operant conditioning is happening. It has also been specially used as a treatment for some disorders.

Token economy. **Ayllon and Azrin (1968)** reported how operant conditioning was used to change the behaviour of psychiatric patients. **Tokens** were given to them whenever they behaved 'normally' or 'adaptively'. These tokens could then be exchanged for reinforcements such as sweets or TV watching. It was found that most patients, even schizophrenics, showed much more 'normal' behaviour.

Autism is a disorder involving extreme social skill impairment. Children show little or no interest in interacting with others, weak attachments and little language development. **Lovaas (1987)** gave autistic children reinforcement (e.g. chocolate) for any **pro-social** act (e.g. making eye contact, imitating a behaviour, making speech sounds). They also received 'aversives' (punishments) for unwanted behaviour. In time, they had to show more of these responses to get reinforcement. Much improvement in their social behaviour was seen.

There are Problems with Behaviour Change Through Conditioning

1) Evidence shows that behaviour change is possible through these therapies, but they do have **limitations**.

- Systematic desensitisation cannot help with some **severe** disorders.
- Aversion therapy may only produce **short-term** improvement.
- Operant conditioning therapies might not produce long-lasting change if the reinforcements aren't **maintained**.
- Conditioning may not be able to change **genetic influences** on behaviour.

2) The therapies also raise **ethical issues** — they may be distressing (e.g. aversion therapy) or involve withholding things of value to later use as reinforcements (e.g. token economy), perhaps violating human rights.
3) **Deliberate attempts** at behaviour change raise ethical issues about **free will and choice**. There may not be such an issue if an individual wanted the behaviour change (e.g. curing a phobia), but there would be a problem if those in power used conditioning to make us behave in more '**socially desirable**' ways. This would reduce our free will. Also those in power might have biased views of what is 'socially desirable'.

Contemporary Issues

There's Debate Over Whether **Role Models** Can Cause **Anorexia**

There are four main characteristics of anorexia:

1) **Anxiety** about getting fat, even when very underweight.
2) A **distorted body image** — **feeling fat**, even when very thin.
3) **Body weight** is less than 85% of what it should be for the person's age, height and build.
4) Female sufferers have further problems — their **periods stop**, or never start, depending on their age. The absence of **three or more** consecutive periods can indicate anorexia.

Models and film stars get loads of **attention** from the public. These celebrities are often pretty **slim**. There's some **vicarious reinforcement** going on here — the **looks** of the celebrities have a **desirable consequence** (the attention they get) and so we're more likely to **imitate** them.

1) If you go on a diet and begin to lose weight, it's likely that you'll be given plenty of **compliments**.
2) You'll start to associate **being thin** (the **stimulus**) with **being complimented** and admired (the **response**).
3) As the compliments keep flooding in, they'll be **reinforcing** the action of losing weight.
4) Also, by **not eating**, the behaviour is again being **reinforced** — but this time it's **negative** reinforcement because not eating **avoids** something undesirable, the anxiety.

There's Also Debate About the Influence of **Advertising** on Behaviour

Learning theory can be applied to advertising too. Advertising is done in such a way as to influence as many people as possible to buy a company's products.

1) Adverts often feature a **celebrity** or someone **admired** by the public.
2) Plenty of people would like to be like this person — for example to have their looks, or their sporting skills.
3) Adverts tend to imply that (for example) the celebrity gets their looks by **using** the particular moisturiser or make-up that's being advertised.
4) People then feel that if they **imitate** by **buying** and **using** the product, they too can gain the good looks.
5) Adverts for sports equipment work the same way. E.g. they try to make the public believe that it's the footballer's **boots** that give him his **skill** and that if you **imitate** by **buying** the same boots, you could be just as good.

Wow... if only I had that style.

Practice Questions

Q1 Explain one way that behaviour change can occur through classical conditioning.
Q2 Explain one way that behaviour change can occur through operant conditioning.
Q3 What is meant by a 'token economy'?
Q4 Give two problems with changing behaviour using conditioning.

Exam Questions

Q1 Describe one example of the deliberate alteration of human behaviour using learning theory. [4 marks]

Q2 Use ideas from social learning theory to explain the influence of role models on anorexia. [8 marks]

Big Issue Sir, Big Issue Miss, Big Issue, Big Issuuuue....

There are so many big issues in psychology that relate to everyday life. Take the two on this page — anorexia and advertising. As you've seen, they can both be explained using social learning theory. But stop right there. Don't think that's the full story. As with everything else, there's plenty of other psychological theories and explanations. Woohoo...

The Psychodynamic Approach

Guess what — Edexcel only again...
Psychodynamic theories like to explain abnormality by talking about unconscious causes — talk about abnormal...

Freud Developed The **Psychodynamic** Approach

'**Psycho**' refers to the mind and '**dynamic**' refers to change or activity.
So, this approach emphasises the **active nature** of mental processes and their role in **shaping personality** and **behaviour**.
This approach was developed by **Sigmund Freud** (1856-1939), in the 18th/early 19th centuries. It assumes that:

1) Human behaviour has **unconscious causes** that we're not aware of.
2) From birth, humans have a need to fulfil basic biological **motivations** — for food, sleep, warmth etc.
3) **Childhood experiences** are a really important influence on the development of adult personality and psychological disorders.

Freud Said There Are Three **Levels of Consciousness**

Freud was interested in '**hysteria**', a disorder involving physical symptoms such as headaches, paralysis and blindness, but with no apparent physical cause. As his patients couldn't give any **conscious** reasons, Freud concluded they had an **unconscious** mind and that's where the cause of the hysteria was. He identified three levels of consciousness:

1) **Conscious**. This is what we are **aware** of at any given time, e.g. what we are seeing, hearing, smelling or thinking.
2) **Preconscious**. This is made up of **memories** that we can recall when we want to, e.g. we can recall our address, phone number, childhood memories or what we did at the weekend.
3) **Unconscious**. This is made up of memories, desires and fears which cause us extreme anxiety and have therefore been '**repressed**' or forced out of conscious awareness. However, the unconscious still influences behaviour. For example, it causes 'Freudian slips' and influences the content of our dreams. This part of our mind can be accessed with the help of a **psychoanalyst**, using the methods that Freud developed (see the next page).

There Are Two **Instincts** That Motivate Our Behaviour

Freud claimed that from birth, two types of **instinct** motivate our behaviour.
The two instincts are in constant **conflict** with each other, and one may **dominate** in a person:

1) **The Life Instinct ('Eros').** This is the need to fulfil basic biological needs, such as for warmth, food or sleep. However, Freud also claimed that infants have the need for **sexual pleasure**, i.e. they obtain pleasure through **erogenous zones** — parts of the body that are sensitive to stimulation. Although this does not involve mature sexual needs, Freud claimed that '**infantile sexuality**' is a major motivation as we progress through the stages of **psychosexual development** (see page 27). The energy of the life instinct is called '**libido**'.
2) **The Death Instinct ('Thanatos').** The death instinct involves the urge to be **aggressive** and **destructive** to others and/or ourselves. This causes violence, war and suicide.

Freud Reckoned **Early Experiences** Influence Development

1) Each stage of psychosexual development focuses on **obtaining pleasure** through that stage's erogenous zone.
2) How parents raise a child affects how much pleasure is obtained through that stage (e.g. how strict they are when potty training, and what type of role models they are).
3) If a child experiences a lot of **conflict** or **anxiety** during a stage of development it becomes '**fixated**' with that stage and will remain, to some extent, attached to that erogenous zone.
4) This experience is all **repressed into the unconscious**, but influences adult personality. Severe fixation could lead to a psychological **disorder**.

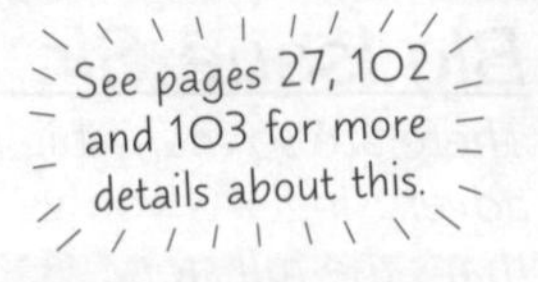

The Psychodynamic Approach

Clinical Interviews and *Symbol Analysis* Reveal Unconscious Problems

Freud did **case studies** on his patients using several **methods** to reveal the **conflicts**, **fears** and **desires** buried in their unconscious mind. These problems could then be faced, allowing the patient to understand and resolve them.

1) In a case study, a lot of **detailed information** about **unique cases** can be collected.
2) However, it's not usually possible to make **generalisations** from the results to the rest of the population.
3) Case studies often rely a lot on **retrospective data** (i.e. from the past) and so if this data is incorrectly recalled, the results become unreliable.
4) Case studies have some **ethical issues** in that some people believe that it's not right to **publish** detailed data about a particular person's problems. However, participants usually remain **anonymous**, are given a **different name**, or are simply referred to by their initials.

Clinical interviews and **symbol analysis** are the main methods of studying the unconscious mind:

Clinical interviews
These are flexible, informal interviews. They may involve:

a) **Free association**. This is where the patient is given a cue and then asked to say whatever comes into their mind, however silly or embarrassing. By analysing what a person does and doesn't talk about, the psychoanalyst can identify unconscious influences, e.g. I say 'revision', and you say 'night out'.

b) **'Freudian slips'**. These occur when we do or say something that we consciously think are mistakes, but which really show our unconscious true feelings. An example given by Freud was how an MP once said, 'the honourable member from Hell', when he really meant 'from Hull'. How very rude. But you have to remember that this was before the Humber Bridge was built. Nowadays the MP would have to say, 'the honourable member from Hull, which does boast the sixth longest single-span suspension bridge in the world, so it's not all bad'.

Analysis of symbols in dreams and culture
Freud believed that the unconscious can reveal itself in the form of symbols. They allow the unconscious fears, desires and conflicts to show themselves or be 'fulfilled'. However, we don't become consciously aware of them, and therefore don't feel anxious or guilty:

a) **Dream analysis**. Freud claimed that dreams involve '**disguised wish fulfilment**'. This means that we use them to 'play out' our repressed wishes — ones which would produce guilt or anxiety if we were consciously aware of them. The images we can recall are the '**manifest content**' (the superficial stuff), but the analyst can interpret the '**latent content**' — the true meaning.

b) **Culture**. Freud claimed that cultural art, theatre and literature are 'manifest content' which symbolically represents the 'latent content' of universal human needs and conflicts.

You should probably bear in mind that all of these methods depend on the **interpretations** of the analyst, so they're **subjective** and **not truly scientific**. Having said that, they still may be useful.

Practice Questions

Q1 Explain the difference between the 'preconscious' and the 'unconscious'.
Q2 Why is early experience important, according to the psychodynamic approach?
Q3 What happens in 'free association'?

Exam Questions

Q1 Describe one assumption of the psychodynamic approach. [6 marks]

Q2 Describe one advantage and one disadvantage of using case studies in the psychodynamic approach. [4 marks]

My favourite subject is (insert Freudian slip here)... Oops — I mean art...

If you've ever called your teacher Mum, or boyfriend Dad, you probably just thought it was a simple mistake. According to psychodynamic theory, you're actually showing your deep-felt desires. Remember, it's not just what you say, but what you think about and what you dream that shows your unconscious mind peeking through — hands up who's scared now...

Gender Development — The Psychodynamic Approach

Just Edexcel again.
Freud had some unusual ideas about how we get our gender behaviour — nothing new there then...

Freud Outlined **Five Stages** of Psychosexual Development

1) Freud believed that we have an **inner drive** that motivates us to seek out pleasure — the **pleasure principle**.
2) This is driven by the id, which works at an **unconscious level** of our minds. We aren't aware of it mentally, but it comes out in our behaviour.
3) Part of this pleasure seeking involves searching for **sexual gratification**.
4) Certain areas of the **body** are associated with this, such as the mouth, anus and genitals. Tee hee.
5) As we develop through early childhood, we **move** from stimulating one area to another. This is what Freud's five stages of development are all about:

0-18 months	**Oral stage**	**The child likes eating, sucking and putting objects in its mouth.**
18-36 months	**Anal stage**	**The child enjoys the pleasure of defecating.**
3-6 years	**Phallic stage**	**The child enjoys the sensation from touching the genitals.**
6 years-puberty	**Latent stage**	**A quiet time, with little bodily focus.**
Puberty onwards	**Genital stage**	**Satisfaction is gained from stimulating the genitals.**

Freud Thought that there are **Three Parts** to Our **Personality**

1) Freud thought that our personalities are made up of the **id**, the **ego** and the **superego**.
2) A **balance** between all three is needed for a person to be healthy — imbalance causes **anxiety**.
3) The id is like an animal, trying to **gain pleasure** at every opportunity.
4) The superego is like a sensible parent — it has **morals** and **lays down rules**.
5) The ego is stuck **in between** — it helps to get what the id wants, but in a way that keeps the superego happy.

The **Oedipus Complex** Explained the Stages of **Gender Development**

1) It was thought that children begin their gender development around the **phallic stage**.
2) In boys, Freud called this development the **Oedipus complex**.
3) In the Oedipus complex, boys associate the pleasure of stimulation of the genitals with their **mother** — she becomes the first **love object**.
4) They're jealous of the father and see him as a **rival**. They **fear** that their father will find out about their feelings for their mother and castrate them — producing **castration anxiety**.
5) To resolve this inner conflict, boys end up **identifying** with their fathers by copying their behaviour — this way, both their mother and father will like them.
6) For **girls**, Freud developed the **feminine Oedipus attitude**, or **Electra complex**. This is where girls come to believe they've been **castrated** by their mother. They then develop **penis envy** and blame their mother for their lack of a penis. They turn to their father as a first **love object**, but then have to resolve their conflict with the mother by **identifying** with her.

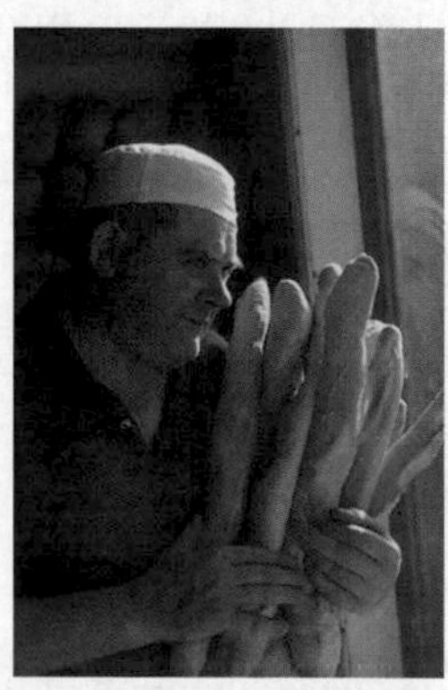

Freud tried to explain Billy's obsession with French bread. It wasn't pretty...

You need to be able to compare this theory with the learning approach (pages 116-117) and also with the biological approach (pages 64-67).

Gender Development — The Psychodynamic Approach

The **Credibility** of Freud's Theory has been Questioned

Masson (1984) criticised Freud's approach for being based on observations taken from patients who may have been the victims of **sexual abuse** by adults. It could be that what Freud believed were unconscious drives might in fact have been a form of recollection of reality.

Masson (1989) also criticised psychoanalysis for creating an **imbalance of power** in the client-therapist relationship — the therapist may be in a position to abuse or take advantage of the client.

Freud Provided Some **Evidence** for the Oedipus Complex

Freud (1909) — The case study of Little Hans

See page 27 for more on this case study.

Method: Freud carried out a **case study** of a child called Hans who had a phobia of horses.

Conclusion: Freud believed that Hans was developing sexual feelings towards his mother. He thought that instead of fearing his father in the way normally seen in the Oedipus complex, Hans had moved his fear on to horses instead. Freud believed that the **horse represented Hans's father** — he had mentioned black bits around the horse's mouth which Freud believed represented the father's moustache. The horse's blinkers were also believed to represent the father's glasses.

Evaluation: This was a **case study**, meaning that it provided lots of detailed data about the subject. The findings provided evidence to support Freud's theories. However, the results were based entirely on observation and interpretation. This means they could have easily been caused by something else. Freud analysed information from Hans's father, and hardly saw Hans himself. This means that the results could be **inaccurate** and **biased**. As this was a study of one person, the results can't be **generalised**.

Freud's Gender Theory Has Had a Lot of **Criticism**

1) Freud has been criticised for being **sexist** — his theories are predominantly based on male gender identity. Even the Electra complex for girls' development includes penis envy.
2) Freud seems to neglect the fact that children brought up in **one-parent families** with no same-sex adult to identify with still develop a normal gender identity.
3) By focusing only on the parents, the theory overlooks all the **other environmental influences** that children are surrounded by — such as friends, media etc.
4) Freud's theories do suggest a biological drive, but they don't account for the discoveries concerning **testosterone** and its effects on behaviour.

Practice Questions

Q1 List Freud's five stages of psychosexual development.

Q2 What is the superego?

Q3 Which case study provided some support for Freud's Oedipus complex?

Exam Questions

Q1 Outline the psychodynamic approach to explaining gender behaviour. [8 marks]

Q2 Evaluate Freud's Oedipus complex. [8 marks]

Id to the left of me, ego to the right — here I am stuck in the middle...

Most of Freud's theories need to be taken with a pinch of salt — they didn't even bother teaching me anything about them in my degree... But unfortunately you still need to know about this one for your exam. Make sure you understand the stages of gender development, and once you've done that, you can start learning all about the theory's many criticisms.

Psychodynamic Theories of Abnormality

Another two pages just for Edexcel.
Freud really had a good go at sorting mental health out with his theories. He developed quite an effective therapy too. Whether it works because his theory is right, or just because it's therapeutic to talk, well that's up to you...

The Psychodynamic Approach Can Explain **Mental Health Problems**

Several different types of mental illness (including anxiety, depression, eating disorders and schizophrenia) can be explained using a psychodynamic approach.

1) The psychodynamic perspective focuses on **unconscious conflicts** starting in early childhood. That's how it tries to deal with mental health problems.
2) Early experiences are seen as very influential, so therapists look for examples of **childhood trauma** to explain adult disorders.
3) Treatment involves bringing the unconscious conflicts into the **conscious mind** to remove the **anxiety** that has been created, e.g. remembering how a trauma felt and talking about it.

Freud Reckoned that **Defence Mechanisms** Reduce Anxiety

Defence mechanisms are used to protect the conscious mind. They tend to occur unconsciously and distort reality.

Repression

1) This is where negative, distressing memories, desires and fears are pushed into the **unconscious mind** to protect the conscious mind.
2) These things don't completely disappear — they can reappear in the form of **abnormal behaviours**, or subconsciously through **dreams**.
3) An example would be if someone had been **abused** by their parents as a child. They might not have any **recollection** of it, but still have trouble **forming relationships**.

Regression

1) This is where the person reverts back to patterns of **behaviour** seen **earlier** in development.
2) In other words, they act like a **child**, rather than acting how a normal adult would in the same situation.
3) You see behaviours from the stage of psychosexual development in which they're **fixated**.

Cramer (1997) Studied **Defence Mechanisms** and **Identity**

	Cramer (1997) — identity, personality and defence mechanisms
Method:	Young adults took part in a **correlational study** into the relationship between identity status and the use of defence mechanisms. Observers classed each participant into an **identity status** — one of four from 'moratorium', 'diffusion', 'achieved' and 'foreclosed'. Distinct characteristics are associated with each status. For example, 'moratorium' and 'diffusion' are characterised by an unpredictable and changeable personality. They have experienced more crises and are more anxious. In contrast, 'achieved' and 'foreclosed' people have a constant personality and have never experienced crisis. As a result, they are less anxious. The scores representing the participants' identity statuses were correlated with their **Defence Mechanisms Manual** (DMM) **defence scores**. The DMM assesses the use of defence mechanisms using a Thematic Apperception Test — participants are shown pictures and are asked to tell a story of what they see.
Results:	A significant **positive correlation** was seen between **moratorium** identities and **use of defence mechanisms**. A significant **negative correlation** was seen between **foreclosed** identities and **use of defence mechanisms**.
Conclusion:	There is a link between identity and personality, and the use of defence mechanisms.
Evaluation:	Although a correlation is seen, you can't say that one thing **causes** the other — another factor may have produced the results. If participants' identity or their use of defence mechanisms had been wrongly classified, the results of the study would have become **unreliable**.

Psychodynamic Theories of Abnormality

Psychoanalytic Therapies Don't Always *Work*

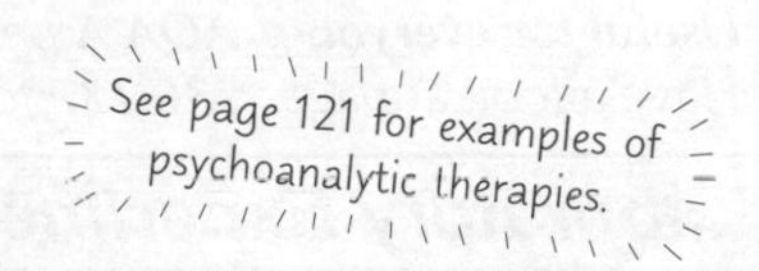

Psychoanalytic therapies are still widely used. However, there's increasing evidence that other therapies might be more effective:

	Durham et al (1994) — effectiveness of therapies
Method:	110 patients suffering from general anxiety disorder were randomly assigned to receive either psychoanalytic therapy or cognitive behavioural therapy (see pages 106-107). They were followed up one year later.
Results:	About two thirds of the patients who had received cognitive behaviour therapy had made a significant improvement. Only a very small number of the patients who had received psychoanalytic therapy had made a significant improvement.
Conclusion:	Cognitive behavioural therapy is more effective than psychoanalysis at treating disorders.
Evaluation:	The **sample size** was quite large, meaning that the results of the study are likely to be reliable. However, the effectiveness of therapies tends to depend on the **disorder** involved. So, it's perhaps not fair to summarise by saying that all disorders can be treated more effectively this way.

Psychoanalytic Therapies Can be *Criticised*

There are a number of problems with psychoanalytic therapy. Still, life goes on...

1) The effectiveness of the therapy depends on the **disorder** — schizophrenia doesn't respond well to psychoanalytic therapy, but disorders such as anxiety and depression often do.
2) Freud said himself that psychoanalytic therapy would **only** work if the person was **willing to change**, **appreciated** that they had a problem, and entered into treatment **voluntarily**.
3) Therapists find it hard to know when to **end** treatment, as the symptoms may have disappeared, but could easily return next time there's a problem.
4) It's hard for the therapist to know whether improvement is actually happening in the person's **everyday** life.
5) At the beginning of therapy, many people **overestimate** their problems to justify needing therapy. At the end, they **underestimate** them to feel like improvement has occurred, to justify the time and expense of therapy. This is the **hello-goodbye effect** — it makes improvement look greater than it really is.

Psychoanalytic therapy doesn't work for everyone.

Practice Questions

Q1 What are defence mechanisms?

Q2 What is meant by repression?

Q3 What is meant by regression?

Q4 Which disorders respond well to psychoanalytic therapy?

Exam Questions

Q1 What did Durham et al's study show about the effectiveness of psychoanalytic therapies? [4 marks]

Q2 Outline the criticisms of psychoanalytic therapies. [6 marks]

There's something stuck on your bum — it's an anal fixation...

Psychoanalytic therapy can actually work. But that doesn't mean all of Freud's theories are right. I mean, who wouldn't feel a bit better if they got to lie on a couch and talk about themselves for an hour three times a week...? And another thing — seeing as Freud suggested a reason for schizophrenia, you'd think his therapy would have some sort of effect... But no

Research Methods

***Useful for everyone. AQA A** people need to know this stuff in relation to the cognitive and developmental approaches. Have a look at pages 136-137 for more on the **ethical issues** surrounding different research methods, if you can take it...*

Laboratory Experiments are Controlled and Scientific

1) An **experiment** is a way of conducting research in a **controlled** way.
2) The aim is to **control** all relevant variables except for **one key variable**, which is altered to see what the effect is. The variable that you alter is called the **independent variable** (see page 129).
3) Laboratory experiments are conducted in an **artificial setting**, e.g. Milgram's study (see page 78).

Advantages

Control — the effects of confounding variables (those that have an effect in addition to the variable of interest — see page 129) are minimised.
Replication — strict controls mean you can run the study again to check the findings.
Causal relationships — ideally it's possible to establish whether one variable actually causes change in another.

Disadvantages

Artificial — experiments might not measure real-life behaviour (i.e. they may lack ecological validity).
Demand characteristics — participants may respond according to what they think is being investigated, which can bias the results.
Ethics — deception is often used, making informed consent difficult.

Field Experiments are Conducted Outside the Laboratory

In **field experiments** behaviour is measured in a **natural environment** like a school, the street or on a train. A **key variable** is still altered so that its effect can be measured.

Advantages

Causal relationships — you can still establish causal relationships by manipulating the key variable and measuring its effect, although it's very difficult to do in a field experiment.
Ecological validity — field experiments are less artificial than those done in a laboratory, so they relate to real life better.
Demand characteristics (participants trying to guess what the researcher expects from them and performing differently because of it) — these can be avoided if participants don't know they're in a study.

Disadvantages

Less control — confounding variables may be more likely in a natural environment.
Ethics — participants who didn't agree to take part might experience distress and often can't be debriefed. Observation must respect privacy.

Natural Experiments Measure but Don't Control Variables

A **natural experiment** is a study that measures variables that **aren't** directly manipulated by the experimenter. For example, comparing behaviour in a single-sex school and a mixed school.

Advantages

Ethical — it's possible to study variables that it would be unethical to manipulate, e.g. you can compare a community that has TV with a community that doesn't to see which is more aggressive.

Disadvantages

Participant allocation — you can't randomly allocate participants to each condition, and so confounding variables (e.g. what area the participants live in) may affect results. Let's face it — you've got no control over the variables so it's ridiculously hard to say what's caused by what.
Rare events — some groups of interest are hard to find, e.g. a community that doesn't have TV.
Ethics — deception is often used, making informed consent difficult. Also, confidentiality may be compromised if the community is identifiable.

Naturalistic Observation — Observing but NOT Interfering

Naturalistic observation involves observing subjects in their natural environment. Researchers take great care not to interfere in any way with the subjects they're studying.

Advantages

Ecological validity — behaviour is natural and there are no demand characteristics, as the participant is unaware of being observed.
Theory development — can be a useful way of developing ideas about behaviour that could be tested in more controlled conditions later.

Disadvantages

Extraneous variables — can't control variables that may affect behaviour.
Observer bias — observers' expectations may affect what they focus on and record. This means the reliability of the results may be a problem — another observer may have come up with very different results.
Ethics — you should only conduct observations where people might expect to be observed by strangers. This limits the situations where you can do a naturalistic observation. Debriefing is difficult. Observation must respect privacy. Getting informed consent can be tricky.

Research Methods

Correlational Research Looks for Relationships Between Variables

Correlation means that two variables rise and fall together, or that one rises as the other falls — but **not** always that one variable **causes** a change in the other, e.g. as age increases so might intelligence, but ageing doesn't **cause** intelligence.

Advantages

Causal relationships — these can be ruled out if no correlation exists.
Ethics — can study variables that would be unethical to manipulate, e.g. is there a relationship between the number of cigarettes smoked and incidences of ill health?

Disadvantages

Causal relationships — these cannot be assumed from a correlation, which may be caused by a third, unknown variable.
Ethics — misinterpretation can be an issue. Sometimes the media (and researchers) infer causality from a correlation.

Questionnaires — Written, Face-to-Face, on the Phone, or via the Internet

Advantages

Practical — can collect a large amount of information quickly and relatively cheaply.

Disadvantages

Bad questions — leading questions (questions that suggest a desired answer) or unclear questions can be a problem.
Biased samples — some people are more likely to respond to a questionnaire, which might make a sample unrepresentative.
Self report — people sometimes want to present themselves in a good light (social desirability bias — see page 135). What they say and what they actually think could be different, making any results unreliable.
Ethics — confidentiality can be a problem, especially around sensitive issues.

Interviews — More Like a Conversation than a Face-to-Face Questionnaire

Structured interviews follow a fixed set of questions that are the same for all participants.
Unstructured interviews may have a set of discussion topics, but are less constrained about how the conversation goes.

Advantages

Rich data — can get detailed information, as there are fewer constraints than with a questionnaire. Unstructured interviews provide richer information than structured interviews.
Pilot study — interviews are a useful way to get information before a study.

Disadvantages

Self report — can be unreliable and affected by social desirability bias (see questionnaires).
Impractical — conducting interviews can be time-consuming and requires skilled researchers.
Ethics — confidentiality can be a problem, especially around sensitive issues.

Case Studies are Intensive Descriptions of a Single Individual or Case

Case studies allow researchers to analyse unusual cases in a lot of detail, e.g. Freud's study of **Little Hans** (page 27).

Advantages

Rich data — researchers have the opportunity to study rare phenomena in a lot of detail.
Unique cases — can challenge existing ideas and theories, and suggest ideas for future research.

Disadvantages

Causal relationships — the researcher has very little control over variables.
Generalisation — only using a single case makes generalising the results extremely difficult.
Ethics — informed consent can be difficult to obtain if the subject has a rare disorder.

Practice Questions

Q1 Describe a disadvantage of studies where correlational analysis is used.
Q2 What are the main advantages of laboratory experiments?
Q3 Why might you get an unrepresentative sample when carrying out questionnaire-based research?

Exam Questions

Q1 Describe what a field experiment is and outline its main advantages and disadvantages. [4 marks]

Q2 Describe the two types of interview a researcher might conduct.
Outline the main differences between them. [8 marks]

Aims and Hypotheses

These pages are for everyone. *When research is conducted, the idea is to carry out an **objective test** of something i.e. to obtain a scientific measurement of how people behave — not just someone's opinion. Well that's what I reckon...*

Research Aims are Important

An **aim** is a statement of a study's purpose — for example Asch's aim might have been:
'To study majority influence in an unambiguous task'. (See page 72 for the detail of Asch's study.)

Research should state its aim **beforehand** so that it's **clear** what the study intends to investigate.

Hypotheses are Theories Tested by Research

Although the **aim** states the **purpose** of a study, it isn't usually **precise** enough to **test**.
What is needed are clear statements of what's actually being tested — the **hypotheses**.

1) **RESEARCH HYPOTHESIS**

   The **research hypothesis** is proposed at the beginning of a piece of research and is often generated from a theory. For example — Bowlby's research hypothesis was that maternal deprivation causes delinquency. (See page 35 for the details of Bowlby's study.)

2) **NULL HYPOTHESIS**

   The **null hypothesis** is what you're going to **assume is true** during the study. Any data you collect will either back this assumption up, or it won't. If the data **doesn't support** your null hypothesis, you **reject** it and go with your **alternative hypothesis** instead.

   Very often, the null hypothesis is a prediction that there will be **no relationship** between key variables in a study — and any correlation is due to **chance**. (An example might be that there is no difference in exam grades between students who use a revision guide and students who don't.)

   (Note: It's quite usual to have something you **don't actually believe** as your null hypothesis. You assume it **is** true for the duration of the study, then if your results lead you to reject this null hypothesis, you've **proved** it **wasn't true** after all. See page 142 for more details.)

3) **EXPERIMENTAL HYPOTHESIS** (or **ALTERNATIVE HYPOTHESIS**)

   If the data forces you to **reject** your null hypothesis, then you accept your **experimental (alternative) hypothesis** instead.

   So if your null hypothesis was that two variables **aren't** linked, then your alternative hypothesis would be that they **are** linked. Or you can be more specific, and be a bit more precise about **how** they are linked, using **directional** hypotheses (see below).

4) **DIRECTIONAL HYPOTHESIS**

   A hypothesis might predict a difference between the exam results obtained by two groups of students — a group that uses a revision guide and another group that doesn't.

   If the hypothesis states which group will do better, it is making a **directional prediction**.

   For example, you might say that students who use a revision guide will get **higher** exam grades than students who don't — this is a directional hypothesis.

   Directional hypotheses are often used when **previous research findings** suggest which way the results will go.

5) **NON-DIRECTIONAL HYPOTHESIS**

   A **non-directional hypothesis** would predict a difference, but wouldn't say which group would do better.

   For example, you might just say that there will be a **difference** in exam grades between students who use a revision guide and students who don't — this is a **non-directional** hypothesis, since you're not saying which group will do better.

   Non-directional hypotheses can be used when there is **little previous research** in the area under investigation, or when previous research findings are **mixed** and **inconclusive**.

Aims and Hypotheses

*Some **Variables** are **Manipulated** by the Researcher — Others Aren't*

A **variable** is a quantity whose **value** can **change** — for example, the time taken to do a task, anxiety levels, or exam results. There are various different kinds of variable.

The Independent Variable is Directly Manipulated

1) An **independent variable** (**IV**) is a variable **directly manipulated** by the researcher.
2) In the example on the previous page about students, exams and revision guides, there are two variables. One is 'whether or not a revision guide is used' (so this variable has only two possible values: yes or no). The other is the 'exam grade' (and this could have lots of possible values: e.g. A, B, C, D, E, N, U).
3) In this case, the **independent variable** is 'whether or not a revision guide is used' — since this is **directly** under the control of the researcher.

*The **Dependent Variable** is Only Affected **Indirectly***

1) The **dependent variable** (**DV**) is the variable that you think is **affected** by changes in the independent variable. (So the DV is **dependent on** the **IV**.)
2) In the exam grades example, the dependent variable is the 'exam grade'. The exam grade is dependent on whether a revision guide was used (or at least, that's what's being **investigated**).

Situation Variables** Can't be **Controlled** but **Might** Still Affect What You're **Measuring

1) Ideally in a study the *only* thing that would influence the **DV** (the thing you're measuring) would be the **IV** (the thing you're manipulating). Usually though, there are other things that will have an effect. This can be due to the **situation** or the **participants** taking part.
2) An **extraneous variable** is any variable (other than the **IV**) that **could** affect what you're trying to measure. If these things **are** actually **influencing** the DV then they're called **confounding variables**.
3) **Situation variables** might include the time of day students sit the exam (tiredness could be important), or whether they used different revision guides when studying (some guides might be better than others, and the study doesn't state that all students have to use the same one).
4) **Participant variables** are things specific to individuals that might also influence the results, such as age, gender, anxiety levels, intelligence or personality.

Operationalisation** is **Showing** How the Variables Will Be **Measured

1) Variables must be **operationalised**. This means describing the **process** by which the variable is **measured**.
2) Some things are easy to operationalise (e.g. **height** might be operationalised as 'the distance in centimetres from the bottom of an object to the top'). Other things are difficult to operationalise (e.g. a mother's love for her newborn baby).
3) **Operationalisation** allows others to see exactly how you're going to define and measure your variables. It also has 18 letters, which is the same as soporiferousnesses, or yaaaaaaawwwwwwwwwn.

Practice Questions

Q1 What is the difference between a directional and non-directional hypothesis?

Q2 When would you reject the null hypothesis?

Q3 What is an independent variable?

Exam Questions

Q1 Bruno is interested in whether taking fish oil supplements every day for a month can improve memory performance. What would an appropriate experimental hypothesis be for his study? [2 marks]

Q2 Identify the dependent variable in Bruno's study. [1 mark]

Aim to learn this page — I hypothesise you'll need it...

Remember, you assume the null hypothesis is true unless your data suggests otherwise — if it does then you quickly switch allegiance to the alternative hypothesis instead. And remember, the IV is deliberately manipulated by the researcher. This might lead to an effect on the DV, but it's often a kind of indirect, knock-on effect. Yep, I agree — that's enough.

Research Design

Useful for everyone. *Once you've got a theory, this is how you'd actually go about researching...*

*The Research Design Must Make the Hypothesis **Testable***

Research example — does the presence of an audience help or hinder people doing the 'wiggly wire' task (moving a loop along a wire without touching it and setting off the buzzer)?
Based on previous research, we expect people to do this better without anyone watching them.

1) The IV (the variable being manipulated) is the presence or absence of an audience.
2) The DV (the variable being measured) is 'how well' the participants do on the task — but it must be testable. You need a **precisely defined** (or **operationalised**) DV, which should be **quantitative** wherever possible. An operationalised DV for this experiment might be 'the time taken to move the loop from one end of the wire to the other without setting off the buzzer'.

*There are Three **Research Designs** that are Used Loads*

1) An **independent groups design** means there are **different participants** in each group.
Here, for example, one group does the task **with** an audience and another group does it **alone**.
This avoids the problem that if all the participants did the test in both conditions, any improvement in performance might be due to them having two goes at the task (which would be a confounding variable).

Advantages

No **order effects** — no one gets better through practice (**learning effect**) or gets worse through being bored or tired (**fatigue effect**).

Disadvantages

Participant variables — differences between the **people** in each group might affect the results (e.g. the 'without audience' group may just have people who are better at the task — so we can't safely compare groups).

Number of participants — **twice as many** participants are needed to get the same amount of data, compared to having everyone do both conditions.

2) A **repeated measures design** is where, e.g., all participants do the task both **with** an audience and then **without**.
You can compare the performances in each condition, knowing the differences weren't due to participant variables.

Advantages

Participant variables — now the same people do the test in both conditions, so any differences between individuals shouldn't affect the results.

Number of participants — **fewer** participants are needed to get the same amount of data.

Disadvantages

Order effects — if all participants did the 'with audience' condition first, any improvements in the second condition could be due to **practice**, not the audience's absence. (But see **counterbalancing** on the next page.)

3) A **matched pairs design** means there are different participants in each condition, but they're **matched** on important variables (like age, sex and personality).
Some studies use **control groups**. These groups have not experienced any of the manipulations of the **IV** that an experimental group might have. This allows the researcher to make a direct comparison between them.
In the example above the group that didn't have an audience would be the control group.

Advantages

No order effects — there are **different people** in each condition.

Participant variables — important differences are minimised through **matching**.

Disadvantages

Number of participants — need twice as many people compared to repeated measures.

Practicalities — **time-consuming** and difficult to find participants who **match**.

*It's Sometimes Good to Run a Small **Pilot Study** First*

1) No piece of research is perfect. To help foresee any problems, a small-scale **pilot study** can be run first.
2) This should establish whether the **design** works, whether **participants** understand the wording in the **instructions**, or whether something important has been **missed out**.
3) Problems can be tackled before running the **main study**, which could save wasting a lot of **time** and **money**.

Research Design

Variables Can Be **'Controlled'** so Their Unwanted Effects are **Minimised**

Counterbalancing (mixing up the order of the tasks) can solve **order effects** in **repeated measures** designs. Half the participants do the task **with** an audience **first** and **then without**. The others do the conditions **the other way round**. Any order effects would then be equal across conditions.

Random allocation (e.g. by drawing names out of a hat) means everyone has an **equal chance** of doing **either** condition. An **independent measures** study with, for example, more men in one group than the other could have a confounding variable. Any difference in performance may be due to **sex** rather than the real IV. Random allocation should ensure groups are **not biased** on key variables.

Extraneous variables can be controlled by:
(i) keeping them **constant** for all participants (e.g. everyone does the task in the same place so distractions are similar),
(ii) eliminating them altogether (e.g. everyone does the task somewhere with no noise distractions — shhhh...).

Standardised instructions should ensure the **experimenters** act in a similar way with all participants. Everything should be **as similar as possible** for all the participants, including each participant's **experience** in such studies.

Researchers have to Consider **Reliability** and **Validity**

Reliability

- If a test is consistent within itself, it has **internal reliability**. The **split-half technique** assesses this. A questionnaire is randomly split in two — if all participants score similarly on both halves, the questions measure the same thing.
- If the measure is stable over time or between people, then it has **external reliability**. This can be assessed by measuring **test-retest reliability** (does the same person always score similarly on the test?) or **inter-rater reliability** (do different assessors agree, i.e. do they both give the same score?).

Validity

- If an experiment shows that the results were caused by the manipulation of the **variables**, rather than the effect of something else, then it has **internal validity**.
- If the findings can be **generalised** beyond the experimental setting (e.g. to different groups of people or different settings), then the experiment has **external validity**.

Research Should be Designed with **Ethical Issues** in Mind

Ethical guidelines assist researchers who have **ethical dilemmas,** and should ensure that research is **acceptable** and participants are **protected**.

Practice Questions

Q1 Give one disadvantage of an independent groups design.

Q2 Give one design that overcomes the disadvantage you identified in Q1.

Q3 What are the main benefits of running a pilot study?

Exam Questions

Q1 Why might a researcher choose to use a repeated measures design instead of an independent groups design? What could the researcher do to minimise any order effects that might influence the results? [6 marks]

Q2 Choose an example of a famous piece of psychological research and identify the design used in the study. Outline any control issues that the researchers would have had to consider before conducting the study. [4 marks]

Inter-test validity, no... split-rater ethics, no... oh sod it.... zzzzzzzzz...

There are a lot of details here, but they're all really important. If you're not really careful when you design a piece of research, the results you get might not be worth the paper you end up writing them down on. And that'd be no good. Spending a little bit of time thinking at the design stage will make it all worth it in the end — trust me.

Observations, Questionnaires and Interviews

Useful for everyone. *This page will tell you everything you need to know about* ***naturalistic observation*** *— the collection of data by observing participants in their natural environments. Oh, and questionnaires. And interviews...*

Researchers can use Participant or Non-Participant Observation

1) **Participant observation** is when the researcher **participates** in the activity under study in an **overt** way (their presence is obvious to the other participants).
   Advantages — The researcher develops a relationship with the group under study, so they can gain a greater understanding of the group's behaviour.
   Disadvantages — The researcher loses objectivity by becoming part of the group.
   — The participants may act differently if they know a researcher is amongst them.
2) **Non-participant observation** is when the researcher observes the activity without getting involved in it. This is a **covert** technique (their presence is unknown to the participants).
   Advantages — The researcher can remain objective throughout the study.
   Disadvantages — The researcher loses a sense of the group dynamics by staying separate from the group.

Sometimes researchers undertake **structured observations**. This is where the behaviour categories that are going to be used are defined in **advance**.
Advantages — It's easier to gather relevant data because you already know what you're looking for.
Disadvantages — Interesting behaviours could go unrecorded because they haven't been pre-defined as important.

Naturalistic Observation Involves Making Design Decisions

There are various ways of organising **structured observations** to make sure no behaviours are missed.

Recording Data	If you want **qualitative data** you could just make **written notes**. But **video** or **audio recording** means that you have a more accurate permanent record.
Categorising Behaviour	You must **define** the behaviours you aim to observe. For example, if you were going to observe children in a school playground to see how many behave aggressively, you'd have to decide **what counts as aggression**. This involves giving an **operationalised definition** (i.e. some **specific**, **observable** behaviours). For example, you might say that *'aggression is any physical act made with the intention to harm another person — such as punching, kicking, etc.'* But you have to be careful not to **miss out** anything important otherwise your definition may not be valid, e.g. aggression can also be verbal.
Rating Behaviour	The behaviours that you're interested in may be things that are a matter of **degree**, so you might need to use a rating scale to classify behaviour. You could put each participant's behaviour into one of several **categories**, e.g. *not aggressive*, *mildly aggressive* or *very aggressive*. Or you could use a **coding system** where each participant is given a **number** (e.g. between 1 and 10) to represent how aggressive they are, where a **higher score** indicates **more aggression**. However, you still have to **define** what kinds of behaviour are included for each number on the scale (e.g. 5 = *pushing* and 10 = *kicking or punching more than once*). Behaviour rated in this way provides **quantitative data** (data in the form of **numbers**).
Sampling Behaviour	You have to decide **how often** and for **how long** you're going to observe the participants. **Event sampling** — this is when you only record particular events that you're interested in (e.g. aggression shown by the children) and ignore other behaviours. Advantages — Researchers know exactly what behaviours they're looking for. Disadvantages — Potentially interesting behaviours could be ignored. **Time-interval sampling** — if the behaviours occur over a long time period you might choose to observe for only set time intervals e.g. the first 10 minutes of every hour. The time intervals could be chosen randomly. Advantages — Very convenient for the researchers to carry out. Disadvantages — If interesting behaviours occur outside the time sample they won't be recorded.
Inter-Observer Reliability	Even after you've **defined** the behaviours you're interested in, you have to make sure that the observers are actually putting each participant in the **right category** or giving the **right rating**. This might involve **comparing** the data from two or more observers to make sure they're giving the **same** scores (i.e. that they are 'reliable').

Observations, Questionnaires and Interviews

Questionnaires *Need to be Designed* ***Carefully***

There are various things you need to consider when designing a questionnaire for a survey.

1) **Type of data** — whether you want **qualitative data** and/or **quantitative data** will affect whether you ask **open** and/or **closed questions**.
   a) **Open questions** are questions such as *What kinds of music do you like?* The participant can reply in **any way**, and in as much detail as they want. This gives detailed, qualitative information, although it may be **hard to analyse**, as the participants could give very different answers.
   b) **Closed questions** limit the answers that can be given, e.g. *Which do you like: Pop, Rock or neither?* They give **quantitative** data that is relatively **easy to analyse** — e.g. you can say exactly **how many** people liked each type of music. However, less detail is obtained about each participant.
2) **Ambiguity** — you have to avoid questions and answer options which are **not** clearly **defined**, e.g. *Do you listen to music frequently?* What is meant here by 'frequently'? — Once a day, once a week?
3) **Double-barrelled questions** — best not to use these, since a person may wish to answer **differently** to each part. For example, *Do you agree that modern music is not as good as the music of the 1960s and that there should be more guitar-based music in the charts?*
4) **Leading questions** — these are questions that **lead** the participant towards a particular answer. E.g. *How old was the boy in the distance?* They might have seen an older person, but by saying *'boy'* you're leading them to describe the person as young. You're also leading them to think that the person was male, but they might not have been sure. (It's really important to avoid leading questions in **eyewitness testimony** — see page 17.)
5) **Complexity** — whenever possible **clear English** should be used, avoiding **jargon**. However, if specialist terms are included, they should be clearly defined. (So the question *Do you prefer music written in unusual time signatures?* probably isn't ideal for most people.)

All of the Above Goes For ***Interviews*** *As Well*

But you also have to consider the following:

1) **How structured** the interview will be: Interviews can be very **informal** with **few set questions**, and new questions being asked **depending on** the participant's **previous answers**. This gives detailed qualitative data, which may be difficult to analyse. Alternatively, they may be more **structured**, with set questions and **closed answers**, giving **less detail** but being **easier to analyse**.
2) Using a **question checklist** — if the interview is structured, a checklist ensures that no questions are left out and questions aren't asked twice.
3) The behaviour or appearance of the **interviewer** — this could **influence** how the participants react.

Practice Questions

Q1 How can behaviour be sampled in observational studies?

Q2 What is 'non-participant observation'?

Q3 Give two ways of rating behaviour in observational studies.

Q4 Explain three of the issues involved in designing questionnaires and interviews.

Exam Questions

Q1 Outline three of the main issues that a researcher must consider when designing a questionnaire. [6 marks]

Q2 What are the advantages of choosing a participant observation design instead of a non-participant observation design? [6 marks]

Big Brother — naturalistic observation at its finest...?

This is all about observing behaviour that's as natural as possible. What you don't want is for people to put on an act just because they're aware that they're being watched — that defeats the object of doing the study in the first place. Makes you wonder about Big Brother — can they keep an act up for all those weeks, or do we actually get to see some natural stuff?

Selecting and Using Participants

Useful for everyone. *Unless you're doing* ***AQA A****, in which case you can pretend that* ***stratified sampling*** *doesn't exist.*

Selecting a **Sample** of Participants Can Be Done in **Three Main Ways**

The part of a **population** that you're interested in studying (e.g. all the people in a particular city, or all people of a certain age or background) is called the **target group**. Usually you can't include everyone in the target group in a study, so you choose a certain **sample** of **participants**.

This sample should be **representative**, i.e. it should reflect the variety of characteristics that are found in the target group. A sample that is unrepresentative is **biased**. There are various methods of selecting a sample:

RANDOM SAMPLING

This is when **every** member of the target group has an **equal chance** of being selected for the sample. This could be done by giving everyone in the target group a number and then getting a computer to randomly pick numbers to select the participants. Sounds like being in a catalogue store. Order number 103 to the collection point...

Advantages: Random sampling is 'fair'. Everyone has an equal chance of being selected and the sample is **likely** to be representative.

Disadvantages: This method doesn't **guarantee** a representative sample — there's still a chance that some subgroups in the target group may not be selected (e.g. people from a minority cultural group). Also, if the target group is large it may not be practical (or possible) to give everyone a number that might be picked. So in practice, completely random samples are rarely used.

OPPORTUNITY SAMPLING

This is when the researcher samples whoever is **available and willing** to be studied. Since many researchers work in universities, they often use opportunity samples made up of students.

Advantages: This is a **quick** and **practical** way of getting a sample.

Disadvantages: The sample is **unlikely** to be **representative** of a target group or population as a whole. This means that we can't confidently **generalise** the findings of the research. However, because it's **quick** and **easy**, opportunity sampling is **often used**.

VOLUNTEER SAMPLING

This is when people actively **volunteer** to be in a study by responding to a request for participants advertised by the researcher, e.g. in a newspaper, or on a notice board.
The researcher may then select only those who are **suitable** for the study.
(This method was used by Milgram — see page 78.)

Advantages: If an advert is placed prominently (e.g. in a national newspaper) a **large number** of people may respond, giving more participants to study. This may allow more **in-depth analysis** and **more accurate** statistical results.

Disadvantages: Even though a large number of people may respond, these will only include people who actually saw the advertisement — no one else would have a chance of being selected. Also, people who volunteer may be more **cooperative** than others. For these reasons the sample is **unlikely** to be **representative** of the target population.

STRATIFIED SAMPLING

This is when the sample **reflects** certain features of the population. For example, if you want a **representative** sample of 18-25 year olds, and you know that 15% of this target population are students, then you'd make sure 15% of your sample were students. You can do this in detail by having more strata.

The students are one **stratum**. Sampling **within** this stratum would then be as **random** as possible.

Advantages: This can be a powerful way of getting a sample that is representative of the larger population.

Disadvantages: A population can be split up in lots of different ways. Sometimes it's difficult to determine exactly which strata are important for the study.

No method can guarantee a representative sample, but you should have confidence that your sample is (quite) representative if you want to generalise your results to the entire target group.

Selecting and Using Participants

*Participants Sometimes **Act Differently** When They're Being **Observed***

Human participants will usually be aware that they are being **studied**. This may mean they don't show their **true response**, and so their data may not be **valid** or **reliable**. Some of these effects are explained below...

THE HAWTHORNE EFFECT: If people are **interested** in something and in the attention they are getting (e.g. from researchers), then they show a more **positive** response, try **harder** at tasks, and so on.

This means their results for tests are often **artificially high** (because they're trying harder than normal), which could make a researcher's conclusions **inaccurate**.

The opposite effect may occur if the participants are **uninterested** in the task.

DEMAND CHARACTERISTICS: This is when participants form an idea about the **purpose** of a study. If they think they know what kind of response the researcher is **expecting** from them, they may show that response to '**please**' the researcher (or they may **deliberately** do the **opposite**).

Either way, the conclusions drawn from the study would be **inaccurate**.

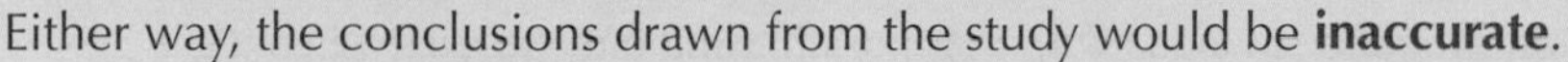

SOCIAL DESIRABILITY BIAS: People usually try to show themselves in the **best possible light**.

So in a survey, they may **not** be completely **truthful**, but give answers that are more **socially acceptable** instead (e.g. people may say they give more money to charity than they really do).

This would make the results **less accurate**.

*The **Researchers** Can **Affect** the Outcomes in **Undesirable Ways***

The **reliability** and **validity** of results may also be influenced by the researcher, since he or she has **expectations** about what will happen. This can produce the following effects:

RESEARCHER (or EXPERIMENTER) BIAS: The researchers' **expectations** can influence how they **design** their study and how they **behave** towards the participants, which may then produce **demand characteristics**. Also, their expectations may influence **how** they take **measurements** and **analyse** their data, resulting in errors that can lead, for example, to accepting a hypothesis that was actually false.

INTERVIEWER EFFECTS: The interviewer's **expectations** may lead them to ask only questions about what **they** are **interested** in, or to ask **leading questions**.

Or, they may **focus** on the aspects of the participant's answers which **fit** their **expectations**.

Also, the participant may react to the **behaviour** or **appearance** of an interviewer and then not answer truthfully.

Practice Questions

Q1 Give a disadvantage of opportunity sampling.

Q2 Give an advantage of volunteer sampling.

Q3 What is stratified sampling?

Q4 What are demand characteristics?

Q5 How might a researcher's expectations affect a study?

Exam Questions

Q1 Describe three ways humans might alter their behaviour if they know they are being observed. [6 marks]

Q2 Outline three sampling strategies that researchers might use when recruiting people for a study. [6 marks]

Volunteers needed for study into pain and embarrassment... (and stupidity)

In a study you could survey everyone in the world, but it might be expensive and time-consuming. This is why in most cases it's better to survey just a sample of participants. But you have to be careful how you choose them. There's no point in going to your local club and surveying all the crazy dancing people, cos I bet down at the old folk's home they'd disagree.

Ethical Issues in Psychological Research

These pages are for AQA A and OCR only. *Ethics are standards about what's right and wrong, so an ethical issue is a dilemma about whether a study is acceptable and justified. Try to imagine yourself as a participant in the studies — ask yourself if you would've been happy taking part, how you'd have felt, and if it would've had long-term effects on you.*

The British Psychological Society (BPS) Produces **Ethical Guidelines**

The **British Psychological Society** (BPS) has developed ethical guidelines to help psychologists resolve ethical issues in research and protect participants. They include advice on **deception**, **consent** and **psychological harm**.

Deception Means Misleading or Withholding Information from Participants

Asch (see page 72) deceived participants about his study's purpose and about the confederates who pretended to be real participants. He argued that without deception the aim of this study could not be achieved. If deception has to be used, participants should be told of the true nature of the research as soon as possible, during the debriefing.

BPS Guidelines for Deception

Deception should be avoided wherever possible and only be used when it's scientifically justified — when the study would be meaningless otherwise.

Deception shouldn't be used if it's likely that the participant will be unhappy when they discover the study's true nature.

Informed Consent Should be Given Where Possible

Giving consent means **agreeing** to participate in a study. When a participant is told the research aim and procedure and then agrees to it, this is **informed consent**. They are fully informed before their decision to participate.
If deception is used, participants **can't** give informed consent until they've been debriefed.
Asch's participants **did not** give informed consent when they agreed to take part.
They were deceived about aspects of the study and didn't have enough information for an informed decision.

BPS Guidelines for Informed Consent

Participants should be given all the information they need to decide whether to participate in research and shouldn't be coerced or pressured.

Some people may not be able to give real informed consent — for example children. In these cases informed consent should be obtained from parents or guardians.

Psychological Harm Means Any **Negative Emotion** (e.g. Stress, Distress, Embarrassment)

Asch's participants may have experienced **stress** and were possibly **embarrassed** about being 'tricked' into conforming.

BPS Guidelines for Psychological Harm

Researchers have a responsibility to protect participants from physical and psychological harm during the study. Any risk of harm should be no greater than what the participant might experience in their normal life.

Researchers Have to Deal with **Ethical Issues in Their Studies**

Deception

Sometimes it's difficult to conduct meaningful research without a bit of **deception**. If participants know exactly what's being studied then their behaviour might change, and the data you get would be useless. Psychologists don't usually tell participants every last detail, but they do try to minimise deception. That way participants aren't likely to be upset when they find out the true nature of the study.
Milgram's experiment (page 76) is an example of a study that would probably not be considered ethical today. He deceived participants about the true purpose of the study and many of them showed signs of **stress** when taking part.

Consent

Gaining consent is central to conducting research ethically. But telling participants they're being observed could **change** the way they **behave**.
Milgram's participants couldn't give informed consent until after they were debriefed. If they'd known about the nature of the study, it wouldn't have worked.

Ethical Issues in Psychological Research

Confidentiality *and* ***Animal Rights*** *are Also* ***Ethical Issues***

Confidentiality means keeping information private.

1) Participants should feel safe that any **sensitive information**, **results** or **behaviour** revealed through research won't be discussed with others.
2) Information obtained during a study should remain confidential **unless** the participant agrees it can be shared with others.
3) The study's report shouldn't reveal information or data **identifiable** to an individual.
4) You shouldn't be able to tell who took part or what their individual data was — these should remain **anonymous**.

Research with non-human animals has caused heated debate.

1) In **support**, people argue that animal research has provided **valuable information** for psychological and medical research. Some **research designs** couldn't have been conducted on humans — e.g. Harlow's study on attachment, where young monkeys were separated from their mothers and reared alone.
2) Some **disagree** with the idea of conducting research with non-human animals. They may argue that it's **ethically wrong** to inflict harm and suffering on animals, and obviously animals can't give consent to take part.
3) Some argue that it's cruel to experiment on animals that have a **similar intelligence** to humans, because they might suffer the same problems we would. It'd be OK to experiment on animals that are far less developed than us, but there is no point because they'll be **too different** from us to give results that apply to humans.

Ethical Guidelines ***Don't Solve*** *All the Problems*

1) There may be researchers who **don't follow the guidelines** properly. Naughty.
2) If a psychologist conducts research in an unacceptable way, they **can't be banned** from research (unlike a doctor who can be 'struck off' for misconduct). But they'd probably be kicked out of their university and the BPS.
3) Even when guidelines are followed, it can be **difficult to assess** things like **psychological harm**, or to **fully justify the use of deception**.
4) Deciding whether the ends (benefits from the study) justify the means (how it was done and at what cost) is not straightforward either. This creates another dilemma for psychologists.

The lasting harm to Milgram's participants was beginning to show.

Practice Questions

Q1 If you have used deception, what should you do immediately after the study?

Q2 What does 'informed consent' mean?

Q3 For the issue of psychological harm, what level of risk is said to be acceptable in research?

Exam Questions

Q1 Identify one strength and one weakness of conducting research on non-human animals. [4 marks]

Q2 Outline the main ethical principles for conducting psychological research, as developed by the British Psychological Society. Indicate how psychologists deal with these issues in their studies. [12 marks]

Q3 Discuss the extent to which ethical objections about social influence research are justified. [12 marks]

Don't let someone debrief you unless you love them very much...

Psychological experiments create many ethical dilemmas. Take Milgram's study — there's no doubting that the results reveal interesting things about how people interact. But do these results justify the possible psychological damage done to the participants? There's no right or wrong answer, but the BPS guidelines are there to address exactly this sort of issue.

Data Analysis

For everybody. *Data analysis may sound vaguely maths-like — but don't run for the hills just yet. It isn't too tricky...*

Data from **Observations** Should be Analysed **Carefully**

1) If you've got **quantitative** data (i.e. numbers), you can use **statistics** to show, for example, the most common behaviours. (Quantitative data can be obtained by **categorising** and **rating** behaviour — see page 132.)
2) **Qualitative** data might consist of a video or audio **recording**, or written **notes** on what the observers witnessed. Analysis of qualitative data is **less straightforward**, but it can still be done.
3) Whatever kind of data you've got, there are some important issues to bear in mind:

a) There must be **adequate data sampling** to ensure that a **representative** sample of participants' behaviour has been seen.

b) **Language** must be used **accurately** — the words used to describe behaviour should be **accurate** and **appropriate** (and must have valid **operationalised definitions**). For example, it might not be appropriate to describe a child's behaviour as 'aggressive' if he or she is play-fighting.

c) Researcher **bias** must be **avoided** — e.g. it's not okay to make notes **only** on events that **support** the researcher's theories, or to have a **biased interpretation** of what is observed.

The Same Goes for Data Obtained from **Interviews**

1) When **closed** questions are used as part of an interview's structure, **quantitative** data can be produced (e.g. the **number** of participants who replied 'Yes' to a particular question). **Statistics** can then be used (see pages 140-149) to further analyse the data.
2) When **open** questions are used, more **detailed**, **qualitative** data is obtained.
3) Again, whatever you've got, there are certain things you'll need to remember:

a) **Context** — the **situation** in which a participant said something, and the way they were **behaving** at the time, may be important. It may help the researcher understand **why** something was said, and give clues about the **honesty** of a statement.

b) The researcher should clearly distinguish **what** was said by the participant from **how** *they* interpreted it.

c) **Selection** of data — a lot of **qualitative** data may be produced by an interview, which may be difficult for the researcher to **summarise** in a report. The researcher must **avoid bias** in selecting what to include (e.g. only including statements that support their ideas). The interviewees may be consulted when deciding **what** to include and **how** to present it.

d) The interviewer should be aware of how *their* feelings about the interviewee could lead to **biased interpretations** of what they say, or how it is later reported.

And Likewise for Data from **Questionnaire Surveys**

1) Like observations and interviews, **surveys** can give you both **quantitative** and **qualitative** data, and so most of the points above are relevant to surveys as well.
2) Again, it's especially important to distinguish the **interpretations** of the **researcher** from the **statements** of the **participant**, and to be **unbiased** in selecting what to include in any report on the research.
3) However, the analysis of **written** answers may be especially difficult because the participant is not present to **clarify** any **ambiguities**, plus you don't know the **context** for their answers (e.g. what mood they were in, and so on).

Data Analysis

Qualitative Data Can Be *Tricky* to *Analyse*

Qualitative data is sometimes seen as 'of **limited use**' because it's difficult to **analyse**. This is why it's often **converted** into **quantitative** data using **content analysis**.

CONTENT ANALYSIS

a) A **representative sample** of qualitative data is first **collected** — e.g. from an interview, printed material (newspapers, etc.) or other media (such as TV programmes).
b) **Coding units** are identified to analyse the data. A coding unit could be, for example, an **act of violence**, or the use of **gender stereotypes** (though both of these must be given valid **operationalised definitions** first — e.g. a definition of an 'act of violence').
c) The qualitative data is then **analysed** to see **how often** each coding unit occurs (or **how much** is said about it, etc.).
d) A **statistical analysis** can then be carried out (see pages 140-149).

ADVANTAGES OF QUANTIFYING DATA

1) It becomes **easier** to see **patterns** in the data, and easier to **summarise** and **present** it (see pages 148-149).
2) **Statistical analysis** allows statements regarding **significance** to be made (see page 142 for more info).

DISADVANTAGES OF QUANTIFYING DATA

1) Care is needed to avoid **bias** in defining **coding units**, or deciding which behaviours fit particular units.
2) Qualitative data has **more detail** (**context**, etc.), which is **lost** when it's converted into **numbers**.

1) Because of the **detail** (and hence the **insight**) that **qualitative** data can give, some researchers prefer to **avoid** 'reducing' it to **numbers**.
2) Instead they analyse the data into **categories** or '**typologies**' (e.g. sarcastic remarks, statements about feelings, etc.), **quotations**, **summaries**, and so on.
3) **Hypotheses** may be developed during this analysis, rather than being stated previously, so that they are 'grounded in the data'.

Audrey was disappointed to learn that she'd been reduced to a number.

Quantitative Data Allows You to Make Statements Regarding *Significance*

1) There's always the chance that results might be due to **chance** rather than the **variables** of interest.
2) One advantage of quantifying data is that it allows you to use **inferential statistics** (see pages 144-145). This allows you to check whether results are likely to be due to chance. If the **probability** of the result being down to **chance** is sufficiently **small**, you say that the finding is **significant**.

Practice Questions

Q1 Distinguish between qualitative and quantitative data.
Q2 Why is data sampling an issue in observation studies?
Q3 Why might survey data be harder to analyse than interview data?
Q4 How is a content analysis done?

Exam Question

Q1 Outline the main differences between qualitative and quantitative data and give one strength and one weakness associated with each. [8 marks]

You must keep an open mind — but just don't let all the facts escape...

It's fairly obvious-ish, I guess, that qualitative data needs to be analysed with an open mind — it's not OK to fit the facts to your theory... you have to fit your theory to the facts. The same goes for analysing quantitative data — it's not just a case of 'doing some maths' — you have to be sure you're not being biased in your interpretations. Keep that mind open...

Descriptive Statistics

Useful for all. *Run for your lives... panic. This really looks like maths... Well, actually, it's not too bad. So calm down.*

Descriptive Statistics — Just Say What You See...

1) **Descriptive statistics** simply describe the **patterns** found in a set of data.
2) Descriptive statistics uses the fancy term '**central tendency**' to describe an **average**. For example, the central tendency (average) for the height of a group of 18-year-old boys might be about 1.70 metres.
3) Measures of **dispersion** describe **how spread out** the data is. For example, the difference in height between the shortest 18-year-old boy and the tallest might be 35 cm.

There are 3 Measures of Central Tendency (aka Average) You Need to Know

The Mean — This is the 'Normal Average'

You calculate the **mean** by **adding** all of the scores in a data set and then **dividing** by the number of scores.

$$\text{Mean} = \bar{X} = \frac{\sum X}{N}, \text{ where } \sum X \text{ is the sum of all the scores (and there are } N \text{ of them).}$$

Σ (pronounced 'sigma') just means you add things up.

Example: If you've got scores of 2, 5, 6, 7 and 10, then $\sum X = 30$ (since all the scores add up to 30), and N = 5 (since there are 5 of them)...

...so the **mean** is $\bar{X} = \frac{30}{5} = 6$.

For example, the scores 10, 40, 25, 20 and 650 have a mean of 149, which is not representative of the central tendency of the data set.

Advantages

a) It uses **all** the scores in a data set.
b) It's used in **further calculations** (e.g. standard deviation — see next page), and so it's handy to work it out.

Disadvantages

a) It can be **skewed** (distorted) by extremely **high** or **low** scores. This can make it **unrepresentative** of most of the scores, and so it may be **misleading**. In these cases, it's best to not use the mean.
b) It can sometimes give an **unrealistically precise** value (e.g. the average home has 2.4 children — but what does 0.4 of a child mean...?)

The Median — The Middle Score When the Data is Put in Order

Example: The **median** of the scores 4, 5, 10, 12 and 14 is **10**.

In this example there was one score in the middle. If there are two middle scores, add them together and then divide by 2 to get the median.

Advantages

a) It's relatively **quick** and **easy** to calculate.
b) It's **not** affected by extremely high or low scores, so it can be used on 'skewed' sets of data to give a '**representative**' average score.

Disadvantages

a) Not **all** the scores are used to work out the median.
b) It has **little further use** in data analysis.

The Mode — The Score that Occurs Most Often

Example: The **mode** (or the **modal score**) of 2, 5, 2, 9, 6, 11 and 2 is **2**.

If there are two scores which are most common then the data set is 'bimodal'. If there are three or more scores which are most common then the data set is 'multimodal'.

Advantages

a) It shows the **most common** or 'important' score.
b) It's always a result from the actual **data set**, so it can be a more **useful** or **realistic** statistic, e.g. the modal average family has 2 children, not 2.4.

Disadvantages

a) It's not very useful if there are **several** modal values, or if the modal value is only **slightly** more common than other scores.
b) It has **little further use** in data analysis.

Descriptive Statistics

Measures of *Dispersion* Tell You How *Spread Out* the Data Is

Range — Highest Score Minus the Lowest Score

Example: The **range** of the scores 6, 10, 35 and 50, is 50 – 6 = **44**

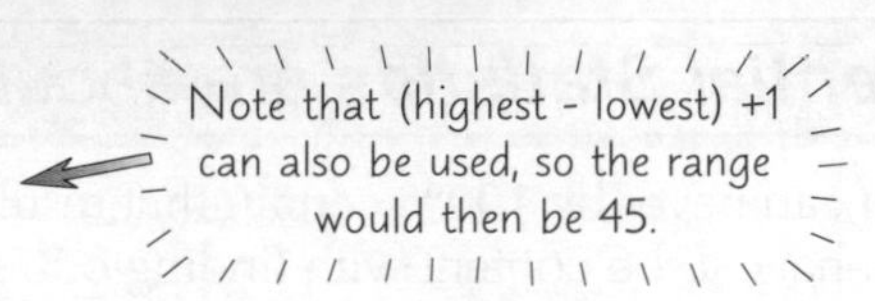

Advantage — it's **quick** and **easy** to calculate.

Disadvantage — it completely ignores the **central** values of a data set, so it can be misleading if there are very **high** or **low** scores.

1) The **interquartile range** (**IQR**) can be calculated to help **avoid** this problem.
2) First the **median** is calculated (this is sometimes called **Q2**).
3) If there's an **odd** number of values then you take the middle number as the median. If there's an **even** number of values then you take the 2 middle numbers, add them together and divide them by 2 to find the median.
4) The **median** of the **lower half** of the data is called the **lower quartile** (or **Q1**). The **median** of the upper half of the data is called the **upper quartile** (or **Q3**)
5) The **IQR = Q3 – Q1**.

Example: 3, 3, **4**, 5, 6, **8**, 10, 13, **14**, 16, 19.
There are 11 values, so median (Q2) = 6th value = 8.
Then Q1 = 4, Q3 = 14, and so IQR = 14 – 4 = **10**.

Standard Deviation — Measures How Much Scores Deviate from the Mean

$$s = \sqrt{\frac{\sum (X - \bar{X})^2}{N}}$$, where s = standard deviation

Example: Scores = 5, 9, 10, 11 and 15. The mean = 10.
So the standard deviation is:

$$s = \sqrt{\frac{(5-10)^2 + (9-10)^2 + (10-10)^2 + (11-10)^2 + (15-10)^2}{5}} = 3.22 \text{ (3 s.f.)}$$

A high standard deviation shows more variability in a set of data.

Advantages — **all** scores in the set are taken into account, so it's **more accurate** than the range. It can also be used in further analysis.

Disadvantage — it's **not** as quick or easy to calculate as the range.

Practice Questions

Q1 Explain how to calculate the mean.

Q2 What is the difference between the mean and the mode?

Q3 How is the range calculated?

Q4 What is meant by 'standard deviation'?

Exam Questions

Q1 Work out the mean, median and mode for the following data set: 2, 2, 4, 6, 8, 9, 10. [4 marks]

Q2 Name two measures of dispersion and outline one advantage and one disadvantage of each. [4 marks]

Dame Edna Average — making stats fun, possums...

These statistics are used to describe a collection of scores in a data set (how big the scores are, how spread out they are, and so on), so they're called... wait for it... descriptive statistics. Don't be put off by the weirdy maths notation either — a bar on top of a letter (e.g. $\bar{X}$) means you work out the mean. And a sigma (Σ) means you add things up. There... not so bad.

Inferential Statistics

Just Edexcel here. *Descriptive statistics say nothing about whether a theory is right or wrong. It's inferential statistics that let you make an 'inference' (or educated guess) about what your results show, or whether they're just due to chance.*

Inferential Statistics are about Ruling Out Chance

1) You can never be 100% certain that results aren't all down to chance. So instead of 'proving' a hypothesis, you have to be content with finding out whether it's **likely** to be true. This is called **statistical significance.**
2) If your results are statistically significant, it means that you can '**read something into**' them — they're unlikely to be just down to chance.
3) If your results are **not statistically significant**, it means they could have happened by chance rather than being the effect of changes in your variable, and you can't really read anything into them.

Use Statistical Tests to find out if your Results Mean Anything

OK, it's not easy, this bit — so stop texting people and concentrate...

1) The first thing you do is write out your **null hypothesis** (see page 128) — this is the theory you want to **test**. In a statistical test, you assume your null hypothesis is **true** (for the time being, at least). (So a null hypothesis might be *"rats that eat poison and rats that eat sugar pellets are equally likely to be ill"*.)
2) Next you choose a **significance level** — this is a '**level of proof**' that you're looking for before you read anything into your results. (The smaller the significance level, the stronger the evidence you're looking for that your results aren't just down to chance.)
3) A significance level is a **probability**, and so is a number between 0 and 1. (Probabilities near 1 mean things are very **likely**, and probabilities near 0 mean things are very **unlikely**.) Significance levels are always **very small** — usually 0.05 (= 5%) or less. (Because a significance level is very **small**, events with probabilities smaller than the significance level are very **unlikely** to happen.)
4) You then turn all your experimental results into a single **test statistic** (fortunately for you, you don't need to know much about this bit for AS Psychology). Then you can find out how likely this test statistic is (and so how likely your results are), **assuming the null hypothesis is true**.
5) If the probability of getting your results (assuming the null hypothesis is true) is **less than the significance level**, then they must be **really unlikely** — and so it's pretty safe to say that your null hypothesis **wasn't true** after all. This is what stats-folk mean when they talk about 'rejecting the null hypothesis'. (If you reject your null hypothesis, you assume your **alternative hypothesis** is true instead — see page 128.)
6) If you reject your null hypothesis, you can proudly shout out that your results are **statistically significant**. (So rejecting the null hypothesis above would mean that *"rats that eat poison and rats that eat sugar pellets are <u>not</u> equally likely to be ill"*.)
7) If you **don't reject** the null hypothesis, it means that your results could have occurred **by chance**, rather than because your null hypothesis was wrong. If this happens, you've proved **nothing**. Hmmphh. (So don't go thinking that not rejecting the null hypothesis means it must be true — cos it doesn't.)
8) Using a significance level of 0.05 (= 5%) is okay for most tests. If the probability of your results is **less** than this, then it's **pretty good evidence** that the null hypothesis **wasn't true** after all. If you use a significance level of 0.01 (= 1%), then you're looking for **really strong evidence** that the null hypothesis is untrue before you're going to reject it.

There are Two Types of Potential Error — Type 1 and Type 2

1) A **Type 1 error** is when you **reject** the null hypothesis when it was **actually true.** The significance level gives you the **probability** of this happening. (This is why significance levels are small.)
2) A **Type 2 error** is when you **don't reject** the null hypothesis when it was **actually false.** This can happen if your significance level is **too small** (e.g. if you want very strong evidence of the need to reject a null hypothesis and so use a 0.001 significance level).
3) Choosing significance levels is a **compromise** — too big and you risk making a Type 1 error, too small and you could make a Type 2 error.

A very small significance level (e.g. 0.01 or 1%) is used when you need to be very confident in your results, like when testing new theories.

Inferential Statistics

There are Different Kinds of **Statistical Test**

The appropriate significance test to use on your data depends on:

1) The **research design** — some tests need **'unrelated'** data from an **independent measures** design (e.g. the heights of 10 different people). Others need **'related pairs'** of data from a **repeated measures** design (e.g. memory scores from people before and after each of them has been trained).
2) The **research aim** — maybe you're looking for a significant **correlation** between 2 variables (see pages 146-147), or a significant **difference** in the scores between 2 groups (like if you're trying a new treatment for an illness).
3) The **type of data** you have and how your data is **measured**. For example, some tests use **ranks** — the position of a score in an ordered list. The scale you see on many **surveys** (strongly disagree, disagree, neutral, agree, strongly agree) is an example of this type of data.

How Your Data is **Measured** is Important

There are **four** levels of measurement that you need to know about:

1) Nominal

Nominal (aka **categorical**) measurement is putting things into **categories** and giving them **category names**. For example, hair colour is measured nominally. There are certain tests that can be used for nominal data, e.g. the **chi-square** test (see p.145).

Simon realised he hadn't covered all the possible hair colours in his survey.

2) Ordinal

Ordinal measurement is ranking things from **highest** to **lowest** (e.g. positions in a race). There are tests that can be used when you have ordinal data, e.g. the **Mann-Whitney U test** for unrelated data (see p.144).

3) Interval

Interval measurements have **equal spacing** between each measurement point, but no **'true' zero point**, e.g. **temperature** is usually measured on an interval scale.

There are tests dealing with interval and ratio data, but luckily for you they're not needed for the exam.

4) Ratio

Ratio measurements are like **interval measurements**, but have a **true zero point**, meaning that you are measuring from 0 upwards. Height is measured in this way.

Practice Questions

Q1 Outline the two types of potential error.

Q2 What is a significance level?

Q3 When would you reject your null hypothesis?

Q4 Describe the four levels of data measurement.

Exam Question

Q1 Why do psychologists use statistical tests, and what are the main issues involved in using them? [12 marks]

Don't be put off by the maths — statistic with it (ahem)...

It's 'statistics this and statistics that' at the moment, I'm afraid. But stick with it, as it's actually not that bad. And it's pretty important as well if you want to interpret the results of an experiment. But you're right — it's probably not quite as exciting as lion-taming, trapeze artistry, sky-diving or even... well... watching paint dry. Sorry, excitement-fiends.

Inferential Statistics

Just Edexcel again.
Now that you know what inferential statistics are, here are some lovely examples. Just what you always wanted...

The Mann-Whitney U Test is Used with Ordinal Data

The **Mann-Whitney U Test** is a test of difference (or of similarity) for **unrelated data**.
It focuses on **ranks** and is used when you have **ordinal** data.
Take a look at the following example:

Two groups took part in a study investigating whether drinking a **vitamin drink** once a day for 4 weeks improved performance on a **verbal memory** test compared to a group who had not had any vitamin drinks.

Number of words recalled								
	Vitamin group	19	13	9	12	21	15	14
	No vitamin group	7	5	10	8	6	11	18

Firstly, the Data Needs to be Ranked

The data is ranked regardless of the group each score is in. Start with the **lowest score** (in the example it's 5) and give it a rank of '**1**'. Then the next lowest score gets a rank of '2' and so on.

Number of words recalled								
	Vitamin group (A) (rank)	19 (13)	13 (9)	9 (5)	12 (8)	21 (14)	15 (11)	14 (10)
	No vitamin group (B) (rank)	7 (3)	5 (1)	10 (6)	8 (4)	6 (2)	11 (7)	18 (12)

If some of the data values are the **same** then you have to use an **average** rank. E.g. if the 3rd and 4th values are the same then you'll use 3.5.

The Ranks for Each Group are then Added Up

Look at the **ranks** associated with the vitamin group's scores and **add** them up.
Then do exactly the same for the no vitamin group.

- Sum of ranks in **vitamin group** (R_A) = 13 + 9 + 5 + 8 + 14 + 11 + 10 = 70
- Sum of ranks in **no vitamin group** (R_B) = 3 + 1 + 6 + 4 + 2 + 7 + 12 = 35

When you think about it, if the vitamin group really did show **better** verbal recall then their scores will be **higher** than the no vitamin group. This means that the **ranks** of the scores in the vitamin group will also be **higher**.
The Mann-Whitney U test then uses the following scary-looking formulas:

$$U_A = N_A N_B + \frac{N_A(N_A + 1)}{2} - R_A$$

$$U_A = (7 \times 7) + \frac{7(7 + 1)}{2} - 70$$

$$U_A = 7$$

$$U_B = N_A N_B + \frac{N_B(N_B + 1)}{2} - R_B$$

$$U_B = (7 \times 7) + \frac{7(7 + 1)}{2} - 35$$

$$U_B = 42$$

N_A is the number of people in group A
N_B is the number of people in group B
R_A is the sum of the ranks for scores in group A
R_B is the sum of the ranks for scores in group B

You need to select the **smaller** of these, 7, and call it '**U**'. Not me, but 'U'.
The observed U must be **less than or equal to** the **critical value** to be **significant**.
Critical values can be found in a table that you'll be given in the exam. In this case, the critical value is **6**, so there's **no significant difference** between the two groups.

Inferential Statistics

The Chi-square Test is Used with Nominal Data and Independent Samples

There's no better way of explaining this than showing you an example. So, hey presto...

Just to throw another spanner in the works, you say "kai", not "chi".

A student is interested to see whether finding reality TV programmes **entertaining** is related to being either **male** or **female**.

The **chi-square test** tests the **null hypothesis**. In this example, the null hypothesis would be that there's **no association** between finding reality TV entertaining and being male or female — this is shown by the **expected frequencies**. Under the null hypothesis, the expected frequencies show that **equal amounts** of men and women find reality TV entertaining, and equal amounts do not.

	Men	Women	Totals
Finds reality TV entertaining	19	35	54
(expected frequency)	(27)	(27)	
Does not find reality TV entertaining	41	25	66
(expected frequency)	(33)	(33)	
Totals	60	60	120

The expected frequencies are worked out using the following formula:

$$E = \frac{\text{row total} \times \text{column total}}{\text{overall total}}$$

You Then Just Have to Put the Numbers into a Formula

The chi-square (χ^2) is calculated using yet another scary-looking equation:

$$\chi^2 = \Sigma \frac{(O - E)^2}{E}$$

O is the observed frequency
E is the expected frequency

So, for each pair of observed and expected frequencies, take the expected score away from the observed score, square this and then divide by the expected score. Do this for all the observed and expected pairs — then add up all your answers (that's what the Σ means).

If you work through this example, χ^2 turns out to be **8.62**.
You can then use a critical value table to see if this is significant (it is, so the null hypothesis is **false**).

Significance tables are tables of values that you can use to look up whether your results are significant.

Practice Questions

Q1 What type of data is a Mann-Whitney U test used on?

Q2 When would a researcher use a chi-square test?

Q3 How do you calculate an expected frequency?

Exam Question

Q1 Ian is interested in whether there is an association between being an only child and having a pet.
Suggest a null hypothesis and a suitable inferential test for this study. [4 marks]

Chi is the Greek letter for X — now isn't that interesting...

...but unfortunately that won't help you much in this exam. What will, though, is knowing what each statistical test is used for. So, the Mann-Whitney U test is for ordinal data and the chi-square test is for nominal data. You could come up with some funny mnemonic (see p.20-21) for remembering those. See, psychology comes in useful sometimes. Isn't it good...

Correlations

***Useful for everyone, I reckon.** You know what they say — correlation is as correlation does. Remember that as you read this page... then you won't go far wrong.*

Correlation Measures How Closely Two Variables are Related

1) **Correlation** is a measure of the relationship between **two variables**, e.g. it can tell you how closely exam grades are related to the amount of revision that someone's done.
2) In a **correlational study** data is collected for some kind of **correlational analysis.**

The Correlation Coefficient is a Number Between –1 and +1

1) To find the correlation between two variables, you first have to collect some **data**.
   For example, you could ask every student in a class how many hours of study they did each week, and note their average test result.

Student	Hours of study	Average test score — %
A	4	58
B	1	23
C	7	67
D	15	89

2) You can then work out a **correlation coefficient** (e.g. Spearman's rho — see next page). This is a number between –1 and +1, and shows:

   a) **How closely** the variables are linked. This is shown by the **size** of the number — if it's **close to +1** or **–1**, then they are **very closely** related, while a smaller number means the relationship is **less strong** (or maybe not there at all if it's close to 0).

   b) The **type** of correlation — a **positive** correlation coefficient (i.e. between 0 and +1) means that the variables rise and fall together, while a negative correlation coefficient (i.e. between –1 and 0) means that as one variable rises, the other falls. (See below for more info.)

Correlation is Easy to See on Scatter Graphs

1) **Positive correlation** — this means that as one variable rises, so does the other (and likewise, if one falls, so does the other).
   Example: hours of study and average test score.
   The correlation coefficient is roughly **0.75** (close to +1).

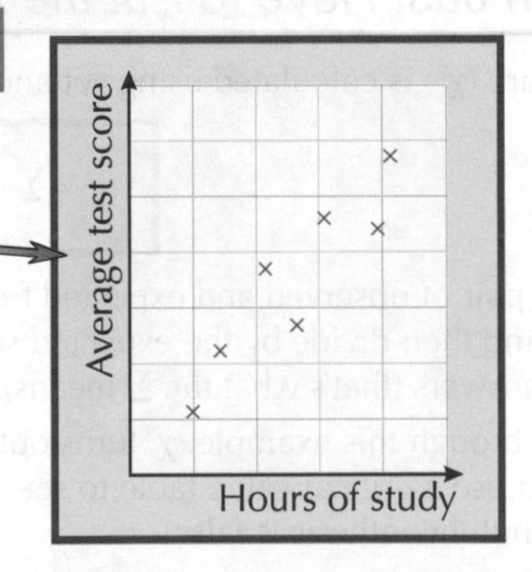

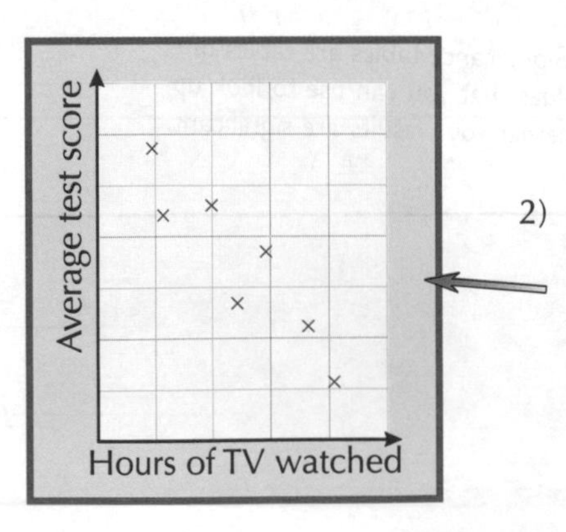

2) **Negative correlation** — this means that as one variable rises, the other one falls (and vice versa).
   Example: hours of TV watched each week and average test score.
   The correlation coefficient is roughly **–0.75** (close to -1).

3) **No correlation** — if the correlation coefficient is 0 (or close to 0), then the two variables aren't linked.
   Example: a student's height and their average test score.
   The correlation coefficient is roughly **0.01** (close to 0).

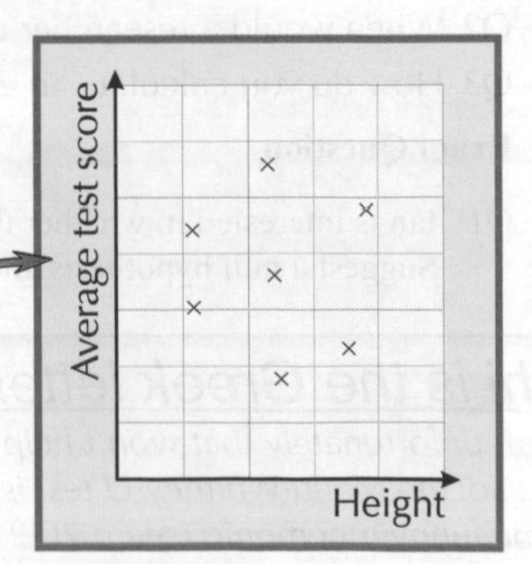

Correlations

Correlational Research has some Advantages...

1) Because correlational research doesn't involve **controlling** any variables, you can do it when (for **practical** or **ethical** reasons) you couldn't do a **controlled experiment**. Handy.
   For example, an experiment into the effects of smoking on humans probably wouldn't be done for ethical reasons, but a correlation between smoking and cancer could be established from hospital records.
2) Correlational analysis can give ideas for **future** research (e.g. biological research on the effects of smoking).
3) Correlation can even be used to test for **reliability** and **validity** (e.g. by testing the results of the same test taken twice by the same people — a good **reliable** test will show a **high correlation**).

...but some Limitations

1) Correlational analysis **can't** establish '**cause and effect**' relationships — it can only show that there's a **statistical link** between the variables.
   Variables can be closely correlated without changes in one causing changes in the other — a **third variable** could be involved. Only a **controlled experiment** can show cause and effect relationships.
2) Care must be taken when **interpreting** correlation coefficients — high correlation coefficients could be down to **chance**. To decide whether a coefficient is **significant**, you have to use a proper **significance test**.

For example, the number of births in a town was found to be positively correlated to the number of storks that nested in that town — but that didn't mean that more storks caused the increase. (It was because more people in the town led to more births, and also to more houses with chimneys to nest on.)

Spearman's Rho is a Correlation Coefficient

To work out (and then test the significance of) **Spearman's rho** correlation coefficient, you need values for two different variables (e.g. hours of revision and average test scores for 10 students).

a) The values for each variable are placed into **rank order** (each variable is ranked separately). The lowest value for each variable gets rank 1 (and in the above example, the biggest value will get rank 10).
b) The **difference** (**d**) in ranks for each student's variables is calculated. (So a particular student may have done the most revision, but got the 3rd best results, in which case the difference in ranks will be d = 3 – 1 = 2.)
c) The value of d for each student is **squared**, then the results are added together (to get $\sum d^2$).
d) Then the special **Spearman's correlation coefficient** calculation is done, which is $r_s = 1 - \frac{6 \times \sum d^2}{N \times (N^2 - 1)}$
   (where N is the number of students, or whatever).
e) To find out whether the result is **significant** (and so whether the variables are linked), you compare the outcome of that nightmarish calculation with a **critical value** that you look up in a **statistics table**.

Practice Questions

Q1 Explain what is meant by correlation.

Q2 What is a correlation coefficient?

Q3 What two things are shown by a correlation coefficient?

Q4 Explain the difference between a negative correlation and no correlation.

Exam Questions

Q1 A study has found a negative correlation between tiredness and reaction time. Explain what this means. [2 marks]

Q2 Outline the limitations of correlational research. [6 marks]

Stats sucks...

Look at the graphs showing the large positive and large negative correlations — all the points lie close-ish to a straight line, which slopes either upwards (positive correlation) or downwards (negative correlation). Just learn the steps involved in working out Spearman's rho — don't try to understand it too much. Well, that's my advice anyway...

Summarising the Data

***This stuff's for all.** It's not very scientific or anything, but the only bit about statistics I don't find mind-numbingly boring is the bit where you get to make all the lovely numbers look pretty... P.S. Ignore me — stats has turned my brain to mush.*

*Data Can Be Presented in **Various Ways***

1) **Qualitative** data from observations, interviews, surveys, etc. (see pages 126-127) can be presented in a **report** as a **'verbal summary'**.
2) The report would contain **summaries** of what was seen or said, possibly using **categories** to group data together. Also **quotations** from participants can be used, and any **research hypotheses** that developed during the study or data analysis may be discussed.
3) When **quantitative** data is **collected** (or **produced** from the data, e.g. by a **content analysis** — see page 139), it can be **summarised** and presented in various ways. Read on...

Tables** are a Good Way to Summarise **Quantitative Data

Tables can be used to clearly present the data and show any **patterns** in the scores.

Tables of **'raw data'** show the scores **before** any **analysis** has been done on them.

Other tables may show **descriptive statistics** such as the mean, range and standard deviation (see pages 140-141).

Edward's data was summarised nicely on his table.

Table To Show the Qualities of Different Types of Ice Cream

	Quality (score out of 10)		
Type of ice cream	Tastiness	Thickness	Throwability
Chocolate	9	7	6
Toffee	8	6	7
Strawberry	8	5	4
Earwax	2	9	8

Bar Charts** Can be Used for **Non-continuous Data

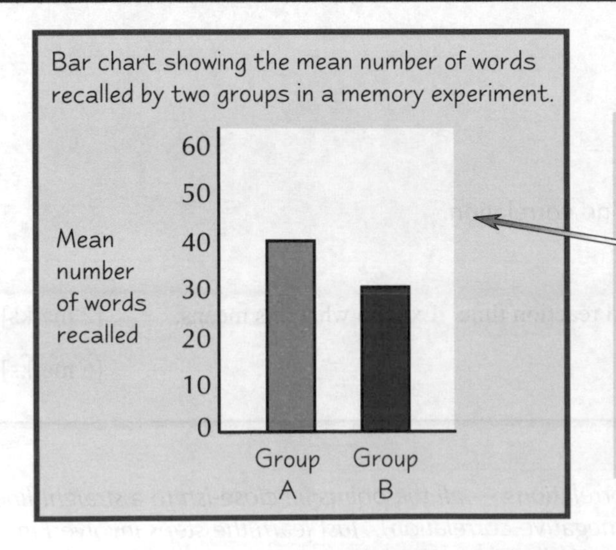

Bar charts (bar graphs) are usually used to present **'non-continuous data'** (like when a variable falls into **categories** rather than being measured on a numbered scale).

This bar chart shows the mean number of words recalled by different groups in a memory experiment.

Note that the columns in bar charts **don't touch** each other. Also, it's preferable to always show the **full vertical scale**, or **clearly indicate** when it isn't all shown (otherwise it can be **misleading**).

Summarising the Data

Nearly done — just a little bit more...

Histograms are for When You Have *Continuous Data*

Histograms show data measured on a '**continuous**' scale of measurement.

This histogram shows the time different participants took to complete a task.

Each column shows a **class interval** (here, each class interval is 10 seconds), and the columns **touch** each other.

It's the **height** of the column that shows the number of values in that interval. (**All** intervals are shown, even if there are **no scores** within them.)

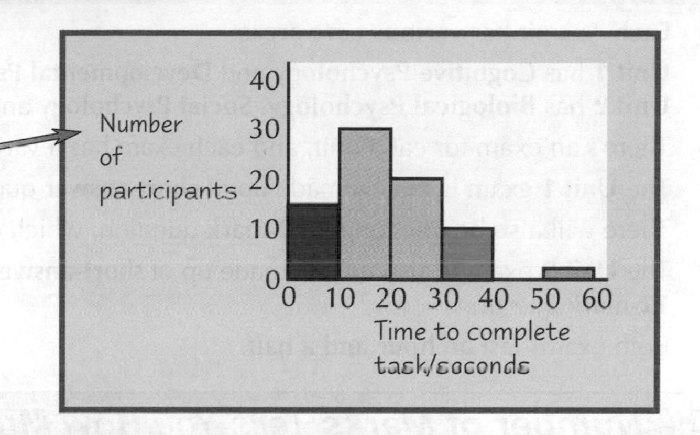

Frequency Polygons are Good for Showing *More Than One* Set of Data

Frequency polygons are similar to histograms, but use **lines** to show where the top of each column would reach.

It can be useful to combine **two or more** frequency polygons on the same set of axes — then it's easy to **make comparisons** between groups.

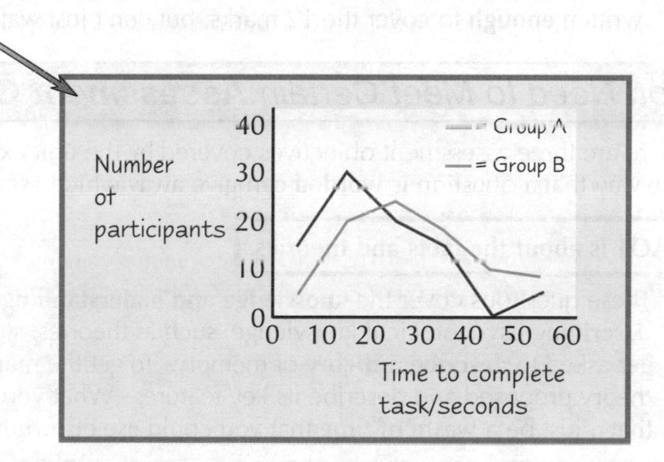

Practice Questions

Q1 What kind of information is typically shown in tables?

Q2 What kind of data is shown on bar charts?

Q3 What type of data do histograms represent?

Q4 What advantage do frequency polygons have over histograms?

Exam Questions

Q1 Describe three ways of summarising quantitative data. [6 marks]

Q2 Sketch a frequency polygon of the data in the table on p.148. [4 marks]

*What goes 'Graph graph graph'? A dog with a sore throat...**

That's it. It's done. The book is finished. Well, apart from that pesky bit about essays. I think you deserve a big cake now. Go and tell your mum I said so. Say you want one of those really big gooey chocolate ones from the freezer department in the supermarket. And then you'll need a cup of tea too. And a night of watching soap operas and stupid American sitcoms.

* Or a crowd at a senior's tennis match. Or a maths teacher. Or my dad coughing in the morning. Or... oh think of your own...

Do Well in Your AQA Exam

These two pages are all about how to do well in AQA A exams. So don't bother reading them if you're not doing AQA.

There are **Two Units** in AQA AS Psychology

1) **Each** AS unit has **various core areas:**
   Unit 1 has **Cognitive Psychology** and **Developmental Psychology**, with some **Research Methods** mixed in for fun.
   Unit 2 has **Biological Psychology**, **Social Psychology** and **Individual Differences**.
2) There's an exam for each unit, and each exam has a variety of **question types**.
3) The **Unit 1** exam is mostly made up of **short-answer** questions.
4) There will also be **one** longer **12-mark** question, which could be in **either** of the core areas.
5) The **Unit 2** exam is also mostly made up of **short-answer** questions, but this time there could be **more than one 12-mark** question.
6) Both exams last **an hour and a half**.

The **Number of Marks** Tells You **How Much to Write**

1) The number of marks that a question is worth gives you a pretty good clue of **how much to write**.
2) You get **one mark per correct point** made, so if a question is worth four marks, make sure you write four decent points.
3) There's no point writing a massive answer for a question that's only worth a few marks — it's just a **waste of your time**.
4) For the longer essay-style questions, make sure that you've written **enough** to cover the 12 marks, but don't just waffle.

Martha suddenly realised that the question was worth 8 marks, not 88.

You Need to Meet Certain **Assessment Objectives**

There are three assessment objectives covered by the unit exams — **AO1**, **AO2** and **AO3**.
The way that a question is **worded** can give away which assessment objective is being tested.

AO1 is about the facts and theories

These questions cover the **knowledge and understanding of science**. You get marks by **recalling** and **describing** psychological knowledge, such as theories, studies and methods. For example, you might get asked to **describe a theory** of memory. To get the marks, you'd simply need to describe what the theory proposed and describe its key features. What you don't need to do is evaluate the theory — that'd just be a **waste of time** that you could use elsewhere, and you **won't get any extra marks**.

AO2 gets you to apply your knowledge

AO2 questions are slightly different in that they get you to **apply your knowledge and understanding of science**. It's likely that these questions will begin with '**analyse**' or '**evaluate**'. Rather than just recalling stuff, e.g. listing relevant experiments, you've got to **apply your knowledge** to the situation in these questions. So, you'd need to use the experiments you've come up with to **support your argument**. You also might have to apply your knowledge to situations you've not come across before. For example, you could be asked to assess the **validity**, **reliability** or **credibility** of a study that's new to you.

AO3 is about 'How Science Works'

'**How Science Works**' focuses on how scientific experiments are carried out.
You need to be able to suggest appropriate **methodology** and know how to make sure measurements and observations are **accurate** and **precise**. You could also be asked to **analyse** and **evaluate** the **methodology** and **results** of a study described in the exam. When you're doing this, don't forget about things like **ethics** and **safety**.

In the **Unit 1** exam, there's an **equal division** of AO1, AO2 and AO3 marks throughout the paper.
In the **Unit 2** exam, there are **fewer AO3 marks** — there's more emphasis on AO1 and AO2.

Do Well in Your AQA Exam

First Things First — Make a Plan

When you're writing your answer, try to **structure** it in an **organised** way. Before you start, it might be worth jotting down a quick **plan** of what you want to write so that you don't end up with a really jumbled answer. If there's one thing that examiners find worse than a load of pointless information, it's being unable to make head or tail of an answer.

An Example Answer to Show You What to Aim for...

This is the sort of answer that would get you full marks.

1 Outline the key features of the multi-store model of memory. *(6 marks)*

The multi-store model proposes that memory is made up of three stores. These three stores are a sensory store, a short-term store and a long-term store. Sensory memory holds the information that is constantly being taken in from the environment, such as visual and auditory information. If you don't pay attention to this information, it will be lost from the sensory store. However, if you do pay attention to it, it will pass into short-term memory. Short-term memory has a limited and temporary capacity, but if the information in it is rehearsed, it will be transferred into long-term memory, which theoretically has an unlimited capacity and duration.

Make sure the information in your answer is relevant and keep it concise.

Don't open with a general or meaningless sentence — get straight into gaining marks.

Stop writing once you've answered the question — don't add irrelevant detail to fill up the space.

The multi-store model has **three features**, and the question is worth **6 marks**. So, logically, you'd just need to write enough about each feature to get you two marks. This answer might look short, but it's all you'd need to write to get you the marks.

... And an Example Answer to Show You What Not to Write...

I repeat... What **NOT** to write...

1 Outline the key features of the multi-store model of memory. *(6 marks)*

Atkinson and Shiffrin proposed the multi-store model. They thought that memory is made up of three stores — a sensory store, a short-term store and a long-term store. Sensory memory holds information from the environment. If you don't pay attention to this information, it gets lost. If you do pay attention to it, it will pass into short-term memory. It's then transferred into long-term memory.

The Primacy Effect has provided some support for this model. The first few items on a list are usually remembered better. This suggests that they have been better rehearsed and have been transferred to long-term memory. Also, if rehearsal of the items on a list is prevented, memory is seen to decline.

This first sentence is a bit irrelevant — it won't get you any marks.

You'd only need to give this detail if the question had asked you to evaluate the model — writing it is just a waste of time.

This would be better if it said what sort of information is taken in from the environment.

This could do with more detail to explain that STM only has a limited capacity, and rehearsal is needed to move information to LTM.

1) The second answer lacks the **detail** of the first answer — it only sketches over the features of the model. It's unlikely that it would earn all the possible marks.
2) Also, there's quite a bit of **irrelevant information** that wouldn't earn you any marks.
3) It's important to remember that it's not just a case of blindly scribbling down **everything** you can think of that's related to the subject. Doing this just **wastes time**, and it doesn't exactly impress the examiner.
4) You only get marks for stuff that's **relevant** and **answers the question**.
5) So, make sure you read over the question a couple of times before you start writing so that you really understand what it's asking.

Do Well in Your OCR Exam

These two pages are all about how to do well in OCR exams. So don't bother reading them if you're not doing OCR.

There are **Two Exams** for OCR

1) There are **two exams** for OCR — **Psychological Investigations** which lasts for one hour, and **Core Studies** which is a two-hour exam.
2) In the **Psychological Investigations** paper, there'll be questions about pieces of research that have been carried out, and also a proposed piece of research. You'll need to use your knowledge of the various research techniques you've learnt about.
3) The paper contains **three sections of compulsory questions** and it's worth **60 marks**.
4) The **Core Studies** paper tests your knowledge of the 15 core studies and related issues that you'll have covered.
5) It contains three sections of questions. You must answer **all** of the questions in the **first** section. In each of the **second** and **third sections**, you'll need to **choose one** question to answer. These questions are worth more marks than those in the first section. In total, **120 marks** are available on this exam paper.

The **Number of Marks** Tells You **How Much to Write**

1) The number of marks that a question is worth gives you a pretty good clue of **how much to write**.
2) You get **one mark per correct point** made, so if a question is worth four marks, make sure you write four decent points.
3) There's no point writing a massive answer for a question that's only worth a few marks — it's just a **waste of your time**.
4) For the longer essay-style questions, make sure that you've written **enough** to cover the marks, but don't just waffle.

You Need to Meet Certain **Assessment Objectives**

There are three assessment objectives covered by the unit exams — **AO1**, **AO2** and **AO3**.
The way that a question is **worded** can give away which assessment objective is being tested.

AO1 is about the facts and theories

These questions cover the **knowledge and understanding of science**. You get marks by **recalling** and **describing** psychological knowledge, such as theories, studies and methods. For example, you might get asked to **describe a theory** of memory. To get the marks, you'd simply need to describe what the theory proposed and describe its key features. What you don't need to do is evaluate the theory — that'd just be a **waste of time** that you could use elsewhere, and you **won't get any extra marks**.

AO2 gets you to apply your knowledge

AO2 questions are slightly different in that they get you to **apply your knowledge and understanding of science**. It's likely that these questions will begin with '**analyse**' or '**evaluate**'. Rather than just recalling stuff, e.g. listing relevant experiments, you've got to **apply your knowledge** to the situation in these questions. So, you'd need to use the experiments you've come up with to **support your argument**. You also might have to apply your knowledge to situations you've not come across before. For example, you could be asked to assess the **validity**, **reliability** or **credibility** of a study that's new to you.

AO3 is about 'How Science Works'

'**How Science Works**' focuses on how scientific experiments are carried out. You need to be able to suggest appropriate **methodology** and know how to make sure measurements and observations are **accurate** and **precise**. You could also be asked to **analyse** and **evaluate** the **methodology** and **results** of a study described in the exam. When you're doing this, don't forget about things like **ethics** and **safety**.

In the **Core Studies** exam, the majority of the marks come from **AO1** and **AO2** questions.
In the **Psychological Investigations** exam, the majority of the marks come from **AO3** questions.

Do Well in Your OCR Exam

An **Example** Core Studies (Section C) Essay That Would Get You **Full Marks**:

1 (a) Outline one assumption of the cognitive approach in psychology. [2]

(b) Describe how the cognitive approach could explain eyewitness testimony. [4]

(c) Describe one similarity and one difference between the Loftus and Palmer (1974) study and any other cognitive approach study. [6]

(d) Describe the strengths and limitations of the cognitive approach using examples from the Loftus and Palmer study. [12]

(a) Cognitive psychology proposes that behaviour is the result of information processing involving perception, language, attention and memory.

The question is only worth two marks, so keep it short and to the point.

(b) We make sense of information in a way that is meaningful to us. This means that we sometimes distort information, or fill in gaps, to help us make sense of something. This means that our memories can sometimes become distorted, leading to inaccuracies in eyewitness testimony.

(c) Another cognitive study was carried out by Bahrick et al in 1975. One similarity between the studies is that they both investigated memory. Loftus and Palmer's study investigated participants' memory of a video of a car crash. Bahrick et al's study investigated participants' memory of the names and faces of their classmates.

The other study doesn't need to be a core study — it can be any cognitive study you like.

However, in contrast to the Loftus and Palmer study, Bahrick et al's study had high ecological validity as it was a field experiment. The Loftus and Palmer study was a laboratory experiment, and used an artificial video, reducing it's ecological validity.

(d) Much of the research in the cognitive approach is carried out using laboratory experiments. This type of research has strengths and weaknesses. In laboratory experiments, the variables can be closely controlled, making the research very scientific and reliable. However, on the downside, laboratory experiments tend to lack ecological validity as they don't really reflect what we do in the real world. This makes it difficult to generalise the results to real-life situations.

Don't waffle — make all information relevant to the question.

Loftus and Palmer's study is an example of this. The study was a laboratory experiment, meaning that the variables could be tightly controlled. This meant that the results were likely to be reliable. Another strength of this study is that the findings have been applied to real life — they led to the development of the cognitive interview techinique, which has helped make eyewitness testimony more reliable. On the other hand, the laboratory setting made it difficult for the researchers to create a real-life situation — the stimulus in the study was a video of an artificial car crash. This may have meant that it was less emotionally arousing than it would be to see a car crash in real life. The experiment could have become one focusing on memory of watching television rather than eyewitness testimony. If this was the case, the results couldn't be generalised to other instances of eyewitness testimony.

Relate your examples of strengths and weaknesses to points of the Loftus and Palmer study.

However, some cognitive psychology experiments do take place in a natural setting. Field experiments, such as the study by Bahrick et al (1975), have more ecological validity as they tend to reflect real life. However, in this type of experiment there's usually less control of the variables.

Problems can be general problems of all studies, not just specific ones.

Sum up your answer with a brief conclusion — don't just repeat everything you've said in your answer.

In conclusion, the strengths and limitations of the cognitive approach depend on the type of research being carried out. Laboratory studies mean that the results are reliable but can lack ecological validity. In contrast, the results produced by field experiments can lack reliability but are usually ecologically valid.

... And Some Pointers About What to **Avoid**...

1) It's important to remember that it's not just a case of blindly scribbling down **everything** you can think of that's related to the subject. Doing this just **wastes time**, and it doesn't exactly impress the examiner.
2) You only get marks for stuff that's **relevant** and **answers the question**.
3) So, make sure you read over the question a couple of times before you start writing so that you really understand what it's asking.
4) When you're writing your answer, try to **structure** it in an **organised** way. If there's one thing that examiners find worse than a load of pointless information, it's being unable to make head or tail of an answer.
5) Before you start, it might be worth jotting down a quick **plan** of what you want to write so that you don't end up with a really jumbled answer.

Do Well in Your Edexcel Exam

These pages are all about how to do well in Edexcel exams. So don't bother reading them if you're not doing Edexcel.

There are **Two Exams** for Edexcel

1) The **Unit 1** exam covers the **Social Approach** and the **Cognitive Approach**.
2) The **Unit 2** exam covers the **Psychodynamic**, **Biological** and **Learning Approaches**.
3) Each exam has **three sections.**
4) The first section of each paper consists of **multiple choice** questions.
5) Section B of the paper is made up of **short answer** questions and Section C is made up of questions requiring a more **extended answer**.
6) These last two sections could also include questions on the **practicals** you'll have carried out during your course. You could be asked to describe or explain some aspects of what you did.

The **Number of Marks** Tells You **How Much to Write**

1) The number of marks that a question is worth gives you a pretty good clue of **how much to write.**
2) You get **one mark per correct point** made, so if a question is worth four marks, make sure you write four decent points.
3) There's no point writing a massive answer for a question that's only worth a few marks — it's just a **waste of your time.**
4) For the longer essay-style questions, make sure that you've written **enough** to cover the marks, but don't just waffle.

You Need to Meet Certain **Assessment Objectives**

There are three assessment objectives covered by the unit exams — **AO1**, **AO2** and **AO3**.
The way that a question is **worded** can give away which assessment objective is being tested.

AO1 is about the facts and theories

These questions cover the **knowledge and understanding of science.** You get marks by **recalling** and **describing** psychological knowledge, such as theories, studies and methods. For example, you might get asked to **describe a theory** of memory. To get the marks, you'd simply need to describe what the theory proposed and describe its key features. What you don't need to do is evaluate the theory — that'd just be a **waste of time** that you could use elsewhere, and you **won't get any extra marks.**

AO2 gets you to apply your knowledge

AO2 questions are slightly different in that they get you to **apply your knowledge and understanding of science.** It's likely that these questions will begin with **'analyse'** or **'evaluate'**. Rather than just recalling stuff, e.g. listing relevant experiments, you've got to **apply your knowledge** to the situation in these questions. So, you'd need to use the experiments you've come up with to **support your argument.** You also might have to apply your knowledge to situations you've not come across before. For example, you could be asked to assess the **validity, reliability** or **credibility** of a study that's new to you.

AO3 is about 'How Science Works'

'**How Science Works**' focuses on how scientific experiments are carried out. You need to be able to suggest appropriate **methodology** and know how to make sure measurements and observations are **accurate** and **precise.** You could also be asked to **analyse** and **evaluate** the **methodology** and **results** of a study described in the exam. When you're doing this, don't forget about things like **ethics** and **safety.**

There's a fairly **even** weighting of AO1, AO2 and AO3 questions in each exam.

Do Well in Your Edexcel Exam

An **Example** of a 12-Mark Essay Question:

1 Describe and evaluate one study into obedience. (12)

In 1963, Milgram was interested in how normal German people followed the orders of the Nazis, leading to their treatment of the Jews. He was interested in whether normal Americans would also blindly follow instructions from authority, even if it led to them hurting other people. Milgram set up a study where participants believed they were taking part in a learning experiment. Each participant was a 'teacher', who read out word pairs to a 'learner' (who was actually a confederate). Every time the learner gave an incorrect response, the participant had to give them an electric shock. With each shock, the voltage was increased up to a final level of 450 V, labelled 'XXX'. At 300 V, the learner pleaded to be let out, saying he couldn't stand the pain. Above 300 V, he was silent. If the participant asked to stop, they were told that the experiment had to continue.

Milgram found that no participants stopped the experiment before 300 V, and 65% actually continued as far as 450 V. Milgram concluded that ordinary Americans obey orders even if it leads to them acting against their conscience and hurting others.

Milgram's experiment was repeated in different situations, leading to different results. When run in normal offices, only 48% of participants gave the maximum shock. This suggests that the original university location made participants more likely to see the researcher as a justified authority figure. Proximity is also an important factor, as when the learner was in the same room as the participant, obedience dropped to 40%. It seemed that participants had lost a buffer protecting them from seeing the consequences of their actions. Likewise, when a confederate gave the shocks instead of the participant, 92.5% of the participants continued to the end of the study — a buffer had been created.

This was a very influential study, which provided great insights into human behaviour. It disproved the 'Germans are different' hypothesis, and led to increased awareness of how easily we can just blindly obey orders, without questioning whether we morally should. However, there are a number of criticisms, including ethical issues and issues of validity.

The participants in Milgram's study suffered a lot of psychological distress. They were also deceived as to the nature of the experiment, which meant they couldn't provide informed consent. Additionally, they were not informed of their right to withdraw, which is now common practice in psychology experiments. Instead, they were urged to continue with the experiment when they asked to stop. This experiment was therefore very ethically questionable, and would never be allowed today. However, Milgram extensively debriefed his participants, including reuniting them with the learner. The participants therefore left understanding that they hadn't hurt anyone. They did, however, leave in the knowledge that they were capable of hurting people, which may have caused them distress.

Milgram's study can also be criticised in terms of external and internal validity. Some people claim that it lacks internal validity — that it wasn't actually measuring obedience rates at all. Perhaps instead, participants were just acting along with the experimenter, not actually believing they were hurting the learner (showing demand characteristics). The experiment has also been criticised in terms of external validity — that it doesn't produce traits that would be shown in the real world, with different people, and different situations. However, similar obedience rates have since been shown in other studies (e.g. Hofling et al), which do have high external validity.

Don't get carried away describing all the details — you just need the aim, and a summary of the method, results and conclusion.

Make sure the study you choose is the one you can describe and evaluate best — not just your favourite.

Don't worry if you can't remember exact figures — just make sure you know the general findings and what they mean.

Interpret findings using sentences beginning with 'This suggests that...' etc.

Evaluations need to include positive points too — not only problems.

Make sure you know the different types of validity — you'll probably need to mention them in any evaluation.

Explain what you mean when you use terms like 'external validity' etc.

... And Some Pointers About What to **Avoid**...

1) It's important to remember that it's not just a case of blindly scribbling down **everything** you can think of that's related to the subject. Doing this just **wastes time**, and it doesn't exactly impress the examiner.
2) You only get marks for stuff that's **relevant** and **answers the question**.
3) So, make sure you read over the question a couple of times before you start writing so that you really understand what it's asking.
4) When you're writing your answer, try to **structure** it in an **organised** way. If there's one thing that examiners find worse than a load of pointless information, it's being unable to make head or tail of an answer.
5) Before you start, it might be worth jotting down a quick **plan** of what you want to write so that you don't end up with a really jumbled answer.

Index

Index

Index